Chinese Legal Tradition
under the Mongols

Studies in East Asian Law
Harvard University

Chinese Legal Tradition under the Mongols

The Code of 1291 as Reconstructed

Paul Heng-chao Ch'en

PRINCETON UNIVERSITY PRESS
Princeton, New Jersey

Copyright © 1979 by Princeton University Press

Published by Princeton University Press, Princeton, New Jersey
In the United Kingdom: Princeton University Press,
Guildford, Surrey

ALL RIGHTS RESERVED

Library of Congress Cataloging in Publication Data will be
found on the last printed page of this book

This book has been composed in Monophoto Baskerville
by Asco Trade Typesetting Limited, Hong Kong

Clothbound editions of Princeton University Press books
are printed on acid-free paper, and binding materials are
chosen for strength and durability.

Printed in the United States of America by Princeton
University Press, Princeton, New Jersey

The Harvard Law School, in cooperation with Harvard's East Asian Research
Center, the Harvard-Yenching Institute, and scholars from other institutions,
has initiated a program of training and research designed to further scholarly
undestanding of the legal systems of China, Japan, Korea, and adjacent areas.
A series of publications has been established in conjunction with this program.
A list of the *Studies in East Asian Law* appears at the back of this book.

TO THE MEMORY OF
my brother,
Professor Hsien-t'ing Peter Ch'en (1930–1977)

CONTENTS

PREFACE

The Yüan dynasty was one of the most important periods in the development of Chinese civilization. It was during the Yüan that centuries of war in China between the Liao, the Chin, and the Sung terminated under a unified empire. For the first time in history, China as a whole experienced a nomadic conquest and was dominated by Mongolian rulers. It was also during the Yüan that the great urban and commercial transformation initiated in the T'ang and expanded in the Sung reached its peak.

As a result of the interaction between the Mongols and Chinese, this great period also confronted Chinese society with new questions. How to react to new situations under the alien rulers became an urgent concern for the Chinese. Conversely, the administration of a vast empire and coexistence with a huge Chinese population became pressing issues for the Mongols. As a result, various adjustments were made to reduce mutual frustrations and to promote the reconstruction of an orderly society. In conjunction with other political, social, and economic measures, these adjustments were reflected concretely in Chinese legal developments during the Yüan. If law is an influence upon many forces in a society, it also responds to the society which creates it. Thus, Chinese legal institutions of the Yüan not only represent the experiences of both the Mongols and Chinese, but also illuminate the trends of changes shaped by law itself and by other forces.

The importance of legal studies for the understanding of human civilization is obvious. In discussing Chinese civilization, however, many historians often neglect, ignore, or underestimate the significance of Yüan legal institutions. Many textbooks and research works jump abruptly from the Sung to the Ming, as if the institutions of the intervening century and a half were of no importance. In some works, Yüan law is only treated briefly, on the apparent assumption that a knowledge of Yüan law is immaterial to our understanding of the Chinese legal tradition in particular and Chinese civilization in general. To be sure, there existed in the Yüan some persistent and predominant features of the Chinese legal tradition which set limits to the range of developmental possibilities and which are by and large known to modern scholars. But there were also changes within the system, and further investigation of these changes will permit us to realize the significance and variety of alternatives within the Chinese legal tradition.

Despite the urgent need to examine the Yüan institutions, to the best of my knowledge only one significant work has been written in a Western language on Chinese law of the Yüan: Paul Ratchnevsky's *Un Code des Yuan*. Ratchnevsky's work is primarily a translation and annotation of the section entitled "Hsing-fa chih" (Treatise on Punishment and Law) in the *Yüan shih* [*Yüan History*], and deals only briefly with other problems of the legal system. Besides, the "Hsing-fa chih" is basically a survey of legal institutions, and, in the strict sense, is not a code. Owing to the nature of the "Hsing-fa chih" and the lack of a thorough discussion of the Yüan legal system in Ratchnevsky's work, this study will present a reconstructed text and annotated translation of the *Chih-yüan hsin-ko* [*Chih-yüan New Code*]—the first substantial code of the Yüan—which was promulgated in 1291, but then lost for centuries. Although the character *ko* may not stand exactly for the word "code," the text of the *Chih-yüan hsin-ko* does contain legal provisions which can be referred to as a code in a broad sense.

The focus of Part One of the present study is on the development of Chinese codes, the penal system, and the administration of justice during the Yüan, and on whether there were significant changes from the legal systems of previous dynasties, and, if so, what they were and how they came about. Since the present work centers on Chinese legal tradition in the Yüan period, the discussion of Part One will be confined to China proper and will not cover other areas of the Mongolian empire. Part One is intended to serve as a background for Part Two, which will be concerned with the reconstruction, translation, and annotation of the *Chih-yüan hsin-ko*. Hitherto, the lack of substantial Yüan legal studies has created a big gap between Sung scholarship and Ming scholarship which has made it impossible for historians to obtain a clear picture of the transformation of Chinese civilization. It is hoped that this study will shed light on some issues concerning the state and society of the Yüan dynasty.

This work is based on my Ph.D. thesis which was written under the guidance of Professor Francis W. Cleaves, whose advice and encouragement were crucial. I would also like to thank Professors Jerome A. Cohen, Benjamin I. Schwartz, and Yü Ying-shih for their support and guidance on specific questions. I am grateful for the kindness of Dr. Glen W. Baxter and for the generous financial support of the Harvard-Yenching Institute and the Harvard Law School. I found my years (1973–1975) as an S.J.D. candidate at the Harvard Law School and Research Scholar at its East Asian Legal Studies under the directorship of Professor Jerome A. Cohen most helpful to my legal training. I am also indebted to Professor Samuel E. Thorne for introducing me to the scholarship of English legal history which has helped me understand Chinese legal tradition through comparative perspectives.

This study has benefited from earlier works in the Yüan field by Professors Abe Takeo, Ch'en Yüan, Iwamura Shinobu, Miyazaki Ichisada, and Niida Noboru. Professor Frederick Mote and other participants of the Yüan Workshop which took place at Princeton University in 1975 under the auspices of the American Council of Learned Societies kindly gave me some suggestions. I am also grateful for the support and encouragement given by Professors Herbert Franke, John Langlois, and other members of the Yüan Conference which was sponsored by the American Council of Learned Societies and held in York, Maine in 1976. As a member of the School of Oriental and African Studies of the University of London, I have benefited from intellectual stimulation from my colleagues there. This study was facilitated by the excellent collection of the Harvard-Yenching Library, and I must thank Mr. George Potter for his kind assistance. Similarly, I was privileged to have access to the collection of the Jimbun Kagaku Kenkyūjo (Research Institute for Humanistic Studies) of Kyoto University during my year (1971–1972) in Japan as a Harvard Travelling Fellow.

Professors Hok-lam Chan and Herbert Franke have given me helpful comments. Also, I am grateful to Mr. Sanford G. Thatcher of the Princeton University Press for his kindness in arranging the publication of this study.

My brother, Peter, and my friend, Professor Don C. Price, inspired me to pursue graduate studies at Harvard University, and I wish to acknowledge their constant advice and help. I am also obliged to my parents, wife, and son for giving me strength and affection.

Harvard Law School   *Paul Heng-chao Ch'en*
Cambridge, Massachusetts
Summer 1977

ABBREVIATIONS

HJAS   *Harvard Journal of Asiatic Studies*

TCTK   *T'ung-chih t'iao-ko* (Kuo-li Pei-p'ing t'u-shu-kuan, Peking, 1930)

YS   *Yüan shih* (*Po-na-pen*, Ming, Hung-wu edition; reprinted by The Commercial Press, Shanghai, 1935)

YTC   *Ta Yüan sheng-cheng kuo-ch'ao tien-chang* (*Yüan tien-chang*) (*Sung-fen-shih ts'ung-k'an* edition, Peking, 1908)

*YTC**   *Ta Yüan sheng-cheng kuo-ch'ao tien-chang* (*Yüan tien-chang*) (Yüan edition; reprinted by National Palace Museum, Taipei, 1972)

YTCHC   *Ta Yüan sheng-cheng kuo-ch'ao tien-chang hsin-chi* (*Yüan tien-chang hsin-chi*) (*Sung-fen-shih ts'ung-k'an* edition, Peking, 1908)

INTRODUCTION

The developments in Chinese history during the thirteenth and fourteenth centuries involved great changes in political thought, intellectual trends, economic activities, and institutional systems. While this period has often been characterized as the "Sung-Yüan-Ming transition" and considered a formative era of modern Chinese civilization, it has not been entirely clear to historians why and how these changes took place at this particular time. Although modern scholarship has tried to explore various aspects of this special period, and to give a satisfactory account for the transformation of Chinese civilization, the effort has encountered great difficulties, mainly because of the unfamiliarity with the innovating role played by the Yüan dynasty (1271–1368).

Among the changes that occurred during the Yüan dynasty, the evolution of its legal tradition is especially striking. While the Yüan dynasty inevitably followed the major historical patterns set by the preceding ones, the Mongolian experiences in China brought new elements into the legal order of the Yüan. The Mongolian rulers, with the participation of the Chinese officials, influenced the course of Chinese law either by hastening the pace of changes which had occurred earlier in the Sung dynasty or by introducing completely novel concepts and institutions to China. Many innovations of the Yüan naturally stood as "important exceptions" to the general patterns of the Chinese legal tradition, and some of them even became standard features in the legal systems of later dynasties.

On the whole, the Yüan innovations were the result of the impact of Mongolian customary law on existing legal institutions and internal changes in these institutions themselves. Mongolian customary law was an important source of law in China during the initial period of the Mongolian conquest, but, as exemplified by the fate of the *Jasaγ*, its role became very limited by the end of the thirteenth century. The *Jasaγ* was a collection of rules and instructions given by Činggis Qan in response to the needs of specific circumstances and was later formally promulgated in 1229. Although it was not a systematically organized legal work, the *Jasaγ* provided the Mongolian ruling clan with guidelines for the administration of government, especially in matters of military discipline and organization.[1] The *Jasaγ* did not apply universally as a code to all tribes under the Mongolian domination, but, by virtue of its authoritative character, it did serve as a principal legal source in China for the period immediately following the fall of the Sung dynasty. Because Chinese society soon proved too complicated for Mongolian customary law to deal with, the application of the *Jasaγ* to Chinese cases diminished gradually, and by the end of the thirteenth century, the *Jasaγ* as a source of law appeared to be of a minimal importance.

As Mongolian customary law began to lose its dominant role in China, efforts were made to establish various Chinese legal codes for the administration of justice and to incorporate Mongolian legal principles into these codes. In addition, the *T'ai-ho lü* [*T'ai-ho Statutes*] of the Chin dynasty (1115–1234) continued to function during the transitional period until a permanent Yüan code was promulgated. In 1271, upon the advice of Liu Ping-chung (1216–1274), Qubilai Qaγan proclaimed the *Yüan* as the name of the reigning dynasty—the concept of the *yüan* being derived from the *I Ching* [*Book of Changes*], referring to the "primal force of the Creative" or "origin of the Universe."[2] The establishment of this national title not only supplied the Mongolian rulers with a new foundation of legitimation but also marked the beginning of a

---

[1] For a fairly recent work on the nature and development of the *Jasaγ*, see Paul Ratchnevsky, "Die Yasa (Ĵasaq) Cinggis-khan und ihre Problematic," *Sprache, Geschichte und Kultur der Altaischen Volker* (Protokollband der XII. Tagung der Permanent International Altaistic Conference 1969 in Berlin) (Berlin. Akademie-Verlag, 1974), pp. 471–487.

[2] For a study of Liu Ping-chung and his contribution, see Hok-lam Chan, "Liu Ping-chung (1216–74): A Buddhist-Taoist Statesman at the Court of Khubilai Khan," *T'oung Pao*, 53 (1967), pp. 98–146.

fresh era in China.[3] As an effective political gesture, along with other practical considerations, the validity of the *T'ai-ho lü* was terminated on the same day that the title of the reigning dynasty was announced. Consequently, the anxiety of the Chinese officials about the lack of a permanent Yüan code was further increased by the abolition of such a standard code as the *T'ai-ho lü*.

The frustration of the Chinese officials who longed for a unified Yüan code was understandably acute, especially in view of the fact that China had had legal codes for centuries and taken pride in her refined judicial system. The codification movement in China started even before the Imperial Period, and as early as 400 B.C. a code known as the *Fa Ching [Cannon of Law]* had been promulgated. The codification effort continued throughout various dynasties, resulting in the establishment of the *T'ang Code* in 653. The *T'ang Code* achieved its final form in 737 and represented an example of excellent legal draftsmanship. The articles of the *T'ang Code* were grouped under twelve sections and covered most legal instances. With the exception of the Yüan experiences, the content and the structure of the *T'ang Code* became by and large standardized in the codifications of subsequent dynasties. For example, the Sung dynasty (960–1271) primarily followed the *T'ang Code* to establish its own *Hsing T'ung [Unified Code]* in 963. Similarly, the *Tai-ho lü* (1201) of the Chin dynasty was also largely a copy of the *T'ang Code*. Although the desires of the Yüan officials for a national code modeled on the *T'ang Code* were partially met by the temporary adoption of the *T'ai-ho lü*, the Yüan dynasty failed to promulgate a national code along the lines of the *T'ang Code*, thus making the Yüan codification experiences very different from those of other dynasties.

With the abolition of the *T'ai-ho lü* in 1271, Chinese officials began to consider formats of codification other than an un-

[3] For a discussion of the Yüan foundation of legitimation, see Herbert Franke, "From Tribal Chieftain to Universal Emperor and God: The Legitimation of the Yüan Dynasty" (paper prepared for the Conference on Legitimation held under the auspices of the American Council of Learned Societies in June 1975, Asilomar Conference Grounds, Monterey, California).

imaginative reproduction of the *T'ang Code*. As a result, codes having statutes of a more casuistic nature and a less unified theme than those of the *T'ang Code* were from time to time established during the Yüan period. Collections of legal cases with decisions were also compiled and made readily available to the Yüan officials so as to provide them with proper judicial guidance. By using various legal codes as a substitute for a national code of the *T'ang Code* type, the Yüan dynasty, with the benefit of numerous legal collections for extensive consultation, managed to reach a compromise between the traditional Chinese reliance on codification and the flexibility of drawing legal authority from precedents. In this respect, the Yüan legal development also departed from the regular practice of previous dynasties.

Although Mongolian customary law gradually became insignificant as a source for law, many Mongolian legal institutions and concepts were adopted into the Chinese codes of the Yüan and became an intergrated part of a new legal order. This trend was clearly reflected in the changes that occurred in the Yüan penal system. The traditional five principal punishments (death, life exile, penal servitude, beating with a heavy stick, and beating with a small stick) underwent modifications in theory and in practice during the Yüan. In addition, for certain offenses, new types of financial and physical punishments were imposed on wrongdoers. As some of these supplemental punishments originated in Mongolian customary law, Mongolian legal institutions and concepts were in substance observed in Chinese law. In short, the Yüan dynasty, although following the traditional patterns of the Chinese legal system, nonetheless made adjustments and innovations in order to strike a balance between the forces of Chinese tradition, Mongolian practice, and new social conditions.

Similarly, with regard to the administration of justice, various steps were taken in the Yüan to reorganize judicial structure and procedure. New regulations were also established to govern legal disputes involving people of different ethnic backgrounds, professional groups, and religious attachments, thus reducing the possible conflict of legal principles and custom. There was an increase in legal professionalism as well during the Yüan period in the sense of dissemination of legal knowledge. Through popular books and education, this occurred both on the bureaucratic level and on the level of the general public. These innovations not only inserted new elements into the Yüan legal system to cushion the clash between Mongolian customary law and Chinese legal principles, but also in the long run had an influence on the law-making processes of the later dynasties.

As most of the Yüan legal codes have not survived, it is extremely difficult to demonstrate in full the significance of the Yüan legal innovations. In studying the historical foundations of English law, S. F. C. Milsom once remarked: "Legal history is not unlike that children's game in which you draw lines between numbered dots, and suddenly from the jumble a picture emerges: but our dots are not numbered."[4] Indeed, our dots for drawing a picture of Yüan legal history are not only unnumbered but are also too scattered. Thus, the reconstruction of the *Chih-yüan hsin-ko* [*Chih-yüan New Code*] in this study is meant to identify a few more of these dots and thereby throw light on the nature of Yüan legal institutions and offer a textual criticism of Yüan legal compilations.

The *Chih-yüan hsin-ko* was drafted by Ho Jung-tsu and promulgated in 1291 as the first substantial code of the Yüan dynasty. It later became one of the most important legal texts and laid the foundation for the compilations of the *Ta Yüan t'ung-chih* [*Comprehensive Institutions of the Great Yüan*] and the *Yüan tien-chang* [*Institutions of the Yüan Dynasty*]. More significantly, fragments of the *Chih-yüan hsin-ko* and the *Ta Yüan t'ung-chih*, along with the complete text of the *Yüan tien-chang*, are the only legal documents which are still available to modern scholars. Fragments of the *Ta Yüan t'ung-chih* were preserved

---

[4] S.F.C. Milsom, *Historical Foundations of the Common Law* (London: Butterworths, 1969), p. xiv.

and printed in 1930 in a text entitled *T'ung-chih t'iao-ko* [*Code of Comprehensive Institutions*], but at that time the full text of the *Chih-yüan hsin-ko* was still lost.

The original text of the *Chih-yüan hsin-ko* had become unavailable by the time of Su T'ien-chüeh (1294–1352). When it was reprinted under the order of the Chung-shu-sheng (Secretarial Council), Su T'ien-chüeh wrote a preface to the new text in which he praised the ability of Ho Jung-tsu and admired the conciseness of the code.[5] Su further pointed out that the code had succeeded in covering all current legal instances by expanding its legal principles beyond a text having no more than several thousand characters. This remark might be an exaggeration, but it nevertheless sheds light on the nature and structure of the code. Aside from Su's preface, unfortunately, this reprint suffered the same fate as its original text and has not survived. The code as reconstructed and presented in Part Two of this study comes from fragments in various Chinese sources. It is hoped that the reconstructed text with the 96 fragments is not far from the original framework of the code.

Throughout this study, owing to the limitations of space, the focus is directed on the changing aspects of the Yüan legal order, thus bypassing those general features which were common to the Yüan and other dynasties.[6] In singling out the innovating and transforming character of the Yüan legal system, this study also hopes to provoke more thought on the role the Mongols played in shaping Chinese history. There has been a common notion among some scholars that the Mongolian contribution to Chinese civilization in general and Chinese legal tradition in particular was extremely limited. For instance, Professors Bodde and Morris have suggested that the Yüan only made some trifling changes in law from the T'ang tradition. In citing V. A. Riasanovsky, they claimed: "Although the Mongols, in view of their very different cultural background,

[5] Su T'ien-chueh, *Tz'u-hsi wen-kao* (*Shih-yüan ts'ung-shu* edition), 6:7b–8a.
[6] I am preparing a more detailed discussion of legal principles and institutions of the Yüan dynasty as reflected in the *T'ung-chih t'iao-ko*. The *T'ung-chih t'iao-ko* study will examine issues of Yuan law which are not dealt with in the present study.

might have been expected to make sweeping changes in Chinese law when they ruled Yüan China, their major 'contribution' seems actually to have been that of using numbers ending in sevens instead of tens when specifying the number of blows of beating or other punishments (7, 17, and so on, in place of 10, 20, 30)."[7] To be sure, the assessment of the scope and significance of a "contribution" often depends on the measure of one's yardstick. In all fairness to the Mongols and their Chinese partners, however, it is obvious that the Yüan contribution to Chinese legal tradition was greater and far more significant than just "that of using numbers ending in sevens" in punishments.

Some of the points made in this study may seem "unconventional." For example, the portrayal of the Yüan leniency in punishment as the "bright" side of the story may admittedly seem too rosy, especially considering the fact that there were brutal aspects of the Mongolian domination in China.[8] But the lenient penal system does not necessarily imply "civilized" court politics, nor a "restrained" political attitude in the power struggles between the Mongolian rulers and their Chinese subjects. In this sense, this study, by examining the Yüan legal order, is meant to supplement other earlier works with a different scholarly approach so as to help contribute to a correct interpretation of the "Sung-Yüan-Ming transition" of Chinese civilization. In any event, because more unnumbered dots in Yüan legal history must still be collected and analyzed, the picture that emerges from the dots drawn in the present study is incomplete and personal.

[7] Derk Bodde and Clarence Morris, *Law in Imperial China* (Cambridge, Mass.: Harvard University Press, 1967), p. 59, n. 19.

[8] For a discussion of the Mongolian domination in China and some brutal aspects of Mongolian politics, see Frederick Mote, "China under Mongol Domination: 1234–1367" (draft prepared for *The Cambridge History of China*, Vol. IV).

THE YÜAN
LEGAL INSTITUTIONS

I. THE DEVELOPMENT OF
CHINESE CODES

During the Yüan dynasty (1271–1368),[1] owing to the expansion of the Mongolian empire, China's territory was especially huge and its population ethnically diverse. To establish a unified code for a population of such ethnic diversity was impractical. Before the establishment of the dynasty, the Mongols already had their Mongolian customary law, which they continued to use throughout the period. At the same time, the *se-mu-jen* (miscellaneous aliens) were mostly Muslim and followed their own Islamic law.[2] Thus it was both impractical and unrealistic to compile a code that would combine traditional Chinese legal principles, Mongolian customary law, and Islamic law. Since there was no intention to promulgate a legal code common to Mongols, Central Asians, and Chinese—and since in reality there was no such code—the development of the legal codes of the Yüan dynasty only involved the codification of Chinese laws. Although these codes in some special instances governed the relations between Chinese and other ethnic groups, they were primarily applied to the Chinese people.

The development of the Yüan codes can be roughly divided

---

[1] On the problem of the dating of the dynasty, see Francis Woodman Cleaves, "The Sino-Mongolian Inscription of 1362 in Memory of Prince Hindu," *Harvard Journal of Asiatic Studies* (hereafter cited as *HJAS*), 12 (1949), p. 38.

[2] The term *se-mu-jen* (miscellaneous aliens) was used in the Yüan period to refer mainly to people from Western and Central Asia. For a discussion of this term, see Yanai Watari, *Mōkoshi kenkyū* [*Studies of Mongolian History*] (Tokyo: Tōkō shoin, 1930), pp. 263–360. See also Francis W. Cleaves, "The Sino-Mongolian Inscription of 1338 in Memory of Jigüntei," *HJAS*, 14 (1951), p. 44, n. 44.

into three stages, although these stages may to some extent overlap one another. The first stage began with the code promulgated by T'ai-tsung (Ögedei Qaγan) in 1229, and ended with the establishment of the Yüan dynasty in 1271. This stage was characterized by strong Mongolian influence. The second stage lasted from 1271 to 1320, during which time changes were undertaken to either restore or create various Chinese institutions that were needed to carry out new administrative functions. In the third period (1321–1368) the cultural accommodation of Mongolian customs to Chinese institutions reached its climax. Efforts begun in the first stage and reinforced in the second stage provided the foundation for the establishment of major new codes in the third stage. During these three stages, various adjustments were made, consciously or subconsciously, to ease the tensions between Mongols and Chinese so as to ensure an effective administration of government. These adjustments were a result of the impact of the Confucian ideal of state and society on the Mongolian rule, on the one hand, and the introduction of Mongolian values and institutions into Chinese society on the other.

THE FIRST STAGE (1229–1270)

The Jasaγ

Before the establishment of the Yüan dynasty in China proper, there existed among the Mongols some legal institutions which later played a part in the development of the Yüan legal system. One of them was the *Ta cha-sa* (*Yeke Jasaγ*). The words *Yeke Jasaγ* mean *Ta fa-ling* (great code) in the Chinese language.[3] The *Ta cha-sa* was known as the Great Code of Činggis Qan and seems to have been promulgated in 1229, when T'ai-tsung was elected to succeed Činggis Qan.[4] Although no complete

---

[3] *Yuan shih* [*Yuan History*] (*Po-na-pen*, Ming, Hung-wu wood-block edition; reprinted by The Commercial Press, Shanghai, 1935) (hereafter cited as *YS*), 2:1b.

[4] *Ibid*

4

version of the code has yet been found, some fragments have been preserved in the records of several early historians (such as Rashid al-Dīn and Makrizi) and in other documents.[5] By using these fragments and records, Western scholars have made extensive studies of the code.[6] Since the subject has been treated and, moreover, since the main concern of this study is with Chinese legal institutions, only some references to the *Jasaɣ* in Chinese documents will be discussed here.

Among the Chinese sources, the *Ta Yüan sheng-cheng kuo-ch'ao tien-chang* (hereinafter abbreviated and cited as the *Yüan tien-chang* or *Institutions of the Yüan Dynasty*)[7] contains one reference to *Ch'eng-chi-ssu huang-ti cha-sa* (i.e., the code of the Emperor Činggis Qan)[8] and thirteen other references to the *Jasaɣ* as such.[9] The former, in a document dated the 19th day of the 8th moon of the 1st year of the Chih-yüan reign [September 10, 1264], deals with a matter endangering the Imperial household. The latter include: 1) a reference in a document

[5] A. V. Riasanovsky, *Fundamental Principles of Mongol Law* (Tientsin, 1931), pp. 25–32. See also George Vernadsky, "The Scope and Contents of Chingis Khan's Yasa," *HJAS*, 3 (1938), pp. 337–339.

[6] For the literature on the subject, see Francis W. Cleaves, "The 'Fifteen "Palace Poems"' by K'o Chiu-ssu," *HJAS*, 20 (1957), pp. 429–430, n. 14. For a fairly recent Western work on this subject, see Paul Ratchnevsky, "Die Yasa (Ĵasaq) Cinggis-khan und ihre Problematic," *Sprach, Geschichte und Kultur der Altaischen Völker* (Berlin: Akademic-Verlag, 1974), pp. 471–487. Chinese and Japanese works are also available. For instance, see Tamura Jituszō, *Chūgoku seihuku ōchō no kenkyū: chū [Dynasties of Conquest in China: Part Two]* (Kyoto: Kyoto University Press, 1971), pp. 387–443.

[7] The text used here is the Shen Chia-pen wood-block edition of 1908. For a detailed discussion of the origin and content of the *Yüan tien-chang* (hereafter cited as *YTC*), see below.

[8] *YTC* 1:2b. An entry in the *YS* also carries the same reference, except that the title *Ch'eng-chi-ssu* is replaced by T'ai-tsu, the Chinese canonization of Činggis Qan. See *YS* 5:22a.

[9] P. Popov notes three references to the code of Činggis Qan in the *Yüan tien-chang*. See P. Popov, "Jasa Čingis-Chana i uloženie Mongolskoj Dinastii," *Zapiski Vostočnogo Otdelenija Russkoga Archeologičeskogo Obščestva*, 17 (1907), p. 0152 (quoted in Vernadsky, "Scope and Contents of Chingis Kahn's Yasa," p. 338). See also Riasanovsky, *Fundamental Principles*, pp. 28–29 and 279. Weng Tu-chien indicates that the *Yüan tien-chang* contains one reference to the *Ch'eng-chi-ssu huang-ti cha-sa* and ten other references to the *cha-sa* as such. See Weng Tu-chien, "Meng-Yüan shih-tai ti fa-tien pien-tsuan" ("The Codification during the Mongol-Yüan Period"), *Yen-ching she-hui k'o-hsueh*, 1 (1948), p. 158.

dated 1280 dealing with counterfeiters;[10] 2) a reference in a *document dated 1278 dealing with military personnel;*[11] 3) a reference in a document dated 1280 dealing with military personnel;[12] 4) three references in a document dated 1286/1287 dealing with military personnel;[13] 5) two references in a document dated 1262 dealing with the postal relay system;[14] 6) a reference in a document dated 1301 dealing with a case of homicide;[15] 7) a reference in a document dated 1272/1273 dealing with a case of performing black magic;[16] 8) a reference in a document dated 1272 dealing with the sale of poison;[17] 9) a reference in a document dated 1297 dealing with the design of an Imperial leather hat;[18] and 10) a reference in a document dated 1321/1322 dealing with the role of the Yü-shih-t'ai (the Censorate).[19]

The above references to the *Jasay*, arranged according to the order of their appearance in the *Yüan tien-chang*, are applied to conduct that infringed on state interests or constituted serious crimes. For instance, Cases 2, 3, and 4 are related to desertions or hiding soldiers. Case 5 considers the function of commissioners and the postal relay system. Case 6 is about the murder of one's own brother; this offense, recorded in the *Yüan tien-chang* under the section of "Pu-mu" (discord in families) was considered one of the *shih-o* (ten abominations) of traditional Chinese law.[20] Case 9 prohibits any reproduction

---

[10] *YTC* 20:20a.

[11] *YTC* 34:20b. This reference to the *Jasay* is, however, not mentioned by Weng Tu-chien in his article.

[12] *YTC* 34:21a.

[13] *YTC* 34:39.

[14] *YTC* 36:8b–9a.

[15] *YTC* 41:8b.

[16] *YTC* 41:30a.

[17] *YTC* 57:40a.

[18] *YTC* 58:16a.

[19] *Yüan tien-chang hsin-chi* (*Sung-fen-shih ts'ung-k'an* edition, Peking, 1908) (hereafter cited as *YTCHC*), "Ch'ao-kang" ("Court Principles"):8b.

[20] According to traditional Chinese legal principles, the *shih-o* (ten abominations) were the most serious offenses and were not subject to an ordinary act of amnesty. For their terms and English translation, see Ch'ü T'ung-tsu, *Law and Society in Traditional China* (The Hague: Mouton & Co., 1961), p. 179, n. 48.

of the color and design of a hat submitted to the Emperor. As a collection of rules and orders given by Činggis Qan, the *Jasaγ* was to provide the Mongolian leaders with guidelines for the administration of government and to supplement Mongolian customary law. Although it was traditionally applied mainly to Mongols, as indicated in the above references, the *Jasaγ* was occasionally applied to Chinese, especially to those having military or official status or whose conduct related to matters in the sphere of state interest.[21]

There are also references to the *Jasaγ* in other Chinese sources. For example, in the *Chan-ch'ih* [*Jamči*] [*On the Postal Relay System*], there are four documents, governing the administration of the postal relay system, that contain references to the *Jasaγ*; the first is dated 1241,[22] the second 1242,[23] the third 1244,[24] and the fourth 1262.[25] In the *T'ung-chih t'iao-ko* [*Code of Comprehensive Institutions*], a document dated 1263, prohibiting soldiers from disturbing common people, there is a reference to the

[21] For convenience, both *Han-jen* (Northern Chinese) and *Nan-jen* (Southern Chinese, i.e., Southern Chinese who became subjects of the Yüan dynasty after the fall of the Sung dynasty in 1279) are referred to as Chinese in this study, unless otherwise indicated. For a detailed discussion of various ethnic groups in the Yüan period, see Yanai Watari, *Mōkoshi kenkyū*, pp. 263–360. See also Meng Ssu-ming, *Yüan-tai she-hui chieh-chi chih-tu* [*Social Classes in China under the Yüan Dynasty*] (Peking: The Harvard-Yenching Institute, 1938), pp. 25–67.

[22] *Chan-ch'ih* [*On the Postal Relay System*] (*Kuo-hsüeh wen-k'u* edition, *Pien* No. 28 & No. 30, Peking, 1936), Vol. 1, p. 14. Professor Cleaves points out three references to the *Jasaγ* in the "Chan-ch'ih" section of the *Yung-lo ta-tien* [*Great Institutions of the Yung-lo Reign*]. See Cleaves, "The 'Fifteen "Palace Poems"' by K'o Chiu-ssu," pp. 429–430, n. 14. Professor Kobayashi also mentions this reference to the *Jasaγ*. However, he incorrectly gives the 12th year of the Chih-yüan reign as the date of this document. The right date is the 12th year of T'ai-tsung. See Kabayashi Takashirō, "Gendai hōseishi zakkō" ("Some Remarks on the Codes of the Yuan Dynasty"), *Kanagawa Kenritsu Gaigo Tankidaigaku kiyō: Jinbun shakai hen* (*Humanities and Social Sciences, Bulletin of the College of Foreign Studies, Yokohama*), 1 (1968), p. 18.

[23] *Chan-ch'ih*, Vol. 1, p. 14.

[24] *Ibid.*, Vol. 1, p. 15.

[25] *Ibid.*, Vol. 2, p. 99. This reference to the *Jasaγ* is also recorded in the *Yüan tien-chang*. See *YTC* 36:9a. The existence of this particular reference is noted by Kobayashi as well, although he incorrectly gives *chuan* 19,429 of the *Yung-lo ta-tien* as the source of the document. *Chüan* 19,424 is the correct citation for the document, and his mistake must be due to a misprint. See Kobayashi Takashirō, "Gendai hōseishi zakkō," p. 19.

Jasay.[26] The *Ta Yüan ma-chang chi* [*On the Administration of Imperial Stud of the Great Yüan*], a document dated 1277, dealing with the punishment of anyone who concealed strong horses, supplies another reference.[27]

Only two of the above references occur after the thirteenth century—a fact that seems to demonstrate the decline of the *Jasay*'s importance and the growing remoteness of Mongolian law to the Chinese people by the end of that century. The *Jasay* served as a major legal source in the initial period of the Mongolian conquest, but after the Mongolian settlement in China, it proved inadequate for the needs of Chinese society because Mongolian law was much simpler and more primitive. On the other hand, the Mongolian rulers became more oriented toward Chinese culture and more interested in developing Chinese law for the governing of the Chinese people. As the society became more complicated and advanced by the end of the thirteenth century, the significance of the *Jasay* naturally diminished in China. This interpretation is substantiated by an observation of V. A. Riasanovsky who claimed that the effectiveness of the *Jasay* as a general legal source for all tribes under the Mongolian domination was short lived and that its importance began to decline at the end of the thirteenth century.[28]

Some proposals submitted by Wang Yün (1227–1304) further illuminate this point. In 1268, when Wang Yün was serving in the Censorate, he memorialized to the throne and suggested that a code be promulgated under the title of the *Chih-yüan hsin-fa* [*Chih-yüan New Code*]. Having foreseen the possible ineffectiveness of such a code, he said:

> If within [this code] there are [items] which cannot effectively function, let us extract [supplements from] the dynastic *cha-sa* (*Jasay*) and, by following the practice of

[26] *T'ung-chih t'iao-ko* [*Code of Comprehensive Institutions*] (Peking: Kuo-li Pei-p'ing t'u-shu-kuan, 1930) (hereafter cited as *TCTK*), 16:27b. For a detailed discussion of this text, see below.
[27] *Ta Yüan ma-cheng chi* [*On the Administration of Imperial Stud of the Great Yuan*] (*Kuo-hsueh wen-k'u* edition, *Pien* No. 49, Peking, 1937), p. 10.
[28] Riasanovsky, *Fundamental Principles*, p. 33.

8

[issuing decrees] of the Chin dynasty, establish [these supplements] separately [under] decree authorization.[29]

In this document Wang Yün recognized the fitness of adopting from the *Jasaɣ* some supplements to improve the effectiveness of the projected new code, and suggested that these supplements should be enacted by issuing decrees.[30] The proposal was submitted, but his plan for the *Chih-yüan hsin-fa* was not carried out. In another proposal dated 1292, Wang Yün once again memorialized:

I humbly suggest that [it is] proper for the established statutes and ordinances to be promulgated as the *Hsin-fa* [*New Code*]. If there are [items] which cannot effectively function [or] thoroughly fit [the situation], let the holy decrees of previous reigns as well as the *t'iao-ko* (articles and codes) from the Chung-t'ung reign to the present be generally deliberated and be used as supplements.[31]

In this second memorial of 1292, significantly enough, Wang Yün does not mention the *Jasaɣ* in his plan for the *Hsin-fa*, and this purposeful omission of the *Jasaɣ* as a legal source reflects his departure from the earlier dependence on Mongolian

[29] Wang Yun, *Ch'iu-chien hsien-sheng ta-ch'üan wen-chi* (*Ssu-pu ts'ung-k'an* edition) (Shanghai: The Commercial Press, 1929), 90:3b. See also Cleaves, "The 'Fifteen "Palace Poems"' by K'o Chiu-ssu," p. 430, n. 14.

[30] During the Sung dynasty, the rigid *lu* (statutes) became increasingly ineffective in dealing with the changing society; therefore more measures were taken and issued in the form of *ch'ih* (decrees) to mete out justice for the new circumstances. Consequently, the importance of the *lu* as a source of law declined. As more decrees of a legal nature accumulated, efforts were made to edit and codify them, and eventually, they became standard laws. This practice was later adopted by the Chin dynasty. For instance, after the promulgation of the *T'ai-ho lü* [*T'ai-ho Statutes*] in 1201, a text containing three *chuan* of decrees was issued under the title of *Hsin-ting ch'ih-t'iao* [*New Codified Decrees*] to supplement the *T'ai-ho lü*. See the *Chin shih* [*Chin History*] (*Po-na-pen*, Yüan, Chih-cheng edition; reprinted by The Commercial Press, Shanghai, 1931), 45:12a. For the importance of the *ch'ih* as a source of law, see Miyazaki Ichisada, "Sō-Gen jidai no hōsei to saiban kikō" ("Law and the Judicial System in the Sung-Yüan period"), *Tōhō gakuhō* (Kyoto), 24 (1954), pp. 115–128. See also Sogabe Shizuo, *Chūgoku ritsuryōshi no kenkyū* [*A Study of the History of Statutes and Ordinances in China*] (Tokyo: Yoshikawa kōbunkan, 1971), pp. 21–46.

[31] Wang Yun, 35:1b–2a. See also *YS* 167:21b–22a.

law. After the succession of Ch'eng-tsung (Temür Qaγan) to the throne in 1294, Wang Yün, in the capacity of *Han-lin hsüeh-shih* (Han-lin academician), submitted to the Emperor another proposal which included a similar plan for the promulgation of a new code to be called the *Yüan-nien hsin-fa* [*First Year New Code*]. He did not mention the *Jasaγ* at all in the last plan submitted to Ch'eng-tsung.[32] A comparison of these three documents clearly indicates the declining importance of the *Jasaγ* in the later years of the thirteenth century; it also suggests that greater attention was gradually being paid to decrees, laws, and ordinances of the traditional Chinese type.

Efforts to establish Chinese institutions in China proper to counteract the Mongolian influence actually started very early. For example, Hsü Heng (1209–1281), the leading scholar of the time, submitted a proposal in 1266 in which he stressed the need for the Mongolian rulers to adopt Chinese institutions, including Chinese laws. He further stated: "That our country should adopt Chinese institutions is beyond any doubt. But should the [Mongolian] national customs of ten thousand generations and the nobility of consecutive reigns be suddenly forced to follow your servant's suggestion and to accommodate themselves to the customs of a perished country, the situation could be extremely difficult."[33] In order to achieve a successful transformation from Mongolian customs to Chinese institutions, Hsü Heng proposed that thirty years be allowed for such gradual changes. It was during this period of gradual transformation that the importance of the *Jasaγ* in the Chinese society declined.

Early Chinese Codes

In the biographical section of Kuo Pao-yü in the *Yüan shih*, it is recorded that in the 6th year of T'ai-tsu (Činggis Qan) [January 17, 1211–February 4, 1212], Činggis Qan followed the advice of Kuo Pao-yü and promulgated the *T'iao-hua*

---

[32] Wang Yun, 79:15b–16a. See also *YS* 167:22a.

[33] Hsu Heng, "Shih-wu wu-shih" ("Five Current Matters"), *Kuo-ch'ao wen-lei* [*Specimens of Our Dynastic Literature*] (Shanghai: The Commercial Press, 1929), 13:1b–4b. See also *YS* 158:9a–10a.

[*Rules*] containing five sections. The *Rules* forbade indiscriminate killing during military campaigns; they also stated that only serious crimes were to be punished by death and that other offenses were to be punished merely by a beating with bamboo sticks.[34] Kuo was a former Chinese general who surrendered to the Mongols after the defeat of his army. After being presented to Činggis Qan, Kuo was consulted on matters of strategy. He advised Činggis Qan that during the initial stage of nation-building it would be proper to promulgate a new code. Although the text of the *Rules* is not substantial, it nevertheless represents the earliest effort by the Mongols to promulgate a Chinese code and marks the beginning of the establishment of Yüan laws.[35] Between the time of the *Rules* and the succession of Shih-tsu (Qubilai Qaγan) in 1260, various ordinances and decrees were issued.[36] Although more Chinese laws were promulgated at the time of Yeh-lü Ch'u-ts'ai (1189–1243),[37] no substantial code was published. As a result, when Shih-tsu came to power, the *T'ai-ho lü* [*T'ai-ho Statutes*] of the Chin dynasty and Mongolian law were still in use.[38]

The *T'ai-ho lü* was promulgated in 1201, at the time when the Chin dynasty had reached its most Sinicized stage under the rule of Chang-tsung (r. 1194–1209). It was divided into twelve sections: "Ming-li" (Terms and General Principles), "Wei-chin" (Imperial Guards and Prohibitions), "Chih-chih" (Administrative Regulations), "Hu-hun" (Families and Marriages), "Chiu-k'u" (Stables and Treasures), "Shan-hsing" (Unauthorized *Corvée* Levies), "Tsei-tao" (Thefts and Violence), "Tou-sung" (Conflicts and Suits), "Cha-wei" (Deceptions and Frauds), "Tsa-lü" (Miscellaneous Statutes),

---

[34] *YS* 149:11.

[35] K'o Shao-min, *Hsin Yüan shih* [*New Yüan History*] (Fu-keng-t'ang edition, Tientsin, 1922), 102:1a.

[36] *Ibid.*, 102:1b–3b.

[37] *YS* 2:4a–5a. See also Igor De Rachewiltz, "Yeh-lü ch'u-ts'ai (1189–1243): Buddhist Idealist and Confucian Statesman," Arthur Wright and Denis Twitchett, eds., *Confucian Personalities* (Stanford: Stanford University Press, 1962), pp. 201–209.

[38] Niida Noboru, *Chūgoku hōseishi kenkyū: keihō* [*A Study of Chinese Legal History: Criminal Law*] (Tokyo: Tokyo University Press, 1959), pp. 453–524.

"Pu-wang" (Arrests and Escapes), and "Tuan-yü" (Trial and Imprisonment). The twelve sections were identical to those of the *T'ang Code*. In the *Chin shih* [*Chin History*] there is a statement that the *T'ai-ho lü* was essentially another *T'ang Code*.[39] The *T'ai-ho lü* followed the *T'ang Code* in style and content, although it had some sixty more entries than the *T'ang Code*.[40]

The complete text of the *T'ai-ho lu* does not survive today. Fortunately, because of the adoption of the code in the early period of the Shih-tsu reign, many fragments have been preserved in the Chinese sources of the Yüan period.[41] Some fragments have even been found in the *Tānksūqnāma-i ilkhān dar fūnūn-i ulūmi-i khitā'i* [*The Precious Work of the Ilkhan on the Various Branches of Khitay Learning*] of Rashid al-Dīn.[42] These materials indicate that the *T'ai-ho lü* influenced the development of the Yüan codes, even after it was officially discontinued in 1271. This code therefore served to transmit the legal principles of the *T'ang Code* first to the Chin dynasty in 1201, and then, when that dynasty was conquered by the Mongols in 1234, the code was adopted and continuously used until the day *i-hai* of the 11th moon of the 8th year of the Chih-yüan reign [December 18, 1271].[43]

---

[39] *Chin shih* 45:11a.

[40] For a comparative study of the *T'ang Code* and the *T'ai-ho lu*, see Niida Noboru, *Chūgoku hōseishi kenkyū: keihō*, pp. 486–521. See also Yō Sen-sho (Yeh Ch'ien-chao), *Kinritsu no kenkyū* [*A Study of the Chin Statutes*] (Tokyo?, 1971?), pp. 21–145. For a Chinese version of the latter book, see Yeh Ch'ien-chao, *Chin-lu chih yen-chiu* [*A Study of the Chin Statutes*] (Taipei: The Commercial Press, 1972).

[41] Some references in the Chinese sources to the *T'ai-ho lu* are mentioned by Professor Niida. See Niida Noboru, *Chūgoku hōseishi kenkyū: keihō*, pp. 460–463.

[42] According to Karl Jahn, the second part of this book deals with the laws of *Tai-khu-lu-lun* (i.e., the *T'ai-ho lu*). This Persian text may be dated at the latest from the year 710 A.H. (A.D. 1310–1311) and was recently examined by Professor Jahn. See Karl Jahn, "Some Ideas of Rashid al-Dīn on Chinese Culture," *Central Asiatic Journal*, 14 (1970), p. 137. Professor Jahn's remark that the *T'ai-ho lü* comprises twenty chapters is not accurate. According to the *Chin shih* and other sources, there are thirty *chüan* in the *T'ai-ho lu*.

[43] *YS* 7:13a.

The explanation given in the *Yüan shih* specifies that the harsh nature of the *T'ai-ho lü* was the reason it was abolished in 1271.[44] In a preface written by Hsü T'ien-lin, to a book entitled *Kuan-min chün-yung* [*Standard References for Officials and Civilians*] we also read that harsh and petty laws were not esteemed in the Yüan dynasty and that therefore, the old precedents of the *T'ai-ho lü* were discontinued.[45] The explanation contained in these two sources seems too superficial, for there would appear to be two more important reasons for the abolition of the *T'ai-ho lü*. In the first place, it was politically unnecessary to continue to use the code of the former dynasty. The *T'ai-ho lü* was abolished on the same day that the title of the reigning dynasty (i.e., *Ta Yüan*) was officially established.[46] The proclamation of the title of the dynasty marked the beginning of a new era and consequently there was no need to perpetuate the code of the previous dynasty. This kind of political sentiment was well demonstrated by Hu Chih-yü (1227–1293) in one of his memorials. Referring to *T'ai-ho lü*, he expressed doubt that the institutions of the defeated Chin dynasty could ever be satisfactory for the court nobility and high officials or be depended upon for deciding legal cases.[47] Second, by 1271 many decisions and precedents had accumulated and it was thought that future legal cases could be decided simply by following these precedents. It was also suggested that decrees be issued to meet new circumstances, whenever the precedents should fail to provide guidelines. For example, Wu Ch'eng (1249–1339), a leading scholar, said:

> The Emperor Shih-tsu of the holy Yüan, after unifying the country, following [the precedent that] the early Sung dynasty did not [continue] using the *Chou lü* [*Chou Code*], issued the decree [ordering] that the *T'ai-ho lü* of the Chin

[44] *YS* 102:1b.

[45] For a brief discussion of this book, see the *Ssu-k'u ch'uan-shu tsung-mu t'i-yao* (Shanghai: The Commercial Press, 1933), 84:27a.

[46] *YS* 7:13b.

[47] Hu Chih-yü, *Tzu-shan ta-ch'üan chi* (Ho-nan kuan-shu-chü, 1932), 12:14b–15a.

dynasty be not used. . . . The holy idea [of Shih-tsu] was the desire to be guided by circumstances for the creation of proper [institutions] and set himself as precedent.[48]

For the above reasons further use of the *Tai-ho lü* was prohibited in 1271. Nevertheless, the code was occasionally consulted even after it was abolished. In the *Yüan shih*, an entry of 1286 reveals that the Chinese authorities still applied the *T'ai-ho lü* to cases every so often, thus disturbing the unity of legal codes.[49] However, with the code officially terminated, a new stage began to develop in 1271.

THE SECOND STAGE (1271–1320)

The Era of Shih-tsu

While applying Mongolian and Chinese laws to Chinese society in the early years of his reign, Shih-tsu in 1262 ordered Yao Shu (1219–1296) and Shih T'ien-tse (1202–1275) to prepare a Chinese code.[50] In 1264 a code was declared,[51] and in the same year another code of 37 items was established upon a proposal by Yeh-lü Chu (1221–1285);[52] in 1271 some further rules were adopted upon a proposal submitted by the Shang-shu-sheng (Presidential Council).[53] Although these codes were not substantial, they nevertheless indicate the attention Shih-tsu paid to Chinese laws.

After the *T'ai-ho lü* was abolished in 1271, Chinese officials were anxious to promote the establishment of a general Chinese code. So Wei Ch'u advocated in a proposal:

[48] Wu Ch'eng, *Wu Wen-cheng kung wen-chi* (1756 edition), 11:25b–26a.

[49] *YS* 14:6a. Since the *T'ai-ho lu* was officially discontinued in 1271, the remark made by Professor Riasanovsky that the code of the Chin dynasty was used in the Yuan period until 1291 is misleading. See Riasanovsky, *Fundamental Principles*, p. 280.

[50] *YS* 5:2a and 158:4b.

[51] *YS* 5:21a. This code of 1264 was not the same code as that proposed by Yao Shu, because as late as 1273, Yao's code had not been established. See n. 55 below.

[52] *YS* 146:11b.

[53] *YS* 7:8a.

I hear [the rumor] that Shih T'ien-tse and other elders have discussed and compiled the *Ta Yüan hsin-lü* [*New Code of the Great Yüan*], and now years and months have passed but [I] have not seen a proposal to promulgate the code. Now [I] thoroughly deliberate [and find that] the Chou dynasty followed [the foundation] of the Yin dynasty, and the latter came after the Hsia dynasty. There were things unchangeable. As to *li* (rites), *yüeh* (music), *hsing* (punishment), and *cheng* (government), they are transitional and are to be modified or expanded according to circumstances nor can they be fixed by a [permanent] code. The *T'ai-ho lü* is not a mere Chin code. It adopted supplements from the Five Classics and institutions of the Three Dynasties [i.e., Hsia, Shang, and Chou—P.C.], Han, and T'ang dynasties. If [we] expunge [from the *T'ai-ho lü*] items esteemed by Chin customs as well as laws established by Chin decrees, and then add decrees and rules issued since the beginning of [our] dynasty as well as the established precedents, then a text can be completed and it will become the *Chih-yüan hsin-lü* [*Chih-yüan New Statutes*]. Furthermore, since law is a tool for the maintenance of a nation, the Censorate especially cannot but regard the establishment of laws as essential.[54]

From this proposal, the code deliberated upon since 1262 by Yao Shu and Shih T'ien-tse came to be known as the *Ta Yüan hsin-lü*. In an entry of November 1273 in the *Yüan shih*, Shih-tsu is recorded as referring the code to his Mongolian ministers, saying: "Recently Shih T'ien-tse and Yao Shu drafted a new code and I personally have read it. It is a usable code but you people must examine it carefully to see if one or two [statutes] may be added or subtracted. Let those items be recorded and discussed for future implementation."[55] Although the *Ta Yüan hsin-lü* prepared by Yao Shu and others was not promulgated, it is significant that more than ten years were

---

[54] Wei Ch'u, *Ch'ing-ya chi* (*Ssu-k'u ch'uan-shu chen-pen ch'u-chi ti-erh-chi* edition) (Shanghai: The Commercial Press, 1934), 4:27.

[55] *YS* 8:6b and 126:2b.

spent in preparing the code and that Shih-tsu personally read the text and expr⌣ssed great interest in it.

Wei Ch'u's proposal was not carried out. On another occasion, in 1274/1275, Chao Liang-pi (1217–1286) advised Shih-tsu that it would be advisable to establish unified laws so as to suppress evil bureaucrats.[56] In 1283 Ts'ui Yü (?–1298), then Minister of the Board of Punishments, also submitted a memorial urging the establishment of unified laws.[57] The desire to have a unified Chinese code became intense during the corrupt years of Sang-ko (Sengge) (?–1291).[58] The most powerful minister at court from 1287 until his death in 1291, Sengge once blocked a draft of regulations prepared and proposed by Ho Jung-tsu to halt the corrupt trend of the government. Ho Jung-tsu resigned in protest but was soon summoned to become the *Shang-shu yu-ch'eng* (Right Vice Minister of the Presidential Council).[59] After the purge of Sengge in 1291, the Shang-shu-sheng (Presidential Council) was changed into the Chung-shu-sheng (Secretarial Council), and Ho Jung-tsu was appointed the *Chung-shu yu-ch'eng* (Right Vice Minister of the Secretarial Council).[60] In his new capacity, Ho drafted a code containing ten sections, including those covering "Kung-kuei" (Public Regulations), "Yü-tao" (Prevention of Thefts), and "Li-ts'ai" (Management of Finances).[61] The code was entitled the *Chih-yüan hsin-ko* [*Chih-yüan New Code*] and was promulgated in the 6th moon of the 28th year of the Chih-yüan reign [June 28–July 26, 1291]. A decree was also issued that ordered all officials and commoners to obey the code. Thus, the *Chih-yüan hsin-ko* became the first substantial code of the Yüan dynasty.[62]

---

[56] *YS* 159:13a.

[57] *YS* 173:6a.

[58] *YS* 205:16b–23a. For a discussion of the life of Sang-ko (Sengge), see Herbert Franke, "Seṅ-ge, Das Leben eines uigurischen Staatsbeamten," *Sinica*, 17 (1942), pp. 90–113. See also Tamura Jitsuzō, *Chūgoku seihuku ōchō no kenkyū: chū*, pp. 572–575.

[59] *YS* 168:19a.

[60] *YS* 16:18b, 85:4a, and 168:19b.

[61] *YS* 16:19a, 102:1b, and 168:19b

[62] *YTC* 2:1a. The entry on the *Chih-cheng t'iao-ko* [*Chih-cheng Code*] in the *Ssu-k'u ch'uan-shu tsung-mu t'i-yao* inaccurately cited the year 1284 as the date of the *Chih-yuan hsin-ko* [*Chih-yuan New Code*]. See the *Ssu-k'u ch'uan-shu tsung-mu t'i-yao*, 84:25b.

The *Chih-yüan hsin-ko* has often been confused by scholars
with the *Chih-yüan hsin-fa* of Wang Yün. Both Niida Noboru
and Kobayashi Takashirō thought these two titles referred to
the same code[63] and failed to notice any difference in the two
codes. The *Chih-yüan hsin-fa*, as mentioned before, was proposed by Wang Yün in 1269.[64] Wang's memorial was submitted during his tenure in the Censorate, and in the *Yüan
shih* Wang Yün is recorded as serving in the Censorate from
1269 to 1272.[65] It becomes clear that at least twenty years sepa-
rated the two codes. In 1292, after the promulgation of the *Chih-
yüan hsin-ko*, Wang Yün was still eager to have his earlier ideas
carried out, and he therefore submitted an almost identical
proposal on the promulgation of a code; however, this time
he called it *Hsin-fa* instead of the original *Chih-yüan hsin-fa*.[66]
After the death of Shih-tsu, Wang Yün once again presented
a similar proposal to Ch'eng-tsung for the promulgation of a
code to be called the *Yüan-nien hsin-fa*.[67] The evidence therefore indicates that the *Chih-yüan hsin-ko* was a separate entity
and should be differentiated from the codes proposed by Wang
Yün.

According to Su T'ien-chüeh (1294–1352), the original text
of the *Chih-yüan hsin-ko* contained no more than several thousand
characters, but it was well constructed by Ho Jung-tsu and
met the needs of the society.[68] The complete text of the *Chih-
yüan hsin-ko* has not survived to the present day. I have collected
96 fragments of the code from various Chinese sources. In
accordance with the ten sections of the code, these fragments
can be divided as follows: 1) "Kung-kuei" (Public Regulations)
—twelve articles; 2) "Hsüan-ko" (Standard of Selections)—
twelve articles; 3) "Chih-min" (Governing of the People)—

[63] Niida Noboru, *Chūgoku hōseishi kenkyū: keihō*, p. 532. See also Kobayashi
Takashirō, "Gendai hōseishi zakkō," p. 2.
[64] Wang Yün, 90:3 and "Fu-lu" ("Appendix"): 12a. Professor Abe's statement that this proposal of Wang Yun was dated 1281 is not accurate. See Abe
Takeo, *Gendaishi no kenkyū* [*Historical Studies on the Yuan Period*] (Tokyo: Sōbunsha, 1972), p. 268.
[65] *YS* 167:19b–20a.
[66] See n. 31 above.
[67] See n. 32 above.
[68] Su T'ien-chueh, *Tz'u-hsi wen-kao* (*Shih-yüan ts'ung-shu* edition), 6:7b–8a.

twelve articles; 4) "Li-ts'ai" (Management of Finances)—eight articles; 5) "Fu-i" (Taxes and *Corvée*)—five articles; 6) "K'o-ch'eng" (Taxes and Levies)—eleven articles; 7) "Ts'ang-k'u" (Warehouses)—twelve articles; 8) "Tsao-tso" (Construction and Manufacturing)—eleven articles; 9) "Fang-tao" (Prevention of Thefts)—six articles; and 10) "Ch'a-yü" (Investigation of Cases)—seven articles.[69]

The text of *Chih-yüan hsin-ko* reflects the importance the Yüan government placed on Chinese legal institutions. It also indicates that the code dealt with many aspects of Chinese society and that most of its provisions were ordinances of a noncriminal nature. The code laid the foundation for the future promulgation of other Chinese codes and was observed throughout the dynasty. It also represented the gradual shift away from reliance on Mongolian customs. Interestingly, it appeared some 25 years after the proposal of Hsü Heng who, it will be remembered, had asked that a period of thirty years be allowed for this shift to take effect. The atmosphere of the society was favorable for the adoption of Chinese institutions, and the fall of Sengge in 1291 directly paved the way for Ho Jung-tsu to establish the *Chih-yüan hsin-ko*. Without these changes, the code might not have been so easily promulgated.

This new atmosphere was clearly reflected in a later document dated 1292 in which officials of the Honan and Fukien branches of the Chung-shu-sheng requested that decrees be written in Chinese. In response to this request, it was ordered that the Mongolian language be used in decrees to Honan, and that the Chinese language be used in decrees to Fukien.[70] The new shift marked a departure from the earlier absolute supremacy of the Mongols. This change was also evident in the 1292 memorial of Wang Yün which did not mention the use of the *Jasaγ* as a supplement to the proposed code. Efforts to establish Chinese laws continued to increase even after the death of Shih-tsu in 1294.

---

[69] For a detailed discussion of the *Chih-yuan hsin-ko*, see Part Two below.
[70] *YS* 17:2a.

The Eras of Ch'eng-tsung, Wu-tsung, and Jen-tsung

Upon receipt of a memorial submitted by one Wang Yüeh, which asked for unification of statutes and ordinances,[71] Ch'eng-tsung commanded Ho Jung-tsu, with the assistance of another colleague, to draft laws concerning the appointment of officials. As a man of vision, Ho Jung-tsu was increasingly entrusted with more power and responsibilities. After he had been appointed a Grand Academician, he was commissioned in 1299 to draft statutes and ordinances.[72] Ch'eng-tsung expressed more interest in Chinese laws and said to Ho Jung-tsu in 1300: "Statutes and ordinances are good institutions. The sooner they are unified the better." Ho answered: "I have already selected 380 articles and each article governs three or four items." The Emperor then remarked: "Between ancient times and the present day there are differences which need not be copied; let what is suitable to the present day be adopted."[73] A code was later completed and given the title of *Ta-te lü-ling* [*Statutes and Ordinances of the* Ta-te *Reign*]. Elder statesmen were summoned to discuss the substance of this code. However, because of the death of his son, Ho had to leave the capital before the conclusion of the meeting. He returned to his native place in Kuang-p'ing (in Ta-ming-hsien, now of Hopei province) where he later died at the age of seventy-nine.[74]

Because the *Yüan shih* does not provide the exact dates of the compilation of the *Ta-te lü-ling* nor of the death of Ho Jung-tsu, it becomes difficult to ascertain when the code was actually compiled and when it was submitted to the throne for discussion by elder statesmen. In a memorial dated 1303 of Cheng Chieh-fu, we read:

Formerly the late Emperor [Shih-tsu] ordered statutes be drafted, but no complete text was compiled in time. Re-

[71] *YS* 178:6a.
[72] *YS* 18:16a, 20:3a, and 168:19b.
[73] *YS* 20:6b.
[74] *YS* 168:19b–20a.

cently the *Ta-te lü* was deliberated, but since wrong people were entrusted with the task, it contains many mistakes. Now it is proper to choose among the Censorate and Secretariat people who have comprehended Classics and methods, understood the essence of government, and conceived priority of circumstances, both by consulting the text of ancient and present statutes and decrees as well as orders issued since the establishment of the reigning dynasty [i.e., *Ta Yüan*] by the late Emperor [Shih-tsu], and by selecting from the proper customs of the South and North, to compile for the dynasty a good code which the authorities can follow and which the common people may respect, thus avoiding committing offenses.[75]

Since Cheng's memorial was written in 1303, the code seems to have been compiled between 1300 and 1303. But it is also recorded that Ho Jung-tsu submitted the code to the throne long after its compilation and that he left for Kuang-p'ing before it could be promulgated.[76] Yet, according to another reference in the *Yüan shih*, Ho was still in the capital in 1305 and involved himself in the discussion about sacrifice to the Imperial ancestors.[77] This reference seems to be his last recorded activity in the capital. Thus, it is most likely that Ho submitted the code in 1305 or so.[78]

[75] Yang Shih-ch'i, ed., *Li-tai ming-ch'eng tsou-i* [*Memorials Submitted by Eminent Ministers in Various Dynasties*] (Ming, Yung-lo, *Nei-fu* edition), 67:26b.

[76] *YS* 168:20a.

[77] *YS* 72·6a.

[78] Professor Niida infers from the *Yüan shih* and the memorial of 1303 by Cheng Chieh-fu that the *Ta-te lu-ling* [*Statutes and Ordinances of the Ta-te Reign*] was compiled between 1300 and 1303 and was probably submitted to the throne in 1302 or 1303. See Niida Noboru, *Chūgoku hōseishi kenkyū: hō to kanshū, hō to dōtoku* [*A Study of Chinese Legal History: Law and Customs, Law and Morality*] (Tokyo. Tokyo University Press, 1964), p. 185. Because of the reference to the activity of Ho Jung-tsu in the capital in 1305, however, the *Ta-te lu-ling* might well have been submitted to the throne after the appearance of Ch'eng's memorial. If this is the case, the date of the memorial does not necessarily make it impossible for the *Ta-te lu-ling* to have been promulgated after 1303. Nor can it support Niida's claim that the text was submitted to the throne in 1302 or 1303.

Despite the arrangements made by Ch'eng-tsung and Ho Jung-tsu, the *Yüan shih* reveals that the *Ta-te lü-ling* was not promulgated before Ho's death. Nor is there any evidence that it was ever promulgated after his death. Although the joint efforts of Ch'eng-tsung and Ho Jung-tsu failed to establish this substantial code at its last stage, a collective text of laws and precedents was compiled during the Ta-te reign (1297–1307), and it was given the title of *Ta-te tien-chang* [*Institutions of the Ta-te Reign*]. Although the exact date of this text is not certain, in a document dated 1303 it is recorded that the authorities of Kiangsi proposed the drafting of a text which would include laws and precedents established between the Chung-t'ung reign and the current day.[79] On the basis of this reference, Niida Noboru has therefore suggested that the *Ta-te tien-chang* was compiled in or after 1303.[80] According to the *Yüan shih*, however, after Wu-tsung (Külüg Qaγan) succeeded to the throne on the 21st day of the 5th moon of the 11th year of the Ta-te reign [June 21, 1307],[81] the Chung-shu-sheng officials submitted a memorial in the 12th moon of that year [December 26, 1307–January 23, 1308] which said:

> Statutes and ordinances are urgent matters for governing the state and are to be modified or expanded in accordance with circumstances. Shih-tsu once issued an edict ordering that the *T'ai-ho lü* of the Chin be not applied and that elder ministers, who thoroughly understand laws, consult [laws of] the ancient and present times so as to establish new [legal] institutions. So far it has not been carried out. We, your subjects, think that statutes and ordinances are serious matters and should not be lightly discussed. [We therefore] request that the *t'iao-ko* put into practice since the succession of Shih-tsu to the throne be examined and

---

[79] *YTC* "Mu-lu" ("Contents"): 1a.

[80] Niida Noboru, *Chūgoku hōseishi kenkyū: hō to kanshū, hō to dōtoku*, pp. 188–189.

[81] *YS* 22:3a. Professor Niida, however, inaccurately cites the 1st moon of the 11th year of the Ta-te reign [February 3–March 4, 1307] as the date of the succession. See Niida Noboru, *Chūgoku hōseishi kenkyū: hō to kanshū, hō to dōtoku*, p. 192.

unified [into one code] so that [it] may be observed and put into practice.[82]

When this plan was proposed, permission was granted to implement it. Therefore, on the basis of this document, it seems logical to assume that the text was compiled in or after the 11th year of the Ta-te reign (i.e., in or after 1307), rather than the year 1303 as suggested by Niida. This interpretation is further supported by two collateral facts. First, since a fragment of the *Ta-te tien-chang* found in the *Yung-lo ta-tien* was dated mid-1302,[83] it is unlikely that the compilation occurred as soon afterward as 1303: a much later date seems more reasonable. Second, the very fact that Ho Jung-tsu was still in the capital in 1305 also suggests that it is unlikely that the *Ta-te tien-chang* would be compiled while the *Ta-te lü-ling* was still under deliberation. It seems more natural that only after the failure to promulgate the *Ta-te lü-ling* and the growing awareness of the technical difficulties in compiling statutes were efforts made to draft a collective text of laws and precedents. The *Ta-te tien-chang* was therefore compiled under these circumstances which led to the publication of the text in or after 1307.[84]

The complete text of the *Ta-te tien-chang* does not survive today, but some fragments have been preserved in the *Yung-*

[82] *YS* 22:19b–20a.

[83] Iwai Hirosato, "Gendai keizaishi jō no ichi shin shiryō" ("A New Historical Document Concerning Economic History of the Yüan Dynasty"), Baikeikai, ed., *Yamashita sensei kanreki tōyōshi ronbun shū* [*Collected Essays on Oriental History in Honor of Mr. Yamashita on the Occasion of His 60th Birthday*] (Tokyo: Rokumeikan, 1938), pp. 163–167.

[84] If my theory is correct, then the *Ta-te lu-ling* and the *Ta-te tien-chang* [*Institutions of the Ta-te Reign*] apparently are two different entities. Consequently, the remark made by Shen Chia-pen that the *Yüan tien-chang* contains many items from the *Ta-te lu-ling* is misleading. It would be more appropriate to say that the *Yüan tien-chang* contains many items from the *Ta-te tien-chang*. For Shen's discussion, see Shen Chia-pen, *Shen Chi-i hsien-sheng i-shu chia-pien* [*Bequested Writings of Mr. Shen Chi-i, First Series*] (Peking, 1929), *Lü-ling* [*Statutes and Ordinances*], 8:5a. Professor Niida, though having no evidence to prove that the *Ta-te lü-ling* and the *Ta-te tien-chang* were identical, did not agree with Shen's remark and therefore suggested that the reference to the *Ta-te lü-ling* be changed to the *Ta-te tien-chang* in this particular remark. See Niida Noboru, *Chūgoku hōseishi kenkyū: hō to kanshū, hō to dōtoku*, p. 189.

lo ta-tien and the *Yüan tien-chang*.[85] According to one reference in the funeral inscription of Mu Wan, the scale of various punishments given in the *Ta-te tien-chang* was not too severe.[86] In view of the failure to establish a permanent code, officials of the Shang-shu-sheng again submitted in 1309 a proposal,[87] saying:

> The territory of [our] country is vast and the people are numerous, exceeding what previous dynasties had. Former and later codes as well as precedents of [our] various reigns are not unified; and law-enforcement bureaucrats impose light or severe [punishments] at will. [We therefore] request that, among 9,000 items of governmental ordinances established since the time of Shih-tsu, multifarious parts be cut out so that they can result in unification and be compiled into a permanent institution.[88]

The proposal was accepted by Wu-tsung, but before a code could be compiled, he died in 1311. It is, however, interesting to note that by the early fourteenth century many ordinances and precedents had been established to meet the changing society and that they had been collected into huge volumes of documents.

Jen-tsung (Buyantu Qaγan) succeeded to the throne on April 7, 1311.[89] He then instructed the Chung-shu-sheng officials to collect codes and regulations.[90] Elder ministers who thoroughly understood the laws were selected to examine and modify those materials so as to unify them into a code.[91] In the same year, Hsieh Jang (1246–1311), the Minister of the Board of Punishments, said to Jen-tsung:

[85] Iwai Hirosato, "Gendai keizaishi jō no ichi shin shiryō," pp. 81–87.

[86] Hsu Yu-jen, *Yüan Hsü Wen-cheng kung Chih-cheng chi* (*Chung-chou ming-hsien wen-piao nei-chi* edition), 59:21a.

[87] The Chung-shu-sheng (Secretarial Council) was changed to the Shang-shu-sheng (Presidential Council) in 1309. See *YS* 23:7a and 85:3b–4b.

[88] *YS* 23:9a.

[89] *YS* 24:6b.

[90] The Shang-shu-sheng was changed back to the Chung-shu-sheng in 1311. See *YS* 24:6b and 85:3b–4b.

[91] *YS* 24:7a.

From ancient times to the present day, those who had the country have all had statutes to supplement their rulings. How could a conscientious holy dynasty like ours have no laws to follow and thus let bureaucrats indulge themselves and people suffer evilness?[92]

Jen-tsung gladly accepted Hsieh's advice and ordered the Chung-shu-sheng to prepare a collection of legal documents; Hsieh himself was appointed to examine and edit those documents. In 1315 Jen-tsung commanded Li Meng (1255–1321) and other officials to classify and edit codes of previous reigns.[93] In addition to his concern about the Chinese codes, Jen-tsung's interest in Chinese institutions was demonstrated by his revival of the traditional Chinese examination system in 1315. Since this was the first such examination to be held during the Yüan dynasty, it not only reflected the significant transformation of Mongolian customs into Chinese institutions, but also represented an effective means for the Chinese people to obtain more power and promote further implementation of various Chinese institutions.

Although no substantial code was compiled from those legal documents during the reign of Jen-tsung, the collection was later edited and expanded into the *Yüan tien-chang* in the reign of Ying-tsung (Gegen Qayan). Meanwhile, another trend relating to the establishment of laws concerning the official disciplines was appearing. In the *Yüan shih*, we read:

After Shih-tsu had conquered the Sung dynasty and the territory was unified, [he] simplified and expunged multifarious and stringent [laws]. For the first time a new code was established and issued to the authorities and entitled *Chih-yüan hsin-ko*. In the time of Jen-tsung, again, the codes, precedents, and regulations concerning official disciplines were classified and compiled into a text entitled *Feng-hsien hung-kang* [*Extensive Principles of Disciplines*]. As to the time of Ying-tsung, [he] also commanded ministers

[92] *YS* 176:13b–14a.
[93] *YS* 25:7b.

24

and Confucian scholar-officials to take hold of the former book [i.e., the *Feng-hsien hung-kang*] and effect modification as well as expansion. The text was completed and entitled *Ta Yüan t'ung-chih* [*Comprehensive Institutions of the Great Yüan*]. The text's outline had three [categories]; the first was *shao-chih* (decretal regulations), the second was *t'iao-ko* (articles and codes), and the third was *tuan-li* (decided precedents). *Shao-chih* comprised 94 items, *t'iao-ko* 1,151 items, and *tuan-li* 717 items. In general, it just compiled the regulations and precedents established since [the time of] Shih-tsu.[94]

The above reference specifies that the *Feng-hsien hung-kang*, compiled during the time of Jen-tsung, was the source of the *Ta Yüan t'ung-chih*. Although the author and the date of its compilation are not mentioned in this reference, the *Yüan shih* records elsewhere, in the biography of Chao Shih-yen (1260–1336), that Chao was the author of the *Feng-hsien hung-kang*.[95] Because Chao's work was completed during the reign of Jen-tsung, its latest date must be 1320, the year in which the Emperor died.[96] In addition, the preface to this work was written by Ma Tsu-ch'ang (1279–1338) at the time when Ma served in the government as a *chien-ch'a yü-shih* (investigating censor).[97] Since the *Yüan shih* records that Ma Tsu-ch'ang became a *chien-ch'a yü-shih* after 1315,[98] and that by 1320 he no longer held this post,[99] the date of the preface must fall between 1315 and 1320. Moreover, because Chao's work dealt mainly with administration and official discipline, and because the preface was also written by a censor, it seems most likely that the *Feng-hsien hung-kang* was compiled by Chao Shih-yen during his service in the Censorate. Furthermore,

[94] *YS* 102:1b.
[95] *YS* 180:9b.
[96] *YS* 26:19b.
[97] Ma Tsu-ch'ang, "*Feng-hsien hung-kang* hsü" ("Preface to *The Extensive Principles of Discipline*"), *Kuo-ch'ao wen-lei*, 36:3a.
[98] *YS* 143:1b.
[99] Ma Tsu-ch'ang became a magistrate in Kai-p'ing when T'ieh-mu-tieh-erh (Temüder) returned to the ministerial post in 1320. See *YS* 143:2a.

Chao himself served as a *yü-shih chung-ch'eng* (Vice Censor-in-Chief) from 1315 to 1316 or 1317.[100] This finding further suggests that the text was probably completed by Chao between 1315 and 1317, thus narrowing the upper and lower limits of its date. Professor Kobayashi has also been interested in the date of this text, but, being unable to ascertain the exact date himself, he simply says that Chao died in 1336 at the age of seventy-seven and that the text had most likely been completed in Chao's later years when his scholarship was mature.[101] However, this argument, linking the author's age and maturity of scholarship to the date of the text, is unrealistic, because such a relationship does not necessarily follow.

In the "*Ta Yüan t'ung-chih* hsü" ("Preface to *The Comprehensive Institutions of the Great Yüan*") by Po-chu-lu Chung (1279–1338), it is stated that soon after the succession of Jentsung to the throne, steps were taken to classify and edit a text which had three categories—namely, *shao-chih*, *t'iao-ko*, and *tuan-li*—and that the text was completed in the 5th moon of the 3rd year of the Yen-yu reign [May 22–June 19, 1316] and was submitted for official discussion. The promulgation of this text was delayed for another eight years, until 1323, when it was finally expanded and published under the title of *Ta Yüan t'ung-chih*.[102] Owing to the expansion of the 1316 text into the *Ta Yüan t'ung-chih*, the text was confused with the *Feng-hsien hung-kang*, for the *Yüan shih* mistakenly regards the latter as the origin of the *Ta Yüan t'ung-chih*. For instance, Professor Okamoto Keiji believes that the text of 1316 was identical to the *Feng-hsien hung-kang*.[103] In a commentary written by Ts'ang Pi-te on the *Yüan tien-chang* (occasioned by the reproduction of its Yüan edition arranged by the National Palace Museum in Taipei in 1972), the *Yüan shih's* remark

---

[100] *YS* 180:7. Although it is not certain whether Chao Shih-yen was still at the Censorate in 1317, he was not a censor in 1318.

[101] Kobayashi Takashirō, "Gendai hōseishi zakkō," p. 11.

[102] Po-chu-lu Chung, "*Ta Yüan t'ung-chih* hsü" ("Preface to *The Comprehensive Institutions of the Great Yuan*"), *Kuo-ch'ao wen-lei*, 36:7.

[103] Kotake Fumio and Okamoto Keiji, eds., *Genshi keihōshi no kenkyū yakuchū* [*An Annotated Translation of the "Treatise on Punishment and Law" in the Yüan shih*] (Tokyo: Kyōiku shoseki, 1962), pp. 17–19.

concerning the origin of the *Ta Yüan t'ung-chih* was also accepted without question, thus perpetuating the common notion that the *Feng-hsien hung-kang* was the source of the *Ta Yüan t'ung-chih*.[104]

There are, however, differences between the *Feng-hsien hung-kang* and the text of 1316. First, the *Feng-hsien hung-kang* was compiled by Chao Shih-yen and published for the public, whereas the text of 1316 was compiled by the officials of Chung-shu-sheng but not published until its revision in 1323. Second, the *Feng-hsien hung-kang* contained legal matters primarily related to official discipline, and the limited nature as well as the size of this book might not have been sufficient to provide a framework for a collection as comprehensive and huge as the *Ta Yüan t'ung-chih*.[105] The text of 1316, on the other hand, included general legal documents from the beginning of the dynasty and also had the same three distintive categories (i.e., *shao-chih*, *t'iao-ko*, and *tuan-li*) as the *Ta Yüan t'ung-chih*. These differences therefore suggest that the *Feng-hsien hung-kang* and the text of 1316 were not identical.

The text of 1316 probably originated in the order of 1311 in which Emperor Jen-tsung commanded the Chung-shu-sheng officials to establish a code. The editors of the "Hsing-fa chih" (Treatise on Punishment and Law) of the *Yüan shih* might have mistaken the *Feng-hsien hung-kang* for the text of 1316 and consequently remarked that the *Ta Yüan t'ung-chih* was derived from the *Feng-hsien hung-kang*. The possible negligence of the *Yüan shih* editors is further illuminated by the fact that Chao Shih-yen, the author of the *Feng-hsien hung-kang*, was not mentioned in the preface to the *Ta Yüan t'ung-chih* written by Po-chu-lu Chung. Po-chu-lu Chung not only took part in the compilation of the *Ta Yüan t'ung-chih* but also was a contemporary of Chao Shih-yen and was himself an Investigating Censor in 1318.[106] Thus, he certainly knew Chao and Chao's

[104] *Ta Yüan sheng-cheng kuo-ch'ao tien-chang* (*Yuan tien-chang*) (Yüan edition; reprinted by National Palace Museum, Taipei, 1972) (hereafter cited as *YTC** in order to distingush it from the 1908 edition of the *YTC*), "Pa":3–4.
[105] Kobayashi Takashirō, "Gendai hōseishi zakkō," pp. 8–10.
[106] *YS* 26:12b and 183:12b–13b.

book well. Should the *Feng-hsien hung-kang* have contributed significantly to the *Ta Yüan t'ung-chih*, Po-chu-lu Chung would have mentioned Chao's name and book in his preface. In any case, the steps taken by the Mongolian rulers and the Chinese officials in preparing various Chinese codes during this second stage succeeded in providing a solid foundation for the further development of codes in the later years of the Yüan dynasty. The gradual implementation of Chinese institutions and the increasingly changing atmosphere of the second stage reached their peak in the third stage, when the Chinese cultural orientation of the dynasty came to full bloom.

The Third Stage (1321–1368)

Ying-tsung succeeded to the throne on April 15, 1320.[107] Being a man of letters, he had great admiration for Chinese culture and respect for Chinese officials such as Fang Hsüanling (578–648) and Tu Ju-hui (589–630) of the T'ang. He also often gave his calligraphy to his ministers.[108] Ying-tsung was very much interested in promoting the establishment of Chinese legal institutions. In 1322 Li Tuan, a censor, suggested to the throne that ordinances should be codified to prevent bureaucrats from committing evil acts and to give the authorities proper guidance. Li's proposal was accepted by Ying-tsung.[109] In 1323 Pai-chu (Baijǔ) (?–1323) also stated in a memorial that the "former code" should be edited and published as the *T'ung-chih* [*Comprehensive Institutions*].[110] This "former code" refers to the text of 1316 which was, as discussed above, originally compiled during the reign of Jen-tsung, but was not promulgated. In response to this memorial, several elder statesmen were summoned by Ying-tsung to arrange the details. The final version of the code was completed and promulgated in 1321 under the title of *Ta Yüan t'ung-chih*.[111]

[107] *YS* 27:4a.

[108] Yoshikawa Kōjirō, *Yoshikawa Kōjirō zenshū dai jūgo kan* [*Collected Works of Yoshikawa Kōjirō, Vol. Fifteen*] (Tokyo. Chikuma shobō, 1969), pp. 240–246.

[109] *YS* 28:8a.

[110] *YS* 137:16a.

[111] *YS* 28:12b. Names of participating statesmen were given by Po-chu-lu Chung. See *Kuo-ch'ao wen-lei*, 36:7b. See also *YS* 176:2b, 178:11, and 183:13b.

The *Ta Yüan t'ung-chih* was one of the most substantial codes of the Yüan dynasty. It had 717 items of *tuan-li*, 1,151 items of *t'iao-ko*, 94 items of *shao-she* (decrees and amnesties), and 557 items of *ling-lei* (miscellaneous ordinances).[112] The *Ta Yüan t'ung-chih* has not survived in its entirety. A Ming edition of its *t'iao-ko* section was, however, preserved and reprinted in 1930 by the National Peking Library under the title of *T'ung-chih t'iao-ko* [*Code of Comprehensive Institutions*].[113] The *t'iao-ko* and the *tuan-li* of the *Ta Yüan t'ung-chih* had 27 and 11 sections, respectively.[114] The titles of the sections and the style of the code resembled the *T'ai-ho lü* so strongly that Abe Takeo suggested that indirectly the origin of the *Ta Yüan t'ung-chih* was the *T'ai-ho lü*.[115] The text marked a mature stage in Yüan legal history because of its substantial content and its adoption of the structure of the Chinese traditional code as represented in the *T'ai-ho lü*. Referring to this code, Wu Ch'eng aptly commented:

> When the ancient code is compared with the new book [i.e., the *Ta Yüan t'ung-chih*], they are different in both sentences and expressions but their meanings are mostly similar. With regard to the ancient code, it is actually used [in the new text] in secret, but is not used openly. The name [of the ancient code] has also been abandoned but the essence has not been abandoned. Why is it so? [It is because] the *chih-shao* and the *t'iao-ko* are equivalent to the former *ch'ih* (decrees), *ling* (ordinances), and *ko-shih* (codes and regulations). The eleven sections of the *tuan-li*, namely, "Wei-chin," "Chih-chih," "Hu-hun," "Chiu-

---

[112] *YS* 28:12b. The number of items in the *ling-lei* (miscellaneous ordinances) category is not recorded in the *Yüan shih*, although the number of other categories is recorded there. See *YS* 102:1b.

[113] This text has 22 *chüan* in 5 *ts'e*.

[114] Shen Chung-wei, *Hsing-t'ung-fu shu* [*Commentaries on the Unified Code in Rhyme*] (*Chen-pi-lo ts'ung-shu* edition, Peking, 1913), p. 4.

[115] Abe Takeo, *Gendaishi no kenkyū*, pp. 290–292. Since the *Ta Yüan t'ung-chih* [*Comprehensive Institutions of the Great Yüan*] came indirectly from the text of 1316 which in turn had adopted legal materials from a series of earlier codes such as the *Ta-te lu-ling* and the *Ta-te tien-chang*, it might have already resembled the *T'ai-ho lü* either through its own choice or through the existing style of the *Ta-te lü-ling* or the *Ta-te tien-chang*. Consequently, in this context, Abe's remark requires some qualifications.

k'u," "Shan-hsing," "Tsei-tao," "Tou-sung," "Cha-wei," "Tsa-lü," "Pu-wang," and "Tuan-yü," are classified and edited according to the same sequence of sections in the ancient code. The ancient code is bound to be followed and therefore, even if [we] wish to be against it, it becomes impossible to be against. Is it not true that [the ancient code] is used in secret but not used openly, and that its name is abandoned but its essence is not abandoned?[116]

Because of its nature and substance, the *Ta Yüan t'ung-chih* was greatly praised by Wu Ch'eng and others for its significant achievement. With regard to the incorporation of Chinese cultural elements into the code, it was under a provision of the *Ta Yüan t'ung-chih* that traditional *wu-fu* (five degrees of mourning) regulations were for the first time officially enforced in the Yüan dynasty.[117] The establishment of the mourning regulations was a significant development. Earlier, Shih-tsu and other Mongolian rulers had simply taken a position of non interference toward this time-honored Chinese custom. Although Chinese officials had been ordered in 1304 to observe the mourning regulations by temporarily resigning from their posts during the mourning periods, the legal provision to enforce compulsory mourning came only at this time, and thereafter Chinese officials were compelled to leave their posts while observing mourning.

During the time of Ying-tsung, there was another achievement, namely, the publication of the *Yüan tien-chang*. Its text was compiled during the reign of Jen-tsung and included codes and regulations issued from the early reign of Shih-tsu to the 4th year of the Yen-yu reign [January 14, 1317–February 1, 1318]. The text, probably compiled by the local government in Kiangsi or by private individuals, was based on the *Ta-te tien-chang* and other recent codifications. By the 2nd year of the Chih-chih reign [January 18, 1322–February 5, 1323] of Ying-tsung, the text was said to have been in circulation for

---

[116] Wu Ch'eng, 11:26.
[117] *Kuo-ch'ao wen-lei*, 42:3b–4a.

years.[118] Since the present version of the *Yüan tien-chang* contains entries dated up to the 7th year of the Yen-yu reign,[119] with some even dated as late as the 11th moon of the year [December 1–29, 1320], the current text must have been compiled no earlier than December 1, 1320, and no later than the 6th moon of the 2nd year of the Chih-chih reign [July 5–August 12, 1322], when the *Yüan tien-chang hsin-chi* [*New Supplements to the Yüan tien-chang*] was compiled.[120] The *Yüan tien-chang hsin-chi* had two functions: one was to compile codes and regulations established since the beginning of the Chih-chih reign; the other was to assemble and classify new precedents heretofore unpublished. It was also planned that later precedents established after the 2nd year of the Chih-chih reign would be subsequently added to the text.

The *Yüan tien-chang* proper has sixty *chüan* and is divided into ten parts: "Shao-ling" (Decrees), "Sheng-cheng" (Holy Government), "Ch'ao-kang" (Court Principles), "T'ai-kang" (Censorate Principles), "Li-pu" (Board of Civil Office), "Hu-pu" (Board of Revenue and Population), "Li-pu (Board of Rites), "Ping-pu" (Board of War), "Hsing-pu" (Board of Punishments), and "Kung-pu" (Board of Public Works). The text consists of a huge collection of codes, ordinances, precedents, cases, and bureaucratic notes, thus reflecting the rich variety of the legal and social life of the Yüan dynasty.[121]

---

[118] *YTCHC* "Kang-mu" ("Outlines"): 1a.

[119] Niida Noboru, *Chūgoku hōseishi kenkyū: hō to kanshū, hō to dōtoku*, pp. 191 and 195, n. 10.

[120] *YTCHC* "Mu-lu" ("Contents"): 11b–12a.

[121] By comparing the number of articles in the *Yüan tien-chang* (2,379 articles) with that of the *T'ang Code* (500 articles), Professor Riasanovsky concludes that the Yüan codification was fuller and more developed than that of the T'ang. See Riasanovsky, *Fundamental Principles*, p. 295. However, it is misleading to compare these two texts in such a manner. To be sure, the *Yüan tien-chang* has a great body of articles. The *T'ang Code*, however, was not the only codification of the T'ang dynasty; indeed, there were several thousand ordinances and regulations issued during the T'ang. Although the Yüan codification may be fuller and more developed, a comparison cannot be made by citing the number of articles in the two texts. Besides, the *Yüan tien-chang* and the *T'ang Code* are also different in nature and style. For the codification of T'ang laws, see Niida Noboru, *Tōryō shūi* [*Remnants of the T'ang Ordinances*] (Tokyo: Tokyo University Press, 1933).

Many items collected in the *Yüan tien-chang* were written in the style of Chinese bureaucratic documents by governmental clerks and bureaucrats who were familiar with administrative and legal matters during the Yüan dynasty.[122] Colloquial language was also prevalent in the text.[123] In addition, many items were translated directly from documents issued in the Mongolian language.[124] Owing to these special features, the *Yüan tien-chang* was often downgraded by traditional Confucian scholars. In one criticism, for instance, we read:

All that is recorded [in the *Yüan tien-chang*] is, however, in the style of bureaucratic documents and, among them, seven- to eight-tenths are also mixed with colloquial language, common sayings, and vulgar expressions distorting the important essence. Its form is furthermore tangled and is loose without trace or order.[125]

Yao Nai (1731–1815), a great Ch'ing scholar, also echoed the above criticism and remarked with contempt that the expressions in the *Yüan tien-chang* were minute, rustic, and confusing.[126] In fact, however, this "unusual" documentary style of Chinese in the *Yüan tien-chang* is basically a special version of a (lost) Mongolian language and is a reflection of Chinese vocabularies arranged according to Mongolian syntax. The narrative and colloquial nature of these documents has, more significantly, provided modern scholars with the most original and thorough information about the state and society of the Yüan dynasty. The very fact that most of the other Yüan legal

---

[122] For a discussion of this particular style of the *Yüan tien-chang*, see Yoshikawa Kōjirō, "Gen tenshō no buntai" ("The Style of Documentary Chinese in the Yuan tien-chang"), *Tōhō gakuhō* (Kyoto), 24 (1954), pp. 367–396.

[123] For a discussion of some colloquial terms in the *Yüan tien-chang*, see Yang Lien-sheng, "Marginalia to the Yuan tien-chang," *HJAS*, 19 (1956), pp. 42–51.

[124] For a discussion of this particular style of the *Yüan tien-chang*, see Yoshikawa Kōjirō and Tanaka Kenji, *Gen tenshō no buntai* [*The Style of Documentary Chinese in the Yuan tien-chang*], pp. 47–161. This book is included as a supplement but in separate book form in Iwamura Shinobu and Tanaka Kenji, eds., *Gen tenshō keibu dai issatsu* [*Board of Punishments in the Institutions of the Yuan Dynasty, Vol. One*] (Kyoto: Kyoto University Press, 1964).

[125] *Ssu-k'u ch'uan-shu tsung-mu t'i-yao*, 83:2b.

[126] Yao Nai, *Hsi-pao-hsien shu-lu* (*Hsi-pao-hsien i-shu* edition, 1879), 2:5b–6a.

32

materials do not survive today has also made the *Yüan tien-chang* an absolutely indispensable text.[127]

After the great achievement of the Yüan leaders in compiling the *Yüan tien-chang* and the *Ta Yüan t'ung-chih*, the trend of codification continued. T'ai-ting Ti (Yesun Temür Qaɣan) ordered in 1324 that copies of the *Ta Yüan t'ung-chih* be distributed to officials, thus giving full recognition to the importance of this Chinese text.[128] In 1328, Wen-tsung (Tuɣ Temür Qaɣan) commanded that the *Ching-shih ta-tien* [*Great Institutions of Statecraft*] be compiled.[129] As a man of letters, Wen-tsung was also very much fascinated by Chinese culture. He followed the earlier practice of T'ai-ting Ti and allowed Mongolian officials to observe their mourning. He also developed excellent taste in Chinese arts such as painting and calligraphy. In 1329 he established the famous Kuei-chang-ko (The Academy of the Kuei-chang Pavilion) to house his scholars as well as his vast collection of paintings, calligraphy, curios, and books. He often attended lectures on the Classics and Confucian learning given at the Kuei-chang-ko and cultivated his own literary skills.[130] It was under these favorable conditions that the compilation of the *Ching-shih ta-tien* was undertaken. Special collective efforts were made by Mongolian and Chinese officials and scholars to expedite the arrangement of the huge number of documents.[131] The whole collection was finally completed in 1331 and was submitted to the throne in the 3rd moon of the 3rd year of the Chih-shun reign [March 27–April 25, 1322].[132]

[127] For a discussion of various editions of the text, see Ch'en Yüan, *Shen-k'o Yüan tien-chang chiao-pu* (Peking: Peking University Press, 1931), "Chuan-shou" (Prologue): 1a–2b. See also Kurata Junnosuke, "Gen tenshō no ryūden" ("Bibliographical Notes on the *Yüan tien-chang*"), *Tōhō gakuhō* (Kyoto), 24 (1954), pp. 443–460.

[128] YS 29:8a.

[129] YS 33:17b.

[130] YS 32:26. For a discussion of the interest Wen-tsung (Tuɣ Temur Qaɣan) had in Chinese culture, see Yoshikawa Kōjirō, *Yoshikawa Kōjirō zenshū dai jūgo kan*, pp. 246–276.

[131] YS 34:1a and 34:3b.

[132] YS 35:16b. See also Ou-yang Hsüan, "Chin *Ching-shih ta-tien* piao" ("Dedication of *The Great Institutions of Statecraft* to the Emperor"), *Kuo-ch'ao wen-lei*, 16:12b–13a.

The *Ching-shih ta-tien* was a documentary survey of various institutions, that followed the pattern of the *Hui-yao [Summaries]* of the T'ang and Sung dynasties. It also symbolized a further acceptance of Chinese culture. Although it is not a legal code, its "Hsien-tien" (Judicial Institutions) is of great importance to Yüan legal history.[133] The editors of the *Ching-shih ta-tien* claimed to have collected as many documents as possible, and the policy for the "Hsien-tien" section was to incorporate the currently existing regulations into the main body of the section and to record all outdated legal materials in its appendix.[134] Pursuant to this policy, the *Yüan tien-chang* and the *Ta Yüan t'ung-chih*, as the complete and existing sources of law of the time, naturally served as the major sources of material for the "Hsien-tien" section. Although no complete text of the *Ching-shih ta-tien* or its original "Hsien-tien" section has survived, it is known that the "Hsien-tien" section comprised 22 subsections and one appendix. The subsections were: "Ming-li" (Terms and General Principles), "Wei-chin" (Imperial Guards and Prohibitions), "Chih-chih" (Administrative Regulations), "Chi-ling" (Ordinances of Sacrifice), "Hsüeh-kuei" (Regulations of Studies), "Chün-lü" (Statutes of Army), "Hu-hun" (Families and Marriages), "Shih-huo" (Food and Goods), "Ta-o" (Grand Abominations), "Chien-fei" (Evilness and Misdeeds), "Tao-tsei" (Thefts and Violence), "Cha-wei" (Deceptions and Frauds), "Su-sung" (Complaints and Suits), "Tou-o" (Conflict and Battery), "Sha-shan" (Homicides and Injuries), "Chin-ling" (Ordinances of Prohibitions), "Tsa-fan" (Miscellaneous Offenses), "Pu-wang" (Arrests and Escapes), "Hsü-hsing" (Leniency of Punishments), "Ping-fang" (Redressment of Wrong Decisions), "She-yu" (Amnesties), and "Yü-k'ung" (Empty Prisons).[135]

The "Hsien-tien" section was almost identical to the text of

[133] For details of the sections in the *Ching-shih ta-tien*, see "*Ching-shih ta-tien hsu-lu*" ("Preface to *The Great Institutions of Statecraft*"), *Kuo-ch'ao wen-lei*, 40:1a–42:19b. See also Yu Chi, *Tao-yuan hsueh-ku lu* (*Ssu-pu ts'ung-k'an* edition), 5:17a–18a.
[134] "Hsien-tien tsung-hsu" ("General Preface to the 'Judicial Institutions'"), *Kuo-ch'ao wen-lei*, 42:1a–2a.
[135] *Ibid.*

the *T'ang Code.* Wen-tsung was so impressed by the similarity that he commented to his officials: "Is it not the *T'ang Code!*"[136] More significantly, the arrangement of the subsections of the "Hsien-tien," with very slight changes, was repeated in the "Hsing-fa chih" of the *Yüan shih.* The "Hsing-fa chih" virtually retained the titles of the first 21 subsections of the "Hsien-tien" as its own subsections.[137] The relation between the "Hsien-tien" and the "Hsing-fa chih" has consequently become a subject of scholarly concern. The "Hsing-fa chih" was regarded by one source as coming from the *Chih-yüan hsin-ko,*[138] but was regarded by other scholars, such as Shen Chia-pen (1840–1913), as coming from the *Ta Yüan t'ung-chih.*[139] It was also often suggested that it derived from the code of 1350.[140] From the interpretation of Professor Abe Takeo, however, it is now well established that the "Hsing-fa chih" derived from the "Hsien-tien" section, just as many other parts of the *Yüan shih* came from corresponding sections of the *Ching-shih ta-tien.*[141]

Besides the important achievement of the "Hsien-tien," there

---

[136] *YS* 181:16b. See also Ou-yang Hsüan, *Kuei-chai wen-chi* (*Ssu-pu ts'ung-k'an* edition), 10:3a.

[137] The "Hsing-fa chih" of the *Yüan shih* contains 21 subsections. For details of these terms, see *YS* 102:2b–105:29b. For French translations of these terms, see Paul Ratchnevsky, *Un Code des Yuan* (Paris: Librairie Ernest Leroux, 1937), p. vi. It is, however, misleading for Ratchnevsky to regard the "Hsing-fa chih" as a code; it is a survey of legal institutions rather than a code in the strict sense.

[138] *Ch'in-ting Hsü Wen-hsien t'ung-k'ao* (Che-chiang shu-chü, 1887), 135:34a–36b.

[139] Shen Chia-pen, *Shen Chi-i hsien-sheng i-shu chia-pen, Lü-ling,* 8:6a. See also Higashigawa Tokuji, *Shina hōseishi ron* [*On Chinese Legal History*] (Tokyo: Rinji Taiwan kyūkan chōsakai, 1916), p. 372.

[140] Asami Rintarō, "Gen no *Keisei daiten* narabini *Genritsu*" ("*The Great Institutions of Statecraft* of the Yuan Dynasty and the *Yuan Code*"), *Hōgaku kyōkai zasshi,* Vol. 41, No. 7 (1923), pp. 13–18.

[141] Abe Takeo, *Gendaishi no kenkyū,* pp. 253–271 and 304–306. It has been established that the *Ching-chih ta-tien* was the primary source of the "Chih" (Treatise) and "Piao" (Table) sections of the *Yüan shih.* See Ichimura Sanjirō, *Shinashi kenkyū* [*A Study of Chinese History*] (Tokyo: Shunjūsha, 1939), pp. 439–458. See also Herbert Franke, *Geld und Wirtschaft in China unter der Mongolenherrschaft* (Leipzig: Otto Harrassowitz, 1949), pp. 25–34, and Herbert Franz Schurmann, *Economic Structure of the Yüan Dynasty* (Cambridge, Mass.: Harvard University Press, 1956), pp. ix–xi.

also existed during this period a small legal text entitled *Ch'eng-hsien kang-yao* [*Essential Outlines of Established Principles*]. It was a concise book for handy reference to current legal materials and precedents. The complete text has not survived, but it is recorded as comprising forty *chüan* in five *ts'e*.[142] Some of its fragments contain references to the *Ta Yüan t'ung-chih*, but there is not a single reference to the *Chih-cheng t'iao-ko* [*Chih-cheng Code*] of 1346. In view of this feature, Abe Takeo claimed that the *Ch'eng-hsien kang-yao* must have been produced before the *Chih-cheng t'iao-ko* but after the *Ta Yüan t'ung-chih*.[143] Since Niida also found some references in the text dated 1323 and 1324, the date of the *Ch'eng-hsien kang-yao* can be narrowed to between 1324 and 1346.[144]

The establishment of the *Chih-cheng t'iao-ko* in 1346 was intended to ease the discrepancy between the changing society and the outdated *Ta Yüan t'ung-chih*. As early as 1333, the inadequacy of the *Ta Yüan t'ung-chih* was pointed out in a memorial to the throne by Su T'ien-chüeh, then a censor, who said:

> The Emperor Ying-tsung ordered the Chung-shu-sheng to codify the *T'ung-chih* and promulgate it to the public, and all officials followed it. Some twenty years have passed between the time of the Yen-yu reign and the present day. Since human affairs have ten thousand situations, how can a precedent govern all of them? Moreover, from time to time, officials have differences in high or low talent which result in the light or heavy punishments proposed in their decisions. Consequently, multifarious articles and fragmentary items increase day by day.... It is proper that the Chung-shu-sheng soon memorialize on the matter and carefully select scholarly officials who have comprehensively studied Classics as well as methods, have understood the essence of government, and have been skillful in civic

---

[142] Ichimura Sanjirō, *Shinashi kenkyū*, p. 517. See also Niida Noboru, *Chūgoku hōseishi kenkyū · hō to kanshu, hō to dōtoku*, p. 198.

[143] Abe Takeo, *Gendaishi no kenkyū*, p. 274, n. 6.

[144] Niida Noboru, *Chūgoku hōseishi kenkyū: hō to kanshū, hō to dōtoku*, pp. 198–199.

affairs, to assemble in conference to listen to or read [the new precedents] so as to select and propose what [precedents] be abandoned or be adopted. Consequently supplements to the *T'ung-chih* should be compiled, printed, and promulgated.[145]

The inability of the *Ta Yüan t'ung-chih* to meet the needs of the society naturally caused great anxiety among senior Chinese officials. Su T'ien-chüeh and others feared that without a new compilation of legal regulations, the common people might commit crimes inadvertently because of their ignorance of new precedents, and that corrupt bureaucrats would take advantage of the intricacies of the laws to pursue their own interests. On April 16, 1338, senior officials cited this plea of the censors and suggested to Shun Ti (Toɣan Temür Qaɣan) that a new code be compiled to meet the circumstances. This proposal was accepted and officials from various branches of the central government were ordered to review both old and new legal materials.

As Ying-tsung was oriented more toward Chinese culture than his predecessors, Shun Ti was in turn more sophisticated in Chinese learning than Ying-tsung. According to one account, the calligraphy of Shun Ti was greatly esteemed.[146] He changed the Kuei-chang-ko into the Hsüan-wen-ko (The Academy of the Hsüan-wen Pavilion) to continue and expand literary activities. In 1334 he issued an edict ordering Mongols and Central Asians in China to observe mourning for their parents.[147] Being aware of the importance of history, he further commanded in 1343 that the histories of the Liao, Chin, and Sung dynasties be compiled. The texts of the "Three Histories" were completed in 1345 and were certainly another reflection of the cultural transformation. When the texts were submitted to the throne, Shun Ti told the ministers about the necessity of learning from historical records the experiences of previous

---

[145] Su T'ien-chueh, *Tz'u-hsi wen-kao*, 26:8a–9a. See also *YS* 183:19a.

[146] For a discussion of the interest Shun Ti (Toɣan Temur Qaɣan) had in Chinese culture, see Yoshikawa Kōjirō, *Yoshikawa Kōjirō zenshū dai jūgo kan*, pp. 276–289.

[147] *YS* 38.9b.

dynasties in order to make a better government.[148] In addition to these various achievements, efforts made by officials to compile a code resulted in the completion of the *Chih-cheng t'iao-ko* on December 8, 1345. The code was later officially promulgated in 1346.[149]

The *Chih-cheng t'iao-ko* contains 150 items of decrees, 1,700 items of articles, and 1,050 items of precedents. The complete text of the code has not survived; it is said to have been divided into 23 *chüan*, with a form similar to that of the *Ta Yüan t'ung-chih*.[150] The text comprised 27 sections, and it seems to have been the last major code to be adopted during the final stage of the Yüan dynasty. The code was mainly a continuation of the *Ta Yüan t'ung-chih* and later became one of the major sources for the compilation of a Korean code in 1391.[151]

After the promulgation of the *Chih-cheng t'iao-ko*, another step was taken to establish the *Yüan Code* which presumably was designed to be the definitive text of the Chinese code of the dynasty. It is recorded in the *Yüan shih* that Ou-yang Hsüan (1283–1357) was commanded to draft a national code, but no specific date is given in this reference.[152] According to another source, Ou-yang Hsüan was assigned this task in the 10th year of the Chih-cheng reign [February 7, 1350–January 27, 1351].[153] The *Yüan shih* also records that in the 11th year of the same reign [January 28, 1351–January 17, 1352] one Ch'en Ssu-ch'ien (1289?–1353) started to compile a national code.[154] Despite the efforts of both Ou-yang Hsüan and Ch'en Ssu-ch'ien, there is no reference to indicate that a national code as such was ever promulgated. It is, however, recorded

---

[148] *YS* 41:7 and 139:13a.

[149] Ou-yang Hsuan, "*Chih-cheng t'iao-ko hsu*" ("Preface to *The Chih-cheng Code*"), *Kuo-ch'ao wen-lei*, 7:8b–9b. See also *YS* 41:8a.

[150] *Ssu-k'u ch'uan-shu tsung-mu t'i-yao* 84:25a.

[151] *Kōraishi* (*Koryŏsa*) [*Korean History*] (Tokyo: Kokusho kankōkai, 1908), Vol. 2, p. 449.

[152] *YS* 182:6b.

[153] Ou-yang Hsüan, *Kuei-chai wen-chi*, "Fu-lu": 12a. Weng Tu-chien, however, claimed that the 10th year of the Chih-cheng reign could be a mistake for the 11th year. See Weng Tu-chien, "Meng-Yüan shih-tai ti fa-tien pien-chuan," p. 173.

[154] *YS* 184:13b.

in the *Yüan shih* that because Liang Chen was critical of the *Chih-cheng tiao-ko*, he selected several people who were familiar with laws to compile a revised text of the *Chih-cheng t'iao-ko*, and that he retired from his official career soon after the completion of the revised text.[155] Since Liang Chen was still an active Right-minister of the Chung-shu-sheng in the 18th year of the Chih-cheng reign [February 9, 1358–January 28, 1359], his new text must have been completed not much earlier than the 18th year of the reign, and the *Chih-cheng t'iao-ko* most likely was at that time still in use. The case of Liang Chen therefore seems to disprove any possible existence of the code of Ou-yang Hsüan or that of Ch'en Ssu-ch'ien.[156]

Whether the text of Liang Chen represented an effort to continue the task initiated by Ou-yang Hsüan and Ch'en Ssu-ch'ien is not clear. Nor is evidence available to indicate whether his text was ever promulgated. By the 18th year of the Chih-cheng reign (1358/1359) the whole nation had already been hurt by a series of uprisings led by Fang Kuo-chen (1319–1374), Liu Fu-t'ung (?–1363), and Hsü Shou-hui (?–1360). In view of these political difficulties and other turmoil, it is highly doubtful whether any special project for the implementation of a new code could have been undertaken. As a result, the *Chih-cheng t'iao-ko* remained the last major code of the dynasty.

In short, there were continuous efforts by Chinese officials and Mongolian rulers to establish Chinese codes during the Yüan dynasty. Mongolian rulers were often considered by scholars such as Chao I (1727–1814) to be ignorant of Chinese culture.[157] The common notion was also held that Mongols, being barbaric and uncivilized, were unable or unwilling to meet the needs of the Chinese people. But evidence proves that Mongolian rulers were not so ignorant and that the cultural achievements of the Yüan dynasty were on the whole

---

[155] *YS* 187:4a.

[156] For a discussion of this issue, see Abe Takeo, *Gendaishi no kenkyū*, pp. 253–260.

[157] Chao I, *Erh-shih-erh shih cha-chi* [*Notes on the Twenty-Two Histories*] (Shanghai: The Commercial Press, 1958), pp. 626–627.

very impressive.[158] As well pointed out by Ch'en Yüan (1880–1971), the Confucian studies and other intellectual activities during the Yüan time were by no means less advanced nor less active than those during other dynasties.[159] Moreover, Mongolian rulers were interested in Chinese institutions, and they made efforts to develop Chinese codes and other institutions to suit the needs of Chinese people and society. Originally, Chinese institutions were adopted in the early stage of the dynasty as an effective means for governing Chinese. But as rulers and their officials became more involved in the government of Chinese people, the establishment of Chinese institutions became an integral part of the dynasty and its society. At the beginning of the Mongolian domination, owing to their earlier contacts with Central Asian culture, the Mongols were not too much in favor of Chinese culture. But after the dynasty had established itself in China proper and after the contacts with Central Asia had significantly decreased, Mongolian rulers, by the beginning of the fourteenth century, were very much exposed to Chinese influences.[160] The speed of their cultural transformation increased as the volume and pace of their contacts with the Chinese increased. At least, after 1320 the cultural accommodation of Mongolian customs to Chinese institutions became evident. Consequently, along with other adjustments, various Chinese legal institutions were established by Mongolian rulers with the help of Chinese officials.

[158] For a study of the acceptance of Chinese culture by Mongols and Central Asians in the Yuan period, see Ch'en Yüan, *Yüan Hsi-yu-jen hua-hua k'ao* [*Studies on the Sinicization of Central Asians of the Yuan Dynasty*] (*Li-yun shu-wu ts'ung-k'o* edition, 1934). For an English translation of this book, see Ch'ien Hsing-hai and L. C. Goodrich, *Western and Central Asians in China under the Mongols* (Los Angeles. University of California Press, 1966).

[159] Ch'en Yuan, *Yuan Hsi-yu-jen hua-hua k'ao*, 8:113a–118a.

[160] For a discussion of the Mongols' contact with Central Asian culture, see Haneda Tōru, "Shina no hokuzoku shochō to kanbunmei" ("La civilisation chinoise et les dynasties barbares du Nord de la Chine"), *Haneda hakushi shigaku ronbunshū jōkan rekishihen* [*Historical Essays of Dr. Haneda, Vol. One: On History*] (Kyoto: Kyoto University Press, 1969), pp. 712–715.

II. THE PENAL SYSTEM

The Yüan dynasty adopted many important legal principles from previous dynasties in establishing its own penal system. The influence of Mongolian law and customs, also provided substantial innovations in the Yüan system. Since the dynasty existed during a period in which the great urban and commercial expansion of Chinese civilization reached its peak, many new principles were institutionalized for the first time in the Yüan legal codes. On the whole, the traditional five punishments (i.e., the *wu-hsing*) remained the major legal penalties, although significant changes, both in content and in form, also occurred. Some of those changes were uniquely Yüan, while others were subsequently adopted by the Ming and the Ch'ing.

In addition to the five punishments, there also existed in the Yüan system some supplemental financial and physical penalties which evolved from a different theoretical framework. They were institutionalized and imposed on persons in addition to the usual penalties. During the Yüan, in general, the supplemental penalties were extensively employed in cases involving such crimes as homicide or injury as well as theft or robbery. Many of the changes and supplemental penalties strongly reflected the influence of Mongolian customary law, and they in turn left their mark on the penal systems of the Ming and the Ch'ing. As a result, through the agent of Mongolian rule, many new legal elements were introduced into the Chinese penal systems of the Yüan and later dynasties.

THE FIVE PUNISHMENTS

The traditional form of the five punishments was adopted in

the Yüan period to designate the major legal penalties, but with modifications and changes. Historically, the standard form of the *wu-hsing* was established in the *Sui Code* of 581–583, although the *wu-hsing* already existed among earlier dynasties. The style and the content of the *Sui Code* were followed and modified by the *T'ang Code* of 653, which became the model for codes of later dynasties. Consequently, through this historical development, the penal system and legal principles of the *T'ang Code* were by and large adopted in the codes of subsequent dynasties.

The standard form of the *wu-hsing* consisted of: 1) death, including *chiao* (strangulation) and *chan* (decapitation); 2) *liu* (life exile), including three degrees from a distance of 2,000 *li* (3 *li* = about 1 English mile) through 2,500 *li* to 3,000 *li*, 3) *t'u* (penal servitude), including five degrees from one to three years (i.e., one, one and a half, two, two and a half, and three); 4) *chang* (beating with a heavy stick), including five degrees from 60 to 100 blows (i.e., 60, 70, 80, 90, and 100); and finally 5) *ch'ih* (beating with a light stick), including five degrees from 10 to 50 blows.

The Yüan dynasty adopted the basic form of the *wu-hsing*, but new arrangements were also made. With regard to the death sentence, the measure of strangulation was replaced by *ling-ch'ih* (death by slow slicing), while decapitation was retained. The punishment of death by slow slicing originally came from practices of the Liao dynasty, and it also occurred in the Sung dynasty as a special measure.[1] The *ling-ch'ih*, as the most severe punishment, was employed against offenders guilty of the most serious crimes, such as treason. It was finally institutionalized in the Yüan as one of two official degrees of punishment by death, and was later adopted by the Ming and Ch'ing codes. According to Shen Chia-pen, the punishment

---

[1] *Liao shih* [*Liao History*] (*Po-na-pen*, Yüan, Chih-cheng edition; reprinted by The Commercial Press, Shanghai, 1931), 112:4, 113:1b–6a, and 114:2. See also Derk Bodde and Clarence Morris, *Law in Imperial China* (Cambridge, Mass.: Harvard University Press, 1967), p. 94. For a discussion of this practice in the Sung period, see Brian McKnight, "Sung Justice: Death by Slicing," *Journal of the American Oriental Society*, Vol. 93, No. 3 (1973), pp. 359–360.

inflicted on the offender eight separate cuts—namely, cuts in the face, hands, feet, breast, stomach, and head. According to Niida Noboru, the cuts could be increased to 24, 36, or 120 in number.[2] In any case, the main purpose of this measure was to make the offender die by a painful and elaborate process.

Decapitation and strangulation, on the other hand, were punishments involving simple death. Strangulation was considered less severe than decapitation, for Chinese belief maintained that the offender in the former case would still preserve his head and thus obtain his rebirth in the next world. However, punishment by strangulation was abolished in the Yüan dynasty, perhaps because the Mongols did not entertain this Chinese belief and saw no significant difference between the two kinds of death.

The offenses legally punishable by death during Yüan times, as recorded in the "Hsing-fa chih" of the *Yüan shih* and much later pointed out by Shen Chia-pen, numbered only 135. This figure was significantly low as compared with the 233 offenses of the *T'ang Code*, the 293 offenses of the *Sung Code* of 963, and the 282 offenses of the *Ming Code* of 1397.[3] Although the "Hsing-fa chih" is not necessarily the most representative document of Yüan law, the figure does indicate the leniency of the penal system of the Yüan dynasty and also contradicts the common notion that the Mongolian rulers employed very harsh punishments against criminal offenders. Professor Derk Bodde, for example, found the figure "particularly striking because of the Mongol reputation for harshness."[4] This notion of harshness exists partly because of prejudice

---

[2] Shen Chia-pen, *Shen Chi-i hsien-sheng i-shu chia-pien, Fen-k'ao [Separate Studies]*, 2:19a. See also Niida Noboru, *Chūgoku hōseishi kenkyū: keihō*, pp. 153–165. For a description of the execution of this penalty in the Yuan period, see the *P'u T'ung-shih yen-chieh (Pak T'ongsa Ŏnhae)* (This text was a handbook used by Koreans to learn the Chinese language and was incorporated in the *Kuei-chang-ko ts'ung-shu*; reprinted in Kyōto?, 1972?).

[3] Shen Chia-pen, *Shen Chi-i hsien-sheng i-shu chia-pien, Ssu-hsing chih su [The Number of Capital Offenses]*, 2a–3a. See also Bodde and Morris, *Law in Imperial China*, p. 102.

[4] *Ibid.*, p. 103.

among Chinese and Western scholars and partly because of the relatively poor development of Yüan scholarship. The "Hsing-fa chih" clearly records that the virtue of the Yüan penal system was in its leniency and that the defect of the system lay in the slow and loose imposition of punishment.[5] This comment was written by Ming scholar-officials who found it necessary to praise the leniency of the Yüan penal system, even though they were political enemies of the Mongolian rulers. Such a generous comment must have a bearing on the nature of the Yüan practice.

The leniency of the system can be further demonstrated by citing the number of people actually sentenced to death. From 1260 to 1307, during the entire rules of Shih-tsu and Ch'eng-tsung, only 2,743 people were put to death. There are about ten years during this period, however, for which we have no statistics, and it cannot be ascertained whether no death sentences were imposed in these years or whether information was simply unavailable. In any case, the number of death sentences can be specifically broken down as follows:[6]

Year	Number
1261	46
1262	66
1263	7
1264	73
1265	42
1266	96
1267	114
1268	69
1269	42
1270	44
1271	105
1272	39

[5] YS 102:2b.

[6] YS 4:22a, 5:11b, 5:17b, 5:24a, 6:5b, 6:14a, 6:17b, 6:21b, 7:7a, 7:15a, 8:30b, 9:15b, 9:23a, 10:13b, 10:26b, 11:10b, 11:19a, 12:25b, 14:12b, 14:22b, 15:15a, 15:27b, 16:12b, 16:26b, 17:15b, 17:23b, 18:11a, 18:21b, 19:19a, 20:16b, 20:22a, and 21:29a.

44

Year	Number
1275	68
1276	34
1277	32
1278	52
1279	132
1280	102
1281	22
1283	278
1285	271
1286	114
1287	121
1288	95
1289	59
1290	72
1291	55
1292	74
1293	41
1294	31
1295	30
1296	24
1297	175
1301	61
1302	3
1303	10
1306	44

These statistics show that the number of people sentenced to death each year was extremely low, considering the certainly vast population of the dynasty. According to another account, those criminals who were sentenced to death during the rule of Shih-tsu were not actually executed but instead imprisoned for life. Owing to this policy, for seventy or eighty years, people so seldom saw an act of execution that they were extremely terrified when they happened to see a corpse's head.[7] This

[7] Sun Ch'eng-tse, *Ch'un-ming meng-yü lu* (*Ku-hsiang-chai hsiu-chen shih-chung* edition), 44:7a.

may be an exaggeration, but it does substantiate the observation concerning the lenient penal system in the Yüan period.

The leniency of the punishment was due in most part to the attitude of the Mongolian rulers. As early as 1260, Shih-tsu stressed to his officials that any case involving a capital offense must be thoroughly reviewed before the death penalty was meted out.[8] Shih-tsu often personally reviewed cases involving the death penalty and acted to spare the criminals' lives by reducing their sentences. In 1287, for example, when some 190 people were to be put to death, Shih-tsu intervened and said: "Prisoners are not a mere flock of sheep. How can they be suddenly executed? It is proper that they be instead enslaved and assigned to pan gold with a sieve."[9] The degree of leniency was further increased by amnesties which set criminals free. To be sure, the practice of granting amnesties was not unique to the Yüan dynasty. The Mongolian rulers, however, tended to grant amnesty more frequently and to respond especially quickly and favorably to requests for anmesty from Buddhist and Lama monks. As a matter of fact, the lenient policy of the Mongolian rulers often provoked criticism from senior Chinese officials. For instance, Chang Yang-hao even proposed to the throne that penalties be made more severe and that the number of amnesties be greatly reduced.[10] The attitude of leniency was, nonetheless, reinforced throughout the dynasty, regardless of criticism.

As during other dynasties, certain extrajudicial types of death punishment were employed against special offenders in Yüan times. In one case, three men were put to death in 1282 for their involvement in murdering A-ho-ma (Aḥmad) and their flesh was pickled.[11] Because of his own earlier political crime, the corpse of Aḥmad was taken from his tomb two months later and cut into pieces.[12] These special punishments

[8] YS 4:1b.

[9] YS 14:15b.

[10] YS 175:23a. See also Chang Yao-hao, *Yuan Chang Wen-cheng kung Kuei-t'ien lei-kao* (1790), 2:7b–9a.

[11] YS 12:3a. For a discussion of the life of A-ho-ma (Aḥmad), see Herbert Franke, "Aḥmad, Ein Beitrag zur Wirtschaftsgeschichte Chinas unter Qubilai," *Oriens*, 1 (1948), pp. 222–236.

[12] YS 12:5a.

were limited mainly to political offenses or those of an unusually evil nature and were not used frequently. Usually, when a person was to be put to death, the execution was carried out after the autumnal equinox and before the vernal equinox. However, criminals who had committed serious offenses, such as those of the "ten abominations," could be executed at any time.[13] For instance, in the *Yüan ch'ü hsüan* [*Selection of Yüan Dramas*], it is stated that one Tou Erh was executed in the hot summer.[14]

The life-exile system of the Yüan dynasty was different from that of other dynasties. Departing from the traditional *liu* of three degrees (from 2,000 *li* to 3,000 *li*), the Yüan exile system only stipulated that Southern Chinese be exiled to Liao-yang and the adjoining northern districts and Northern Chinese be sent to Hu-Kuang (i.e., Hunan and Hupeh).[15] Similarly, Jurchen and Korean criminals were also exiled to Hu-kuang under this arrangement.[16] At the exile stations, the criminals were assigned to cultivate the land or serve the postal relay system. Being nomadic, Mongols were used to mobile, pastoral patterns of life and therefore did not develop strong ideas about the restriction of freedom as a measure of punishment. Especially in cases where a tribe had to move from one pastoral land to another, it became technically impractical to restrict criminals to a confined area. As a result, the Yüan practice of life exile was transformed from the deprivation of personal freedom to the imposition of physical pain and the utilization of labor, although it still preserved the traditional goals of revenge, intimidation, prohibition, and rehabitation.[17]

[13] *YTC* 39:6.
[14] *Yüan ch'ü hsüan* [*Selection of Yuan Dramas*] (*Ssu-pu pei-yao* edition; reprinted by Chung-hua shu-chü, Taipei, 1968), Vol. 4, 7b–9b.
[15] *YS* 102:3.
[16] *YS* 103:12b–13a.
[17] In giving the rationale for punishment, Blackstone once wrote: "The public gains equal security, whether the offender himself be amended by wholesome correction, or whether he be disabled from doing any further harm; and if the penalty fails of both these effects, as it may do, still the terror of his example remains as a warning to other citizens." Sir William Blackstone, *Commentaries on the Laws of England* (London: John Murray, 1857), IV, 10. In the *Yuan tien-chang* it is also clearly stated that exiling criminals to Liao-yang to cultivate the land would teach malevolent people to fear law and punishment. See *YTC* 39:5a.

In addition to the life-exile system, the Yüan dynasty also developed two other measures: one was *ch'u-chün* (banishment to serve in the army); the other was *ch'ien-hsi* (forced removal from one's residence). As an adjunct to standard life exile, the punishment of *ch'u-chün* was occasionally employed against criminals in cases of salt smuggling or theft so as to put these offenders into military service.[18] The measure of *ch'u-chün* was adopted by the Ming dynasty and, under the new name of *ch'ung-chün*, was expanded into a systematic and important punishment.[19] The Yüan measure of *ch'ien-hsi* came from the T'ang prototype of *i-hsiang* (removal from village), and it was often employed against undesirable elements in the villages by moving them from their homes to distant places.[20] This measure was different from standard exile, but after the Ming dynasty inherited it from the Yüan, it was changed to a part of punishment by exile.[21]

Like punishment by exile, penal servitude in the Yüan also lost its original significance in terms of the restriction of personal freedom. The dynasty imposed five degrees of penal servitude: 1) one year plus 67 blows with a heavy stick; 2) one and a half years plus 77 blows; 3) two years plus 87 blows; 4) two and a half years plus 97 blows; and 5) three years plus 107 blows with a heavy stick. Criminals sentenced to penal servitude were assigned mainly to the mines or salt wells where they were fettered and put to work during the day. Each criminal was kept under surveillance, and the amount of work he did was calculated daily.[22] Since both physical pain and forced labor were emphasized in this system of penal servitude, the traditional significance of restriction of freedom began to decline during the Yüan dynasty. The spirit of Yüan penal servitude was continued in the Ming dynasty, and persons

---

[18] *YTC* 22:41a and 50:3b. See also *YTCHC* "Hsing-pu" (Board of Punishments):3a.

[19] Shen Chia-pen, *Shen Chi-i hsien-sheng i-shu chia-pien, Ch'ung-chün k'ao* [*Studies on Military Exile*], Part One:2a.

[20] *YTC* 39:4a–5b.

[21] In the Yüan period, the measure of *ch'ien-hsi* (forced removal from one's residence) was a supplement to the system of punishment by exile rather than a formal part of the system itself.

[22] *YS* 103:12b–13a and 104:12a.

were sent to join the iron-works or salt wells for a specific period of time and were required to produce a certain amount of iron or salt in accordance with a daily quota.[23] Another innovation of the Yüan system of penal servitude was the change it created in the relationship between penal servitude per se and the beating attached to it. Originally, the beating was only an auxiliary aspect of the punishment of penal servitude proper. During the Yüan dynasty, owing to the new attitude toward the restriction of freedom and the emphasis on forced labor, beating in a case of penal servitude was considered more painful and substantial than the principal penalty. Consequently, penal servitude per se became supplemental to the beating, thus adding a new significance to the relationship between these two measures.[24]

The traditional system of punishment by beating with a heavy or light stick also underwent transformation during the Yüan. Ever since the *Sui Code*, the punishments of *ch'ih* and *chang* both had had five degrees, and the number of blows had been calculated in units of ten. In contrast, the Yüan dynasty had six degrees of punishment with a light stick (7, 17, 27, 37, 47, and 57) and five degrees of punishment with a heavy stick (67, 77, 87, 97, and 107).[25] Various scholars have given reasons why the blows were calculated in units of seven. For example, Yeh Tzu-ch'i explained that the odd numbers were the result of the clemency of Emperor Shih-tsu who ordered a reduction of one blow each "for Heaven, for Earth, and for myself."[26] Although such an explanation is not entirely impossible, it does seem too romantic. It would be more realistic to suggest that the establishment of the units of seven came from the Mongolian custom of using odd numbers.[27] As

[23] *Ta Ming hui-tien* [*Institutions of the Great Ming Dynasty*] (1587 edition; reprinted in Taipei, 1963), 61:27b–28b.

[24] Wu Shih-tao, *Wu Li-pu chi* (*Hsü Chin-hua ts'ung-shu* edition), 19:16b. See also Miyazaki Ichisada, "Sō-Gen jidai no hōsei to saiban kikō," pp. 216–217, n. 8.

[25] *YS* 102:3a and *YTC* 39:1a.

[26] Yeh Tzu-ch'i, *Ts'ao mu tzu* (original preface dated December 17, 1378; reprinted in 1762), 3:28b–29a.

[27] Iwamura Shinobu, *Mongoru shakai keizaishi no kenkyū* [*Studies in the Social and Economic History of the Mongols*] (Kyoto: Kyoto University Press, 1968), pp. 552–556.

pointed out by the Persian historian, Waṣṣāf, the number of blows administered by the Mongols in punishment was always odd (3, 5, and so forth, up to 77).[28]

This system of punishment was reported by Marco Polo. In his *Travels*, for instance, we read:

> It is true that when a man has taken some little things for which he ought not to die, they condemn him to be beaten. There is given him by the government at least seven blows with a rod or, if he has stolen two things, seventeen blows or, if three things, twenty-seven blows or thirty-seven or forty-seven, and in this way it goes up sometimes to a hundred and seven, always increasing by ten blows for each thing which is stolen, according to what he has taken and the measure of the crime. And many of them die of this beating.[29]

The practice of calculating blows in units of seven did not exist before 1260. As early as 1264, however, a decree prohibiting walking in the capital after a certain hour at night mandated that the offenders be punished by a beating of 27 blows with a light stick.[30] Thereafter, calculations in terms of seven were performed throughout the dynasty, although in most offenses related to the monopoly of salt, tea, and other items of economic value, the number of blows imposed on wrongdoers was still calculated in units of ten.[31] The Ch'ien-lung edition of the *Yüan shih*, however, changed the number of blows with a heavy stick from 70 to 77 for such offenses as salt and tea smuggling as well as concealing taxable items. Apparently, with regard to this particular reference, the Ch'ing editors of the text wrongly changed the number of blows in order to maintain the consistency of the unique Yüan practice of calculating blows in units of seven, and this mistake was,

[28] Hammar Purgstall, *Geschichte der Ilchane*, I, 37; quoted in Henry Yule, *Travels of Marco Polo* (London: John Murray, 1929), I, 277.

[29] A. C. Moule and Paul Pelliot, *Marco Polo: The Description of the World* (London: George Routledge & Sons Ltd. 1938), I, 175.

[30] *YTC* 57:23a. See also Miyazaki Ichisada, "Sō-Gen jidai no hōsei to saiban kikō," pp. 215–216, n. 7.

[31] *YS* 104:1a–5a.

unfortunately, followed by Shen Chia-pen in his writings.[32] In any event, the Yüan stipulated that the diameter of the light stick for the imposition of beating be 0.27 Chinese inches at the large end and 0.17 inches at the small end, and that the heavy stick be 0.32 inches at the large end and 0.22 inches at the small end.[33] These specifiations were different from those given by other dynasties, and Professor Bodde, in remarking that the diameters of sticks from the T'ang dynasty through the Ming dynasty were uniformly fixed, seems to have been unaware of such differences.[34]

Despite these changes and modifications, the Yüan dynasty nevertheless utilized the traditional Chinese format of the "five punishments" in its penal system. To the extent that many Mongolian customs were reflected in the penal system, the Yüan experience represented elements of innovation within the Chinese legal tradition. These elements can be further discovered in the supplemental penalties of the Yüan dynasty.

Supplemental Financial Penalties

As a form of penalty, redemption has always been important in conciliation and private settlement of legal disputes. Historically, however, from as early as the beginning of the Han dynasty, it was well established in China that a murderer should be executed and one who injured or robbed be punished accordingly, thus allowing little room for the practice of redemption. In accordance with the T'ang Code, the "five punishments" were meted out as the major form of substantial (as opposed to supplemental) penalties against offenders, and the state succeeded in monopolizing the power of sanctions with regard to criminal offenses. As a result, only in exceptional cases would redemption be accepted.

During the Yüan dynasty, as in previous dynasties, in some

---

[32] Shen Chia-pen, *Shen Chi-i hsien-sheng i-shu chia-pien, Yen-fa k'ao* [*Studies on the Salt System*], 8b–9a. For a discussion of this mistake, see also Abe Takeo, *Gendaishi no kenkyū*, pp. 264–265.

[33] *YTC* 40:1a.

[34] Bodde and Morris, *Law in Imperial China*, pp. 80–81.

offenses certain types of wrongdoers were permitted to make redemption to avoid the actual implementation of substantial penalties. These categories included people who could not bear physical punishment, such as persons seventy years old or more, children fifteen or younger, persons crippled or injured, and very sick people.[35] In these cases, each blow of beating was to be computed as one *kuan* (string) of a *Chung-t'ung ch'ao* (Chung-t'ung note).[36] However, if a boy of fifteen or younger committed a sexual offense with a girl of ten or younger, he would not be allowed to make redemption; the prohibition was also applied to a man of seventy or older who committed such a sexual offense.[37]

Unlike previous dynasties, the Yüan dynasty developed two other types of financial compensation in its formal penal system. Funeral expenses—namely, *shao-mai-yin* (silver for the burning and burying expenses)—were to be paid by the wrongdoer to his victim's family. The other type of compensation was payment of "nourishment expenses" for medication and treatment of the injured person. These two measures were of Mongolian origin. Like many other nomadic tribes, the Mongols used the institution of redemption extensively to maintain justice and to prevent revenge. In a fragment of the *Jasaɣ*, for example, we read: "In case of murder (punishment for murder) one could ransom himself by paying fines which were: for a Mohammedan—40 golden coins (Balysh); and for a Chinese—one donkey."[38]

The practice of redemption was certainly not unique to the Mongols, for it has also been observed by many other Asian tribes and was reflected in the *Wergeld* (man money) of the ancient Germanic and early English laws.[39] The practice,

[35] *YS* 102:6b.

[36] *YS* 105:28 and *YTC* 39:3a. For a discussion of the *Chung-t'ung ch'ao* (Chung-t'ung note), see Yang Lien-sheng, *Money and Credit in China* (Cambridge, Mass.: Harvard University Press, 1952), p. 63. See also P'eng Hsin-wei, *Chung-kuo huo-pi-shih* [*History of Chinese Money and Credit*] (Shanghai: Jen-min ch'u-pan she, 1965), pp. 557–560 and 587–593.

[37] *YS* 104:9b.

[38] Riasanovsky, *Fundamental Principles*, p. 85.

[39] Nakada Kaoru, *Hōseishi ronshū dai ikkan* [*Collected Studies of Legal History*,

however, came to play a significant role for the first time in Chinese law through the impact of Mongolian customary law on the Yüan code. Among many references to the *shao-mai-yin* as a form of redemption in the Yüan documents, one typical example reads:

> Any person who murders shall be executed. [The authorities] shall also exact from the person's relatives fifty *liang* (taels) of the *shao-mai-yin* for the *k'u-chu* (victim's family). In cases of no silver, ten *ting* (ingots) of Chung-t'ung notes shall be exacted instead. If the person be pardoned by amnesty, [the sum] shall be doubled.[40]

Another example reads: "Any elder brother who beats a sister-in-law and causes her to die from the injury shall be punished 107 blows by beating with a heavy stick. The *shao-mai-yin* shall be exacted."[41]

In both instances, the victim's family was given the *shao-mai-yin* regardless of the fate of the wrongdoer. In other words, it was compulsory for a wrongdoer or his family to pay the funeral expenses in addition to whatever punishment was meted out. The sum was normally fixed at fifty taels of silver or its equivalent, but in certain cases, when special considerations warranted, the amount could be reduced to 25 taels. If the full payment of the amount could not be met, the balance was to be made up in personal service or by surrendering a member of the wrongdoer's family (such as his daughter) to the victim's family to work as a slave.[42] The Yüan system of redemption differed somewhat from that of Mongolian law and

---

Vol. One] (Tokyo: Iwanami shoten, 1926), pp. 732–733. See also Niida Noboru, *Chūgoku hōseishi kenkyū: keihō*, pp. 301–372. For a discussion of this practice in Germanic law, see Heinrich Brunner, *Deutsche Rechtsgeschichte* (Leipzig: Verlag von Duncker & Humblot, 1906), I, 119. For a discussion of this practice in early English law, see Frederick Pollock and Frederic Maitland, *History of English Law*, 2nd ed. (Cambridge: Cambridge University Press, 1968), II, 241–245 and 449–451.

[40] *YS* 105:10a.

[41] *YS* 105:12b.

[42] *YTC* 43:9a–10a. For the special cases in which the penalty of imposing funeral expenses could be totally waived, see *YTC* 43:13b–17a.

the Germanic *Wergeld* practice, for the latter two systems would spare the wrongdoer from suffering the principal punishment after the submission of redemption.

This Yüan feature was also applied to the imposition of "nourishment expenses" which were to be paid to the injured party by the wrongdoer in addition to the principal punishment. In this sense, the practice of "nourishment expenses" was also different from the traditional redemption in Mongolian law or the *Busse* (redemption) in the Germanic laws. The feature is clearly demonstrated in the following typical case:

> Any person who injures with an instrument another person and makes [the victim] crippled or seriously sick shall be punished 77 blows by beating with a heavy stick. [The authorities] shall also obtain [from the wrongdoer] ten *ting* of Chung-t'ung notes to give the injured person as "nourishment expenses."[43]

The imposition of the *shao-mai-yin* or the "nourishment expenses" in addition to the principal punishment seems on the surface to place a harsh burden on the wrongdoer. In reality, however, since the principal punishment for the offense was less severe in the Yüan than in previous dynasties, the principal punishment and the "redemption" imposed in the Yüan system were no more harsh than the simple principal punishment of other systems. To be more specific, the punishment imposed for an offense where the victim was crippled or made seriously ill was three years' penal servitude in the *T'ang Code*; the *Ming Code* or the *Ch'ing Code* specified that the offender be given 100 blows with a heavy stick plus three years' penal servitude. By contrast, the penalty for the same offense in Yüan law was only 77 blows with a heavy stick plus ten *ting* of Chung-t'ung notes. To give another example, as punishment for beating one's sister-in-law and causing her to die from the injuries, the Yüan system required the payment of funeral expenses in addition to a principal punishment of only 107 blows with a

[43] *YS* 105:8a.

heavy stick; strangulation was the punishment for the same offense in the T'ang, Ming, and Ch'ing dynasties. In short, the imposition of financial burdens on wrongdoers made it necessary for the Yüan penal system to reduce the severity of principal punishments for various offenses so that an ideal balance between the two measures could be maintained. This balance resulted in a compromise between the traditional Chinese principle of substantial state-imposed penalties and the Mongolian custom of accepting redemption. The fact that the measure of redemption was easily blended with the traditional Chinese sanctioning system and that the *shao-mai-yin* and "nourishment expenses" were calculated in monetary terms seem to reflect a rising money economy in the Yüan dynasty. The practice of imposing a financial burden on the wrongdoer was later adopted in the Ming dynasty. Unlike Yüan law, the *Ming Code*, in exacting the *mai-tsang-ch'ien* (cash for burying expenses), did not reduce the principal punishment proportionally, thus making the punishments more severe than those of the Yüan.

Owing to the influence of Mongolian customary law, there also existed in the Yüan dynasty the legal principle of *noxae deditio*, a feature similar to the practice in Roman law. If a slave committed an offense such as theft or robbery, or caused damage or injury, his master, by virtue of this principle, could elect either to pay the damages or surrender the slave. One case in point reads:

> In the case of a male or female slave or servant who has stolen a person's ox or horse and has been convicted and punished, [the slave or the servant] shall be given to the owner [of the stolen item]. If the master wishes to make redemption, let him do so.[44]

According to this reference in the *Yüan shih*, the master could either surrender the slave to the owner of the stolen animal or elect to make redemption and keep the slave, thus giving himself two options for his liability for his slave's misdeed.

[44] *YS* 104:20b–21a.

Although this principle existed in the Roman and some other legal systems,[45] it was only during the Yüan dynasty that the principle was institutionalized in China under the influence of Mongolian law. This Mongolian practice was observed in later days. For instance, in the *Mongol-Oirat Regulations* of 1640, one reference reads: "If one wife killed another wife, her husband was obliged to pay a heavy fine (as for homicide) to the relatives of the victim, or cut off the ear(s) of the killer and give her in marriage to another at his discretion."[46]

The provision "at his discretion" in this context refers to the option given to the killer's husband. In other words, the husband of the wrongdoer could either pay redemption and keep her or give her in marriage to the victim's husband. This particular reference was earlier recorded and translated into Russian by Golstunskij in his *Mongolo-Oiratskije Zakony* in 1880. By comparing the Russian version and the English translation made by Riasanovsky, Tayama Shigeru concluded that "at his discretion" refered to the option for the victim's husband rather than the killer's husband.[47] Tayama's view was adopted by Niida Noboru in their discussion of this problem,[48] and it was further accepted without reservation by Shimada Masao in one of his writings.[49] Although both Golstunskij and Riasanovsky did not mention explicitly that the killer's husband had the right of selection, such an inference is nevertheless reasonably valid from the contexts of both the Russian and English versions. This view, unlike that of the three Japanese

[45] For reference to this principle in Roman law, see William Alexander Hunter, *A Systematic and Historical Exposition on Roman Law*, 3rd ed. (London: Sweet & Maxwell Limited, 1897), p. 166. For other systems, such as the Assyrian, see Harada Keikichi, *Kusabıgata mojı hō no kenkyū* [*Study of Cuneiform Law*] (Tokyo: Kiyomizu kōbundō shobō, 1967), pp. 271–272 and 349.

[46] Riasanovsky, *Fundamental Principles*, p. 103.

[47] Tayama Shigeru, *Mōko hōten no kenkyū* [*Study of Mongolian Codes*] (Tokyo· Nihon gakujutsu shinkōkai, 1967), p. 143.

[48] Niida Noboru, *Chūgoku hōseishi kenkyū: keihō*, pp. 336–337.

[49] Shimada Masao, "Mindai Mōko no hōkanshū" ("Legal Customs of the Mongols ın the Ming Dynasty"), Nihon daigaku hōgakkai (Society of Legal Studies, Japan Univ.), ed. *Hōseıshıgaku no shomondaı* [*Varıous Problems Concerning the Scholarship of Legal Hıstory*] (Tokyo: Nihon daigaku hōgakkai, 1971), pp. 648 and 651, n. 2.

scholars, is in accord with the original Roman principle, for in Roman law it was the master of the slave rather than the victim himself who elected to pay redemption or to surrender the wrongdoer.[50] Since these Japanese scholars all consider that the above reference reflects the principle of *noxae deditio*, it would be logical for them to interpret "at his discretion" as meaning that the killer's husband could either pay a heavy fine or give her in marriage to the victim's husband, unless they understand the original Roman theory differently.

According to the principle established in the *T'ang Code*, officials and their wives were allowed to commute the usual penalties for misdeeds other than major offenses to redemption or forfeiture of salary over a given period of time, or to official reduction in rank or dismissal from the civil service.[51] This practice was adopted in the Yüan dynasty, but for certain offenses prescribed in Yüan codes, the actual penalties, as well as the above special measures, were to be imposed on the officials. When dealing with the case of attempted rape, Yüan law provided: "Any official who commits an unsuccessful act of rape against the wife of his subordinate shall be punished by 107 blows with a heavy stick and be dismissed from the civil service."[52]

The measure of punishment in this particular reference indicates that the traditional privilege of exemption from the actual penalties was not extended to officials in cases of this nature. This policy naturally created resentment among officials. For instance, Wang Yün protested on the grounds that the tradition was that penalties should not be applied to gentry-officials, whereas *li* (rites) were not to be extended to

[50] Hunter, *Exposition on Roman Law*, pp. 166–167. See also Sheldon Amos, *The History and Principles of the Civil Law of Rome* (London: Kegan Paul, Trench & Co., 1883), p. 354.

[51] For a discussion of the privilege of officials to make redemption, see Tai En-fui (Tai Yen-hui), "Tōritsu ni okeru jomen tōzokuhō" ("The Provision for 'the Expulsion-Dismissal and Atonement' in T'ang law"), *Hōseishi kenkyū*, 13 (1962), pp. 53–92. For a detailed discussion of the scope and significance of the redemption practice in the *T'ang Code*, see Tai Yen-hui, *T'ang lü t'ung-lun* [*On the General Principles of the T'ang Code*] (Taipei: Cheng-chung shu-chu, 1970), pp. 216–280 and 303–307.

[52] *YS* 104:9b–10a.

common people.[53] The request of Wang Yün was not honored and consequently, aside from cases of public negligence in which officials were permitted to ransom themselves for misdeeds occurring during the performance of their duties, officials were in most cases punished by both the usual penalties and such special measures as forfeiture of salary, reduction in rank, or dismissal from the civil service.[54]

In addition to these new features of redemption, the Yüan penal system developed the ninefold fine as a supplemental financial penalty for the theft of cattle. For instance, in one reference we read:

> Any person who steals a camel, horse, ox, ass, or mule shall, for each one [stolen], compensate with nine. In a case of stealing a camel, for the first offense, the ringleader shall be punished with 97 blows with a heavy stick plus two and a half years' penal servitude, and the accomplice with two years' penal servitude; for the second offense, one degree of punishment shall be increased; and for the third offense, regardless whether he be the ringleader or accomplice, he shall be punished with 107 blows and be exiled for military service.[55]

The practice of imposing a ninefold fine upon a cattle thief was an innovation in the formal Chinese penal system, and it certainly originated in Mongolian law. In a reference in the *jasay* we read:

> The man in whose possession a stolen horse is found must return it to the owner and add nine horses of the same kind; if he is unable to pay this fine, his children must be taken instead of the horses, and if he has no children, he himself shall then be slaughtered like a sheep.[56]

The Mongols, being a nomadic people, regarded the theft of cattle—their basic form of property and essential means

[53] Wang Yün, 87:5a–6a.
[54] *YS* 102:6b.
[55] *YS* 104:13a and *YTC* 49:21a–24a.
[56] Riasanovsky, *Fundamental Principles*, p. 85.

of existence—as a serious offense. They naturally regulated in the *Jasay* the imposition of a heavy fine on a cattle thief. Marco Polo also remarked upon this practice of Mongolian law in his *Travels:*

> And if the man steals 15 oxen so that it would come to exceed 107 blows [or] a horse or other thing for which he ought to lose life he is cut in two with a sword and killed; so, truly, that if he who steals can pay and will give nine times as much as the value of that which he has stolen he escapes from death and they do not despatch him with the sword.[57]

The Mongolian law of the ninefold fine not only existed in the times of the *Jasay* and Marco Polo, but also continued in practice in the *Mongol Oirat Code* of 1640, the *Khalkha Djirom* [i.e., *Qelqa Jirum*], and the law of the Kalmucks.[58] The custom of ordering a thief to repay several times the value of the stolen item is not uniquely Mongolian, for it existed in some other legal systems, such as the *Dezimalsystem* (decimal system) and *Duodezimalsystem* (duodecimal system) in the Germanic laws.[59] It was, however, only through the influence of Mongolian law that the measure was for the first time institutionalized in China. Unlike the Mongolian and Germanic laws, Yüan law imposed the ninefold fine on the cattle thief and subjected him to the usual penalties as well. The combination was again a compromise between the traditional Chinese punishment and the Mongolian practice of redemption.[60]

For some other types of theft, Yüan law also developed a scale of twofold fines. For example, it is recorded in one refer-

---

[57] Moule and Pelliot, *Marco Polo*, 1, 175.

[58] Riasanovsky, *Fundamental Principles*, pp. 104, 124, and 158.

[59] Heinrich Brunner, *Deutsche Rechtsgeschichte* (Münich and Leipzig; Verlag von Duncker & Humblot, 1928), II, 802.

[60] For a general discussion of the Mongolian practice of redemption, see Paul Ratchnevsky, "Die mongolische Rechtsinstitution der Busse in der chinesischen Gesetzgebung der Yuan-Zeit," Herbert Franke, ed., *Studia Sino-Altaica, Festschrift für Erich Haenisch zum 80. Geburtstag* (Wiesbaden: Franz Steiner Verlag GMBH, 1961), pp. 169–179.

ence: "Any estimate of the value of stolen goods shall use *Chih-yüan ch'ao* (chih-yüan note) as the standard. Besides the original stolen item, the thief shall be assessed twofold goods for repayment."[61] The original term in this reference for "twofold goods" in Chinese was *pei-tsang*, which means, according to one Yüan annotation, "to steal one but to be assessed two for repayment."[62] As a rule, the ninefold fine was employed against a cattle thief, but the twofold repayment was sufficient punishment for thefts of a different nature; this practice probably resulted from the feeling that it was less serious to steal items other than cattle. In some cases, if special relations existed between the thief and the victim, or if the circumstances deserved any special consideration, the imposition of the twofold fine could be waived, thus subjecting the thief to the

[61] *YTC* 49:8a. The *Yüan shih* also records the same reference, but the character *tsei* is a misprint for the character *tsang*(a). See *YS* 104:12a. The *Chih-yüan ch'ao* (Chih-yüan note) is an abbreviation of *Chih-yüan t'ung-hsing pao-ch'ao* (circulating precious note of the Chih-yüan reign). For a discussion of this circulating note, see Yang Lien-sheng, *Money and Credit in China*, p. 64. See also P'eng Hsing-wei, *Chung-kuo huo-pi-shih*, pp. 561–562.

[62] Hsu Yüan-jui, *Li-hsüeh chih-nan [Guidance to Bureaucratic Studies]* (original preface dated 1301; reprinted and incorporated in the *Chu-chia pi-yung shih-lei ch'uan-chi hsin-chi*, Ming, *Ssu-li-chien* edition), 32a. Professor Niida notes that the character *tsang*(a) was wrongly printed as *tsang*(b) in the Japanese version of the text. See Niida Noboru, *Chūgoku hōseishi kenkyū: keihō*, p. 566, n. 64. Although Niida did not give any citation for the place and date of publication of this Japanese version, his text seems to be the Shōkakudō (Kyoto) edition of 1673. In another Japanese text entitled *Rigaku shinan* (i.e., the *Li-hsüeh chih-nan*), however, there is no such misprint. The *Rigaku shinan* is a manuscript and gives no date or place of publication. The Harvard-Yenching Library has the above two Japanese texts in addition to the microfilm of the *Ssu-li-chien* edition. In Japan, Professors Miyazaki Ichisada and Naitō Kenkichi each have a different version of the Japanese texts, one of which is the Shōkakudō edition. Kyoto University also prepared in 1951 a revised edition of the text by copying the Ming edition. A recent revised edition has also been published in Taiwan (Ta hua yin-shu-kuan, Taipei?, 1969?). Although Niida points out the misprint of the Shōkakudō edition, the characters *tsang*(a) and *tsang*(b) are, however, used interchangeably on several occasions in the *Ssu-li-chien* edition. The *Li-hsüeh chih-nan* is of great importance for Yüan studies, and I am indebted to Professor Francis W. Cleaves for calling my attention to the Japanese manuscript of the *Rigaku shinan*. For a general discussion of the significance of this Yüan work, see Okamoto Keiji, "*Rigaku shinan no kenkyū*" ("Study of *Li-hsüeh chih-nan*—The Historical Significance of Law in the Yüan Dynasty"), *Tōkyō kyōiku daigaku bungakubu kiyō (The Bulletin of the Tokyo Kyoiku University Literature Department)*, 36 (1962), pp. 1–31.

normal penalty and the duty of restoring the stolen goods. To be more specific, if the thief and the victim were both slaves of the same master, the twofold fine would not be imposed on the thief, for they were considered as members of a family and were therefore governed by a special relationship. According to traditional Chinese law, theft among relatives was considered less grave than theft among people of no relation, because it was assumed that all relatives had at least a moral obligation to help one another in case of financial need and that family harmony and solidarity should be maintained regardless of the theft. Pursuant to this principle, theft among relatives during the Yüan period was also treated much more leniently than theft committed by outsiders. Consequently, the special relations between the thief and the victim would allow the former to avoid the twofold payment penalty, although he nevertheless had to suffer the usual punishment.

These transformations provided a new direction for the Chinese penal system. While the traditional types of simple fine and confiscation did not entirely disappear as punishments for other offenses,[63] the new penalties of redemption, ninefold fine, and twofold fine were used extensively in cases of homicide, injury, and theft. Such supplemental financial penalties came to function effectively in the formal penal system of the Yüan period.

SUPPLEMENTAL PHYSICAL PENALTIES

Along with the supplemental financial penalties, Yüan law also developed some supplemental physical penalties, notably the imposition of *talio* (retaliatory punishment) on certain classes of wrongdoers. *Talio* is a Latin word referring to punishment of injury by an act of the same kind, as an eye for an eye, a limb for a limb. It is a means of taking revenge proportional to the degree of injury inflicted by the offender. As indicated in the Bible and the *Code of Hammurabi*,[64] the practice of *talio*

---

[63] Shen Chia-pen, *Shen Chi-i hsien-sheng i-shu chia-pien, Fen-k'ao* 12:23b–24a. For an example of confiscation in Yüan law, see *YS* 104:7b.

[64] For a discussion of the *talio* principle in the Bible, see Akai Setsu, "He-

was not uncommon among ancient peoples. It was also fixed by the *Twelve Tables* of Roman law that the penalty for inflicting a disabled limb upon a victim was the imposition of the same injury on the wrongdoer. In China this practice was not unfamiliar to ancient thinkers. For example, Mencius once remarked:

> From this time forth I know the heavy consequences of killing a man's near relation. When a man kills another's father, that other will kill his father; when a man kills another's brother, that other will kill his elder brother. So he does not himself indeed do the act, but there is only an interval between him and it.[65]

In spite of the reflection of *talio* in Chinese ancient thought and legal proverbs, the traditional penal system did not substantially develop this type of punishment. This was due to the fact that by the time of the *T'ang Code* the penal system had already moved beyond the early primitive form of revenge or *talio* and had achieved a much more sophisticated stage of public penalties fixed by the state. Among a few remaining examples of *talio* in the traditional penal system was the punishment meted out for the offense of false accusation. It was stipulated in the *T'ang Code* that a person who made a false accusation should be punished by the same penalty fixed for the offense named in such an accusation. This principle was continuously observed by later dynasties, including the Yüan. One reference to the Yüan practice reads:

> Any person who accuses someone of [committing] a crime shall clearly indicate the year and the month of the event and shall state the truthful facts rather than ambiguous suspicion. Any person who falsely accuses shall himself atone for the crime and suffer retribution.[66]

---

buraihō ni okeru dōgai hōkuku no keibatsu ni tsuite" ("Lex Talionis in the Pentateuch"), *Hōseishi kenkyū*, 5 (1954), pp. 32–78.

[65] James Legge, *The Chinese Classics* (Hong Kong: Hong Kong University Press, 1960), II, 266.

[66] *YS* 105:5a.

Historically, when a physical penalty of a retaliatory nature was imposed upon a criminal, the law tended to reflect, in the punishment meted out, the type of crime in the given case. In other words, when a penalty was applied, the penalty itself would automatically reflect the crime committed. In the Yüan sources, there are some references to this type of penalty. For example, in 1290 a proposal was submitted to Shih-tsu recommending that any official of a public warehouse who stole or embezzled funds or grain be branded by tattooing and have his hand(s) cut off. But Shih-tsu, thinking that this sort of hand-cutting penalty had its origin in Islamic law, rejected the proposal.[67] Although this particular penalty was not institutionalized to punish corrupt officials, a similar measure was employed against other types of offenders. In one reference we read: "He who beats a Lama monk shall have his hand(s) cut off; he who curses [such a monk] shall have his tongue cut out."[68]

The penalty of hand-cutting was also commented upon by Marco Polo: "Indeed if a man strikes with steel or with a sword, whether he hits or not, or threatens one, he loses his hand. He who wounds must receive a like wound from the wounded."[69] As indicated in these references, such retaliatory penalties as hand-cutting were adopted in the Yüan period to supplement the traditional form of "five punishments." Another retaliatory measure in a modified form, namely, the penalty of tz'u-tzu (writing with a stylus, i.e., branding a criminal by tattooing) was institutionalized in the Yüan dynasty and applied extensively in cases of theft and robbery. This measure originated in the Sung in 1181/1182, when a decree ordered that the two characters ch'iang-tao (robbery) be inscribed on the forehead of a robber.[70] When such characters were tattooed on the offender, they automatically reflected

---

[67] *YS* 16:7b.

[68] *YS* 202:6b. Since the victim in this particular type of offense was a Lama monk, the special penalty of cutting off the hand(s) or removing the tongue might have been influenced by Central Asians of Islamic background or have even originated in Hindu law.

[69] Moule and Pelliot, *Marco Polo*, I, 175.

[70] Ma Tuan-lin, *Wen-hsien t'ung-k'ao* (Che-chiang shu-chü, 1896), 167:39a.

the nature of his crime and informed the public of the crime, thus giving a warning to others and at the same time subjecting the offender to discrimination. In this sense, the penalty of tattooing was also a form of retaliatory punishment.

Tattoos in the Yüan period were placed on the arm or neck instead of on the forehead. After being tattooed, the criminal was further required by Yüan law to serve as a *ching-chi-jen* (person on alert, i.e., auxiliary police) and inform the authorities of other thieves or undesirable elements. This new measure was established on August 26, 1264, in the following decree:

> A robber who is not put to death and a thief, besides being sentenced for the principal penalty, shall, for the first offense, be tattooed on the right arm with the characters *ch'iang ch'ieh-tao i-tu* (robbery or theft once). A robber, for a second offense, shall be sentenced to death. A thief, for a second offense, shall be sentenced for the offense and be also tattooed on the neck. (If an amnesty should be granted, the characters are still to be branded.) In either case, the person shall register with the local authorities and serve as a *ching-chi-jen*.[71]

As stipulated in this provision, in case of theft or robbery, the supplemental penalty was to be employed against the criminal in addition to the principal penalty such as beating with a heavy stick or penal servitude. More significantly, the obligation of serving as a *ching-chi-jen* was also a standard punishment imposed on such a wrongdoer, and thus it became an outstanding feature of the Yüan penal system. In the *Chou li*, there is a similar measure. According to this Chou reference, a *ssu-li* (commissioner of enslaved persons) was to lead his imprisoned slaves to arrest robbers and thieves.[72] The function of a slave in this context was similar to that of a *ching-chi-jen* insofar as both were entrusted with the task of helping the authorities arrest other criminals. In the Sung dynasty, some

[71] *YTC* 49:47a.
[72] *Chou-li chu-shu* (*Ssu-pu pei-yao* edition, 1930), 36:8b–9a.

wrongdoers were ordered to register their names in a record, with the understanding that if they proved that they had repented, and if they maintained good behavior for a specific period of time, their names would be erased from this record.[73] In spite of these similarities, the institution of *ching-chi-jen* as a supplemental penalty and as an "auxiliary police" function was for the first time established in China by Yüan law. A *ching-chi-jen* was required by law to register with the local authorities and to inform neighbors of his whereabouts. Whenever he left his residence for an extended period of time or moved to another place, he had to report his destination. If he did not commit any other crime for five years, he was to be recommended and guaranteed jointly by his village-head and the neighbors and then released from his *ching-chi-jen* status. Besides keeping a *ching-chi-jen* under close control, this measure also utilized the criminal's knowledge.[74] Being an ex-thief or ex-robber, the former wrongdoer might have information concerning the various criminals in his district. He was therefore expected to give information or clues leading to the arrest of other criminals. As the main function of a *ching-chi-jen* was to help in arresting criminals, it is proper to define this person as an "auxiliary policeman."[75]

The Yüan authorities adopted other measures to suppress those wrongdoers who either stole the property of another person or took the same by force. To encourage the cooperation of the *ching-chi-jen*, the Yüan dynasty also set up a reward

[73] Li Yüan-pi, *Tso-i tzu-chen* (*Ssu-pu ts'ung-k'an hsü-pien* edition, original preface dated 1117; reprinted by The Commercial Press, Shanghai, 1934), 30b–31a.

[74] For a discussion of the meaning of this term, see Hsüeh Yün-sheng, *T'ang Ming lü ho-pien* [*A Combined Text of the T'ang and Ming Codes*] (*Wan-yu wen-k'u* edition, The Commercial Press, Shanghai, 1937), IV, 482–483.

[75] It is interesting to note that Yoshikawa Kōjirō, in defining a *ching-chi-jen* as "a man being watched by the authorities," seems to have overlooked this significant function of the Yüan institution. See Yoshikawa Kōjirō, *Yoshikawa Kōjirō zenshū dai jūyon kan* [*Collected Works of Yoshikawa Kōjirō, Vol. Fourteen*] (Tokyo: Chikuma shobō, 1968), pp. 457–458. For a discussion of similar control of wrongdoers in the Ch'ing, see Fu-mei Chang Ch'en, "Local Control of Convicted Thieves in Eighteenth-Century China," Frederick Wakeman, Jr. and Carolyn Grant, eds., *Conflict and Control in Late Imperial China* (Berkeley and Los Angeles: University of California Press, 1975), pp. 121–142.

system. If a *ching-chi-jen* accused and helped arrest one thief, his five-year term would be shortened to only four years. But if one robber was arrested, the five-year term would be shortened to three years; and for two robbers arrested, the wrongdoer would no longer be required to serve as a *ching-chi-jen*. On the other hand, if a *ching-chi-jen* committed another crime during his five-year term, he was to be registered in the same status for his lifetime.[76] In order to ensure the proper functioning of this measure, three steps were prescribed in Yüan law to supervise a *ching-chi-jen*. In the first place, after serving his principal penalty, a thief or robber was to be sent back to his hometown as a *ching-chi-jen* to uncover other local criminals, a step that was known as *chuan-fa yüan-chi* (dispatch back to one's native place). Second, the name of such a *ching-chi-jen* and the nature of his offense were to be announced publicly and then written in red paint on a wall which was to be erected in front of his residence, thus subjecting him to both discrimination and surveillance in the village. Third, once in the first half of every month and once in the second half, he was to present himself to the local authorities and report his activities. His neighbors, village-head, and other security officials were also ordered to see him frequently in order to prevent him from escaping to another place; if he should escape and commit an offense in another district, these people were to be punished for their negligence.[77]

The original methods of branding criminals by tattooing were modified on January 25, 1302, in the "General Precedents concerning Robber and Thief." The new provision reads:

Any thief shall be tattooed for the first offense by placing characters on the left arm. (This refers to the person who has already obtained goods by stealing.) For the second offense, he shall be tattooed on the right arm; and for the third offense, the neck. A robber shall be tattooed for the first offense on the neck. [Both of them] shall also serve

[76] *YTC* 49:47a.
[77] *YTC* 49:47b–48a.

as *ching-chi-jen.* The authorities shall examine and inspect [them] in accordance with the old methods [i.e., methods prescribed in the decree of 1264—P.C.]. If a Mongol shall commit [such a crime] or a woman shall commit [it], the offender is not to be dealt with pursuant to the regulations concerning branding by tattooing.[78]

This version was, with slight changes, later recorded in the "Hsing-fa chih" of the *Yüan-shih,*[79] and the supplemental penalties of branding a thief or robber by tattooing and of requiring the person to become a *ching-chi-jen* were standardized. Under certain special circumstances, however, a thief or robber was exempted from being tattooed and from serving as a *ching-chi-jen.* For example, if the thief was a near relative of the victim, he would not be branded by tattooing because of the traditional legal principle which treated a theft among relatives less severely than one committed by an outsider. Nor would a person who stole grain or rice owing to hunger in times of scarcity of food be branded. This exemption was further extended to a Buddhist monk or Taoist priest who stole from his religious teacher, because the wrongdoer and the victim were regarded as members of the same family.[80] Outside these special circumstances, the supplemental physical penalties were extensively applied in cases of theft and robbery during the Yüan period. These various innovations, in conjunction with the supplemental financial penalties, contributed significantly, especially through the legal principle of *talio,* to the development of a formal Chinese penal system.

[78] *YTC* 49:7b–8a.
[79] *YS* 104:11b–12a.
[80] *YTC* 49:33a–41a.

III. THE ADMINISTRATION
OF JUSTICE

A well-constructed judicial system was established in the Yüan period to carry out the administration of justice. Although the Yüan system retained the major features of the Chinese judicial framework, it did introduce new legal institutions to China. Institutions such as the joint conference of judicial and administrative officials and censorial supervision, which were established in the Yüan dynasty, not only gave bureaucrats a means of dealing with legal matters, but also provided the public with more effective protection against bureaucratic abuse.

Because different ethnic groups observed different legal principles and customs, conflicts of law and issues of jurisdiction became extremely pressing in the Yüan. An elaborate scheme was therefore developed to settle legal disputes involving different ethnic groups. Special arrangements were also made to adjudicate cases involving members of some professions such as musicians, medical doctors, and salt-refining households. Similarly, under some circumstances, special jurisdiction was extended to people of different religious affiliations. Because the large population of the dynasty consisted of subjects with so many different ethnic backgrounds, religious contacts, professional functions, and household registrations, it was essential for the Yüan rulers to develop this type of elaborate judicial system.

Legal professionalism was significantly increased during the Yüan and was reflected both in formal trials and informal legal settlements. Many officials and clerks in the bureaucracy were given legal training. In addition, numerous books on legal matters were published, thus enabling the common

69

people to become more familiar with legal matters. The expansion of legal professionalism eventually contributed greatly to the administration of justice in the Yüan dynasty.

JUDICIAL STRUCTURE AND PROCEDURE

During the Yüan dynasty, below the Chung-shu-sheng of the central government, there existed ten Hsing Chung-shu-sheng (abbreviated as Hsing-sheng [Regional Secretarial Council]), whose jurisdiction corresponded roughly to that of the provincial governments in the West.[1] Under the Hsing-sheng, there were four administrative divisions: *lu, fu, chou,* and *hsien.* In general, the *lu* controlled the *chou* which in turn controlled the *hsien.* In some instances, the *fu* existed between the *lu* and *chou* in the administrative hierarchy. Also, there were *fu* and *chou* which were placed under the direct supervision of the Hsing-sheng, thus bypassing the jurisdiction of any intermediate *lu.*[2] On the whole, the *lu, fu,* and *chou* divisions were all equivalent to the *chou* of the Sung dynasty, and the *hsien* remained the basic administrative unit.

There appeared in the Yüan dynasty another basic administrative unit, the *lu-shih-ssu.* In a *hsien* in which the government of a *lu* or *fu* was located, a special district of the *hsien* was designated the *lu-shih-ssu,* which was under the direct control of the *lu* or *fu* rather than that of the host *hsien. Lu-shih-ssu* and *hsien* were often referred to jointly as the *ssu-hsien* —the basic administrative division in the Yüan period. In addition to these regular divisions, there were special bodies such as the Hsüan-wei-ssu (Bureau of Pacification) and the

---

[1] For the structure of the Hsing-sheng (Regional Secretarial Council), see *YS* 91:1a–4a. If the Cheng-tung Hsing-sheng (Regional Secretarial Council for Eastern Expedition) is also included, the total number of the Hsing-sheng in the Yüan period becomes eleven. See *YS* 58:2a.

[2] For the structure of the *lu, fu,* and *chou,* see *YS* 58:2b and 91:13b–16b. See also Otagi Matsuo, "Gendai toshi seido to sono kigen" ("L'état et l'origine du système municipal dans la Chine sous les Mongols"), *Tōyōshi kenkyū,* 3 (1938), pp 269–270. For a general discussion of the Yüan administrative units, see Yang P'ei-kuei, *Yüan-tai ti-fang cheng-fu* [*Local Governments in the Yüan Period*] (Taipei: Hao-han ch'u-pan she, 1975).

chün (army) which were related to the military establishment of the Yüan dynasty.[3]

These administrative divisions roughly corresponded to the various divisions of judicial structure. A case involving an offense punishable by a beating of 57 blows or less with a light stick was to be decided simply at the *ssu-hsien* level. If the penalty involved 87 blows or less with a heavy stick, the case was to be decided at the *fu, chou,* or *chün* level. If the penalty was 107 blows or 97 blows with a heavy stick, the case was to be decided at the *lu* or Hsüan-wei-ssu level. If the penalty involved penal servitude, life exile, or death, the decision required the approval of the higher authorities.[4]

Under such delegation of responsibility, the *hsien* became the basic judicial division. Depending upon the total number of households in its jurisdiction, a *hsien* was ranked as upper, medium, or lower. Officials of an upper *hsien* included a *ta-lu-hua-ch'ih (daruɣači)*, a *hsien-yin* (magistrate), a *hsien-ch'eng* (assistant magistrate), a *chu-pu* (record-keeper), a *hsien-wei* (police commissioner), and two *tien-shih* (record officials). A medium or lower *hsien* did not have any *hsien-ch'eng*, but had the other members of the staff.[5] Responsibility for maintaining public order in a *hsien* was normally entrusted to the *hsien-wei*. The police commissioner was given the authority to patrol the area and to arrest suspects; he was relieved of other administrative burdens in the district government.[6] Under his leadership, a group of *kung-shou* (archers, i.e., police) was organized to implement the task of maintaining local security. For every 100 households in the district, a household with an average income was selected to provide one male adult to serve as a *kung-shou*. In return for this service, the other 99

[3] For the structure of the Hsuan-wei-ssu (Bureau of Pacification), see *YS* 91 : 4b–5b. See also Paul Ratchnevsky, *Un Code des Yuan*, p. 93, n. 1 and Yanai Watari, *Mōkoshi kenkyū*, pp. 916–918. A *chün* (army) was established in a remote frontier area and its status was equivalent to a lower *chou*. See *YS* 91 : 16a.

[4] *YS* 39 : 2a.

[5] *YS* 91 : 15b–16a.

[6] Ch'en Yüan, *Shen-k'o Yuan tien-chang chiao-pu*, "Chüeh-wen" ("Omitted Entries"), 1 : 35a.

households were to split the *corvée* obligation of the *kung-shou* so as to distribute the burden evenly.[7]

Since the duty of an archer was to prevent crime from occurring as well as to arrest criminals, he became more of a local policeman than a military serviceman. His main concern was to capture thieves and robbers. For failure to arrest a thief or a robber within a month, he was to be punished with seven or seventeen blows with a light stick, respectively; for two months, seventeen or 27 blows, respectively; and for three months, 27 or 37 blows, respectively. On the other hand, he was to be rewarded for arresting a thief or robber within the deadline.[8] To perform his task successfully, an archer often received assistance and information from the *ching-chi-jen* who were former thieves or robbers. Under the supervision of the *hsien-wei*, the archers of each locality formed the basic police force for the enforcement of law and order.

A wrongdoer, whether he was arrested by an archer or whether he voluntarily turned himself in to the authorities, was to be tried by the *hsien-yin*, for neither an archer nor a *hsien-wei* had the authority to conduct a trial.[9] If, after a brief interrogation, the wrongdoer was reasonably suspected of having committed a serious crime, he was to be transferred to a higher authority in the *lu*, *fu*, or *chou* where he was to be jailed to await trial. This was necessary because a *hsien* normally had no authority to decide such a case and stocked only a very limited supply of rations for inmates.[10] On the other hand, if the cases were of a less serious nature—such as disputes over land, marriage, family property, debt, assault, or other miscellaneous offenses punishable only by beating with a light stick—they were to be decided by the magistrate in the *hsien*. Although defendants and witnesses normally were not jailed in these types of cases, they were obliged to present themselves immediately upon receiving a summons.[11] Trials for these

[7] *YTC* 51:2a.
[8] *YTC* 49:8b–9a.
[9] *YTC* 51:12a.
[10] *YTC* 39:7a and 51:12a.
[11] *YTC* 40:10a. See also Hu Chih-yu, *Tzu-shan ta-ch'uan-chi*, 23:3b–4b.

civil cases and petty criminal offenses were scheduled between the first day of the 10th moon of the year and the first day of the 3rd moon of the following year so that each party or witness would not be kept from his agricultural work.[12] Since a magistrate was required to observe holidays, perform social obligations, and inspect district affairs, the number of working days for judicial matters within the above period was further reduced to only fifty or sixty days per year.[13]

Since judicial authority at the *ssu-hsien* level was relatively limited, officials at the *lu, fu,* or *chou* level naturally functioned more actively than the more junior officials at the local level. The official organizations of the *lu, fu,* and *chou* were on the whole similar to one another. Unlike a *hsien,* each had a well-staffed jail to receive offenders transferred from the subordinate *hsien.* In addition, the government at the *lu, fu,* or *chou* level was also better staffed than that of a *hsien.*

The administration of the prison system in the Yüan period differed from that of the earlier dynasties. Since the penalties of exile and penal servitude in the Yüan dynasty stressed the utilization of labor, the function of the jail during the Yüan was not to deprive an offender of freedom per se, but rather to put a suspect in custody before or during a formal trial or to detain a sentenced person before the final imposition of a sentence. Moreover, in the Yüan period, jails were headed by a *ssu-yü* (prison commissioner) who was under the direct supervision of the Su-cheng lien-fang ssu or, before 1291, T'i-hsing an-ch'a ssu (Surveillance Bureau, a Branch of the Censorate). As a result, the *ssu-yü* was not immediately supervised by the chief executive at the *lu, fu,* or *chou* level, although his various responsibilities were shared by an official appointed as the *t'i-k'ung lao-yü kuan* (prison intendent) on a monthly basis by the executive members of the *lu, fu,* or *chou* government.[14] The appointment of the *ssu-yü* was made by a *t'ui-kuan* (judge), but the *ssu-yü* was at least theoretically independent of the influence or the direct control of the chief executive. Meanwhile, censors in

[12] *YTC* 53:36a–37b.
[13] Hu Chih-yü, *Tzu-shan ta-ch'uan-chi,* 23:25a–27a.
[14] *YTC* 40:21a–23a.

the Su-cheng lien-fang ssu, through their links with the office of the *ssu-yü*, effectively extended their inspecting power to the judicial matters of a provincial or local government. On the other hand, through the activities of the *t'i-k'ung lao-yü kuan*, other officials could maintain close contact with the functions of the jail and the work of the *ssu-yü*. A kind of system of "checks and balances" was therefore successfully designed and observed in the Yüan judicial system.[15]

The sole responsibility of the *ssu-yü* was to administer the affairs of the jail. These affairs included: 1) seeing that the cells and cangues were cleaned; 2) providing clothes and food regularly to inmates; 3) personally inspecting sick inmates; and 4) directly reporting inmates' grievances to the Su-cheng lien-fang ssu.[16] Of these, the last item was especially important, for censors could quickly restore justice and impeach officials upon a direct report from the *ssu-yü*. For instance, one Liu Chi saved several people by apprising himself of their grievance while he was a *ssu-yü*.[17] This special function of the *ssu-yü* justified and reinforced the need that he be independent and not controlled by other officials in the *lu*, *fu*, or *chou* government.

The *ssu-yü* was usually assisted by a *yü-tien* (prison clerk) and several *chin-tzu* (jailers) or *lao-tzu* (jailers).[18] The post of *yü-tien* required some legal knowledge and was usually filled by clerks from either a branch of the provincial government or from the Su-cheng lien-fang ssu.[19] The post of *lao-tzu* required physical training; *lao-tzu* who were fast runners would be encouraged to participate in an annual race of 180 *li* in the capital for a prize that was awarded by the Emperor himself.[20] Members of the jail staff were responsible for preventing inmates from escaping. Serious offenders were forced to wear

---

[15] Since censors often visited various localities, they could seek out cases of injustice, thus aiding in the effective administration of justice.

[16] *YTCHC* "Hsing-pu": 7.

[17] Huang Chin, *Chin-hua Huang hsien-sheng wen-chi* (*Hsü Chin-hua ts'ung-shu* edition), 31:1.

[18] *YTC* 12:66 and *YS* 85:29b.

[19] *YS* 83:34b.

[20] T'ao Tsung-i, *Cho-keng lu* (Shih-chieh shu-chu edition, Taipei, 1963), p. 34. See also the *P'u T'ung-shih yen-chieh*, pp. 241–243.

a *chia* (wooden cangue or collar). Its length ranged from five to six Chinese feet and its width was from 1.4 to 1.6 Chinese feet. Its weight varied according to the nature of the offense: 25 catties for a capital offense; 20 catties for an offense punishable by penal servitude; and 18 catties for an offense punishable by beating with a heavy stick. A male criminal who had committed a capital offense would be ordered to wear a pair of *niu* (wooden handcuffs); the length of these handcuffs ranged from 1.6 to 2 Chinese feet, while their width and thickness were 3 and 1 Chinese inches, respectively. There were also other instruments used in the Yüan period, such as the *suo* (chain) and *liao* (fetters). A *suo* was used to tie a person around the waist and its length was between 8 and 12 Chinese feet; the *liao* were used to attach the feet of a criminal and weighed 3 chatties.[21] Although such instruments were regulated by Yüan law, more painful and illegal instruments were occasionally employed, despite strict prohibitions, to torture criminals.

On the whole, the government at the *lu*, *fu*, or *chou* level was well staffed. For instance, a *lu* government was theoretically headed by a *ta-lu-hua-ch'ih* (*daruɣači*) who was a Mongolian official. The actual administration was managed by a Chinese *tsung-kuan* (chief administrator) who was in turn assisted by a group of *cheng-kuan* (principal officials), including the *t'üng-chih* (associate prefect), *chih-chung* (assistant prefect), *p'an-kuan* (commissary of records), and *t'ui-kuan* (judge). Below these principal officials was a group of *shou-ling-kuan* (chief officials) who were in charge of various clerks and functionaries. Since the *ta-lu-hua-ch'ih* (*daruɣači*) was merely a nominal head of the administration, major administrative and judicial matters were jointly decided by the *tsung-kuan* and the principal official in a conference. Although the Sung dynasty had earlier developed a summary system of conference, the structure of conference was further modified and refined in the Yüan period to facilitate various functions of government.

The *t'ui-kuan* was in charge of judicial matters in the *lu*

[21] *YTC* 40:1a and *YS* 103:13.

government and was free from other administrative burdens. He was to investigate a case, conduct the trial, and submit his findings to other principal officials in the joint conference for final decision. Unless approval was given by the joint conference, the findings and recommendation of a *t'ui-kuan* had no binding force. Since his preliminary decisions of cases had to be reviewed by fellow officials, a *t'ui-kuan* was unable to abuse his power with regard to judicial matters. To be sure, the reviews in the joint conference might be no more than routine formalities. The procedure, however, served as an effective bar to possible misconduct of the *t'ui-kuan* (albeit perhaps at the expense of judicial independence). The position of *t'ui-kuan* required comprehensive legal knowledge. During the preliminary trial, the *t'ui-kuan* had to study every detail of the case carefully and interrogate the wrongdoer and witness thoroughly. Every bit of evidence had to be examined so that injustice might not occur.

Because of the traditional emphasis on the importance of a suspect's confession as evidence, Chinese authorities often tortured an accused in order to extract his confession. During the Yüan dynasty, however, a special mechanism was developed to prevent the *t'ui-kuan* from imposing excessive torture on a suspect. It was stipulated in Yüan law that only when a wrong-doer was reasonably suspected and the supporting evidence was also clear, could the *t'ui-kuan* impose torture. And the *t'ui-kuan* still had to consult his fellow officials in the conference before authorizing any torture. If there was no supporting evidence, a suspect could not be tortured at all.[22] A *hsün-chang* (interrogation stick) was normally used to carry out the torture. It was 3.5 Chinese feet in length and 0.55 Chinese inches in diameter at the large end, tapering to 0.25 inches at the small end.[23] Occasionally, some harsher types of torture were applied despite the strict prohibition against them, and consequently, suspects were forced to confess to crimes which they had not committed.[24] But in general, the regulations concerning the

[22] *YTC* 40:17.
[23] *YTC* 40:1a.
[24] *YTC* 40:2b–8a.

joint conference and torture became important features of the Yüan judicial system and provided suspects with an additional measure of protection.

If the penalty that was meted out after the joint conference had reviewed and approved the findings submitted by the *t'ui-kuan* was no heavier than 107 blows with a heavy stick, the wrongdoer would be so punished and the case closed. If the penalty involved death, exile, or penal servitude, then an affidavit of acceptance of the findings had to be obtained from the wrongdoer in front of his family and the public, thus allowing the wrongdoer and his family an opportunity to express any objection or grievance in the court.[25] When the decision was not contested, the affidavit had to be personally signed by the wrongdoer by impressing his fingerprints upon it. In this method of signature, the tip of the index finger (usually that of the left hand for a male and that of the right hand for a female) and the back of its first and second joints were inked and then pressed beneath the person's name at the end of the document in question. The impression consisted of three ink spots, the mark made by the finger tip being at the bottom. As the width of the index finger and the distance between its joints differ from person to person, forgery was impossible.[26] For example, Yao Sui records a legal case involving the authenticity of a legal document that was decided solely on the basis of the evidence of such marks.[27]

The wrongdoer's affidavit, along with other documents of his case, was then sent to the Su-cheng lien-fang ssu for review. If the wrongdoer refused to sign an affidavit or his family members challenged the validity of the findings, the case had to be reported at once to the Su-cheng lien-fang ssu which in turn was required to order a nearby official to conduct a new trial. Also, if the censors in their review found mistakes in the

[25] *YTC* 12:18.

[26] For a discussion of this method of legal authentication, see Niida Noboru, *Tō-Sō hōritsu bunsho no kenkyū* [*The Critical Study on Legal Documents of the T'ang and Sung Eras*] (Tokyo: Tokyo University Press, 1937), pp. 37–60.

[27] Yao Sui, *Mu-an chi* (*Ssu-pu ts'ung-k'an* edition, The Commercial Press, Shanghai, 1929), 22:14b–15a.

affidavit or other documents sent by the *lu* government, a new trial would be ordered so as to restore justice.[28] On the other hand, if no mistakes were found during the review, the Su-cheng lien-fang ssu would give its consent to the findings. Upon such consent, if the penalty was only penal servitude, the *lu* government could implement the decision and officially close the case. If the penalty involved exile or death, the *lu* authorities were required to report the case to the Hsing-sheng which in turn was to transmit it to the central government for final review. Only after final approval had been received from the central government could the *lu* authorities impose the penalty of exile or death on the wrongdoer and officially close the case.[29]

Before 1271 the judicial structure of the central government was divided into three levels: the Fa-ssu (Bureau of Law), Hsing-pu (Board of Punishments), and Tu-sheng (capital *Sheng*, i.e., the Chung-shu-sheng or Shang-shu-sheng).[30] The Fa-ssu was dissolved when the *T'ai-ho lü* was abolished in 1271. The judicial functions of the Hsing-pu and the Tu-sheng, however, remained important throughout the Yüan dynasty. The Hsing-pu reviewed cases involving punishment by exile or death and clarified ambiguities in the application of law and punishment.[31] Since the office of the Ta-li-shih (Grand Court of Revisions) of previous dynasties did not continue into the Yüan period, the traditional judicial authority and function of the Ta-li-shih as the highest legal organ began to shift to the Hsing-pu. This transformation was another significant feature of Yüan judicial structure, and the superior position of the Hsing-pu was subsequently observed by later dynasties. The decisions of the Hsing-pu were subjected to final modification by the Tu-sheng. Normally, decisions drafted by the Hsing-pu were rarely questioned; in some major cases, however, the Tu-sheng could modify controversial decisions by obtaining a mandate from the Emperor. When a final decision was made,

[28] Miyazaki Ichisada, "Sō-Gen jidai no hōsei to saiban kikō," p. 165.
[29] *Ibid.*
[30] Ratchnevsky, *Un Code des Yuan*, p. 23, n. 3.
[31] *YS* 85:28b–29a.

the Tu-sheng would transmit it to the Hsing-pu which in turn would relay it to the Hsing-sheng. Upon the arrival of the final decision, the Hsing-sheng would send it to the *lu* government for actual implementation and thus conclude the case entirely.

Judicial function and structure at each level of Yüan government were so well defined that persons who ignored the procedures and bypassed the proper authorities would be punished.[32] On the other hand, if a case was not justly handled by the authorities or if there was any grievance, the victim or his family was allowed to report the matter directly to the censors in order to restore justice.[33] For some exceptionally grave injustices, the victim and his family were encouraged to submit the case directly to the Emperor by beating the drum which was set up in the Imperial palace for reporting great injustice to the throne.[34] On the whole, Yüan judicial structure and procedures extended more effective protection to the people than did the structure and procedures of previous dynasties. The clear delegation of judicial authority at each level of government limited the danger of abuse of power and at the same time protected the rights of suspects. Since more serious cases were automatically tried or reviewed by more experienced officials at higher levels of government, the Yüan system therefore afforded suspects more substantial chances to have a just trial. For example, capital offenses were entitled to a final review by the central government. In contrast to this, capital offenses during the Sung were not necessarily reviewed by the central government, owing to the distinction between *ying-tsou* (should be memorialized) and *pu-ying-tsou* (need not be memorialized) cases. The *pu-ying-tsou* category referred to cases in which the evidence was clear, the application of law was correct, and the finding was accepted by the accused. Such cases were not to be memorialized to the central government; only cases within the category of *ying-tsou* were entitled to central government review. By contrast, the mandatory re-

[32] *YTC* 53:23b–24a.
[33] *YTC* 53:19a–21b.
[34] *YS* 8:22b.

view system of the Yüan required that every capital offense case be submitted to the central government for approval of the punishment. Undoubtedly, some Yüan institutions, such as the joint conference and special censorial supervision, in practice might have jeopardized absolute judicial independence or delayed the final settlement of a case. Thus the delay caused by the review system was severely criticized by Hu Chih-yü who proposed that some adjustments be made.[35] In order to avoid the long delay, it was established that if a suspect was arrested for involvement in a serious crime and if no substantial evidence could be gathered against him within three years, he was to be released.[36] Although some exceptional cases might be delayed for more than three years or might be sent back and forth by authorities of different judicial bodies,[37] the judicial system of the Yüan dynasty was well constructed and effectively prevented officials from abusing their power.

Special Jurisdiction and Conflict of Laws

Historically, the status of foreigners was always a matter of concern to the Chinese. Politically, the Chinese sometimes took pacific views toward foreigners and sometimes militant stands.[38] Morally, the Chinese tended to feel superior to foreigners, measuring them against the Confucian criteria of high cultural and moral standards.[39] Legally, however, disputes between foreigners and Chinese or between foreigners themselves involved differences in customs and legal principles and could not be solved by political or moral criteria alone. Consequently, a concrete set of legal formulae on jurisdiction and conflict of laws was always needed.

[35] Hu Chih-yü, *Tzu-shan ta-ch'uan-chi*, 21:30b–32b.

[36] *YS* 33:20b and 37:3b.

[37] For instance, it is recorded in the *Yuan shih* that two persons had been jailed for more than ten years before they were finally released after trial. See *YS* 131:22b.

[38] Yang Lien-sheng, "Historical Notes on the Chinese World Order," John K. Fairbank, ed., *The Chinese World Order* (Cambridge, Mass.: Harvard University Press, 1968), pp. 24–28.

[39] Benjamin I. Schwartz, "The Chinese Perception of World Order," *ibid.*, pp. 277–278.

As early as the T'ang dynasty, Chinese authorities had begun to establish principles to deal with cases involving foreigners. Thus if a *hua-wai-jen* (person outside the culture, i.e., a foreigner) had a legal dispute with a fellow foreigner of the same ethnic group, his case was to be decided according to the criteria of the law of his own group—in effect, according to a kind of "personality principle." On the other hand, if the two parties were of different ethnic backgrounds, the case was to be governed by Chinese law. To be more specific, disputes between a Korean and a Japanese in China were to be decided by neither Korean nor Japanese law but rather by Chinese law. If two parties were both Koreans or Japanese, their case was to be tried by Korean law or Japanese law, respectively, rather than by the law of the host country. This T'ang practice reflects the traditional convention in China that "When one enters a new territory, one inquires about its prohibitions; when one enters a new state, one inquires about its customs."[40] The practice, with some minor modifications, continued in existence in the later dynasties.[41] However, it became much more complicated and elaborate in the Yüan period because of the existence of several major ethnic groups in China proper.

The three main ethnic groups were the Mongols, the Central Asians, and the Chinese. The division, as suggested by Yanai Watari, was made on the basis of the distinct differences in political treatment, ethnic background, language, customs, historical origin, and geographic location of the three groups.[42] This division was later modified by Meng Ssu-ming, who proposed a classification of four categories—Mongols, Central Asians, Northern Chinese, and Southern Chinese.[43] Since the above groups in China were all under the domination of the Mongolian rulers, theoretically they were not foreigners in the strict sense. They were, however, so different from one another

[40] For a discussion of the traditional ideas concerning this principle in China, see Niida Noboru, *Chūgoku no nōson kazoku* [*Chinese Peasant Families and Clans*] (Tokyo: Tokyo University Press, 1952), pp. 3–4.
[41] Niida Noboru, *Chūgoku hōseishi kenkyū: keihō*, pp. 398–452. See also Kuwabara Jitsuzō, *Kuwabara Jitsuzō zenshū dai go kan* [*Collected Works of Kuwabara Jitsuzō, Vol. Five*] (Tokyo: Iwanami shoten, 1968), pp. 76–81.
[42] See Ch. I, n. 21 above.
[43] See Ch. I, n. 21 above.

that criteria had to be formulated for settling disputes arising between people of these different ethnic groups. The need for such criteria was strongly felt in the early period of the dynasty. For instance, Hu Chih-yü advocated: "To rule Chinese people Chinese law must be used; to rule Northern people [i.e., Mongols and Central Asians as contrasted with Chinese] Northern law must be applied."[44] Behind this policy was a basic awareness that Chinese and non-Chinese could not both be governed by a single set of legal principles. He had said on an earlier occasion:

> To force the South to follow the North is impractical, and to force the North to follow the South is more impractical. Matters in the South are complicated; and when matters are complicated, laws are complicated. Matters in the North are simple; and if the matters are simple, laws are simple. To force the complicated [laws] to follow the simple will make it impossible to rule. To force the simple [laws] to follow the complicated will make people suffer nuisance and bitterness.[45]

The policy proposed by Hu Chih-yü of establishing legal criteria prevailed very early. By 1272 the Ta Tsung-cheng-fu (Grand Bureau for the Affairs of the Imperial Clan) was entrusted with the responsibility of deciding cases of Mongols alone, thus relinquishing its former jurisdiction over Chinese cases.[46] This division was further applied to Central Asians, and cases brought by them were placed solely under the jurisdiction of the Tu-hu-fu (Bureau of Guardianship).[47] Under this arrangement, Mongols and Central Asians were tried according to their own Mongolian or Central Asian laws, and Chinese were tried according to their Chinese laws. For instance, in a case of theft or robbery, a Chinese offender was tattooed in addition to the imposition of principal punishment, whereas such punishment by tattooing was not imposed on a

[44] Hu Chih-yü, *Tzu-shan ta-ch'uan-chi*, 21:19a.
[45] *Ibid.*, 21:7.
[46] *YS* 87:1a.
[47] *YS* 89:33b.

Mongol or a Central Asian.[48] If a judge should have a Mongol tattooed, he himself was to be punished by a beating of 77 blows with a heavy stick and removed from his official post; in addition, the tattoo on the Mongol was to be erased.[49] The formal differences in punishment (such as tattooing in the above instance) were often cited by scholars as a reflection of Mongolian discrimination against Chinese. For example, Meng Ssu-ming used the evidence of the tattooing practice to support his theory that in the Yüan dynasty Mongols and Chinese were obviously treated unequally.[50] The difference in tattooing, however, was not an intentional discrimination but rather a result of observing norms of the various ethnic groups. There was no provision for the penalty of tattooing in Mongolian or Central Asian customary law, and as a result, Mongols or Central Asians were not to be tattooed for their offenses of theft or robbery. By the same token, if a person of an ethnic group that did not follow the custom of *levirate* married the widow of his deceased brother, he was to be punished.[51] Consequently, a Chinese who married his brother's widow was subjected to punishment, whereas a Mongol who did so would be free from any legal sanction.[52]

Legal disputes between Chinese, Mongols, and Central Asians were usually decided in a joint conference attended by the representatives of the ethnic groups involved. In 1328 it became well established that in the Ta-tu and Shang-tu areas, legal disputes arising between persons of different ethnic backgrounds were to be decided by the Tsung-cheng-fu (Bureau for the Affairs of the Imperial Clan),[53] while disputes occurring in the *lu, fu, chou,* or *hsien* elsewhere were to be decided by the authorities at each respective level under the jurisdiction of

[48] *YTC* 49:7b–8a and *YS* 38:10a and 104:21b.
[49] *YS* 103:11b.
[50] Meng Ssu-ming, *Yuan-tai she-hui chieh-chi chih-tu,* p. 55.
[51] *YS* 34:23a.
[52] *YS* 8:18a and 187:2a.
[53] The Ta Tsung-cheng-fu (Grand Bureau for the Affairs of the Imperial Clan) changed its name to the Tsung-cheng-fu (Bureau for the Affairs of the Imperial Clan) in the time of Jen-tsung (Buyantu Qaγan). See *YS* 92:4a.

the Hsing-pu.[54] In general, the "personality principle" was the guideline for deciding a case involving a conflict of laws. In cases where there were extreme difficulties in applying the guideline, supplemental regulations were provided. For example, if there were ambiguities in the application of law in a case of intermarriage, the disputes were to be adjudicated according to the husband's law. If the wife was a Mongol, however, the disputes automatically were to be decided by Mongolian law. Consequently, Mongolian law prevailed where a party to the intermarriage was a Mongol, be the person husband or wife.[55]

The Yüan dynasty further developed a system of combined courts to deal with cases involving persons with special status such as soldiers or members of specific professional groups. Disputes between Mongolian soldiers themselves over marriage, slaves, debts, assaults, and other civil matters, sexual offenses, or other miscellaneous matters were to be decided by the officers at the ao-lu (a'uraɣ) (camp).[56] If the case was of a more serious nature—such as homicide, an important public offense, theft, robbery, or counterfeiting—it was to be decided by the officer and the civilian official in a combined court.[57] It was also provided that a case involving a civilian and a Mongolian soldier in adultery, robbery, fraud, deceit, or other serious criminal offense was to be decided by the civilian official alone. If the disputes between them were only matters of land ownership, assault, marriage, slaves, family property, debt, or inheritance, they were to be decided by the officer and the civilian official in a combined court.[58] The arrangement of being tried in a combined court was, however, not made for

---

[54] YS 87·1b.

[55] Niida Noboru, Chūgoku hōseishi kenkyū: keihō, p. 412. See also Hu Chih-yü, Tzu-shan ta-ch'uan-chi, 21:7b.

[56] For a discussion of this term, see Francis W. Cleaves, "The Sino-Mongolian Inscription of 1362 in Memory of Prince Hindu," p. 50, n. 92. While Pelliot identified this term as aɣrug, it was identified incorrectly as aul by Professors Shiratori Kurakichi and Iwamura Shinobu. See Iwamura Shinobu, "Gen tenshō keibu no kenkyū" ("Criminal Procedure under the Yuan Dynasty"), Tōhō gakuhō (Kyoto), 24 (1954), pp. 19–21.

[57] YTC 39:8b.

[58] YTC 53:32 and YTCHC "Hsing-pu": 52. See also YS 102:19a.

a soldier who had legal disputes with a civilian residing in a neighboring *hsien* or *chou*. In this situation, the case was to be decided by the authorities who had jurisdiction over the defendant. If the authorities should refuse to try the case, the plaintiff would be allowed to complain to the higher authorities, and the negligent lower authorities would be investigated.[59]

The presence of the officer in the combined court was intended to help the civilian official expedite the judicial procedure as well as maintain the authority of military jurisdiction. In practice, however, officers often failed to attend, either through negligence or arrogance. As a result, trials were often delayed and sometimes evidence was even destroyed. In order to arrest this trend of irresponsibility, it was mandated in 1308 that if an officer failed to participate in a combined court after being notified three times, the case would be automatically decided by the civilian official alone.[60]

It is recorded in the *Yüan shih* that if a Mongol beat a Chinese during a quarrel, the latter could not fight back.[61] The reference has often been interpreted by modern scholars as obvious discrimination by Mongols against Chinese. A passage in the *Yüan tien-chang*, however, gives an account of background behind the *Yüan shih* provision; in the *Yüan tien-change* it is stated that Chinese often refused to supply Mongolian garrison officers or other officials with food and accommodations during their missions, and that such refusals frequently resulted in disputes and accidents. It was, therefore, established in 1283 that civilians had to provide food and accommodations so as to avoid disputes with the Mongolian officers, and that if a Mongolian officer should beat a Chinese, the latter should present witnesses and file suit with the local authorities instead of beating the officer in return.[62] From this document it becomes clear that, far from oppressing the Chinese with this provision, the Mongols were actually providing them with recourse for legal satisfaction, even in cases where they had

[59] *YTC* 53:14a and *YS* 102:19a.
[60] See n. 58 above.
[61] *YS* 105:5b–6a.
[62] *YTC* 44:8a. See also *Chan-ch'ih*, 1, 50.

refused food and accommodations to garrison officers. Thus the Mongols in prohibiting the Chinese from fighting back were not denying them recourse of satisfaction but rather insisting that they seek it in a different forum. To be sure, there were various kinds of political discrimination against Chinese. However, it is misleading to interpret the above reference as evidence of discrimination by Mongols against Chinese, because the provision in this particular document was used to enforce the practice of separate jurisdiction according to the above-described "personality principle" rather than to encourage discrimination against Chinese.[63]

The arrangement of special jurisdiction was also extended *to Central Asians who were associated with special organiza-tions.* For instance, disputes between an Uighur who was affiliated with the I-tu-hu (Iduqut) and a Chinese civilian were to be tried by a combined court made up of the head of the Uighur group and the appropriate civilian official.[64] This arrangement was further sustained in 1319, so that a minor case between a Chinese and an Uighur might be decided by the civilian official and a leader of the Iduqut in a combined court. Serious offenses between them were nevertheless to be decided by the civilian official alone. If the Uighur was not associated with the Iduqut, he was to be tried by the civilian official alone, regardless of the nature of his case.[65]

This special arrangement was extended to several categories of Chinese whose household registrations were different from those of common people. These categories included Buddhist monks, Taoist priests, soldiers, and *chan-hu* (households of the postal relay system). Buddhist monks are a case in point. In 1313 it was established that if a monk committed an offense of a serious nature, such as a sexual offense, robbery, fraud,

---

[63] For a discussion of this issue, see Iwamura Shinobu, "Gen tenshō keibu no kenkyū," pp. 73–75.

[64] *YTC* 53:31b–41a. For a discussion of the term *Iduqut*, see Francis W. Cleaves, "The Sino-Mongolian Inscription of 1362 in Memory of Prince Hindu," p. 43, n. 28 and p. 100, n. 28.

[65] *YTCHC* "Hsing-pu": 54. For a discussion of special jurisdiction over Central Asians in China, see Iwamura Shinobu, "Gen tenshō keibu no kenkyū," pp. 66–69 and 90–93.

deceit, or homicide, he was to be tried by the civilian official alone. With regard to other minor legal disputes between monks themselves, the head monk of their temple was authorized to decide the cases. Minor disputes between a monk and a layman were decided by the head monk and the civilian official in a combined court.[66] If a monk should accuse the head monk of committing a crime or vice versa, the case would be decided by the head monk of a neighboring temple.[67] Like a Buddhist monk, a Taoist priest was also entitled to a similar arrangement. But the arrangement was not applicable to a Confucian scholar, since his registration was not different from that of other secular people.[68] On the other hand, if a Confucian scholar, a Buddhist monk, and a Taoist priest should quarrel among themselves, their cases were to be tried jointly by the leaders of their groups, and civilian officials were asked not to involve themselves in such matters.[69]

Disputes between laymen and members of some special professional groups were governed by similar special jurisdictional arrangements. For instance, in 1295 it was ordered that disputes between a medical doctor and a layman be decided jointly by the civilian official and the leader of the medical association.[70] In 1299 it was also established that a musician's disputes with a layman were to be decided by the civilian official and the head of the musician's group.[71] This arrangement was further extended in 1302 to members of *tsao-hu* (salt-refining households), so that disputes between members and civilian or military personnel were to be tried jointly by the authorities of the Salt Bureau and the civilian official or the military officer.[72]

The extension of special jurisdiction to these ethnic or professional groups was not due to the fact that they commanded any special social or political privilege. On the contrary, the

[66] *YTC* 53:12a–13a.
[67] *YTC* 53:11b–12a.
[68] *YTC* 53:10b–11a.
[69] *YTC* 53:30.
[70] *YTC* 53:30b.
[71] *YTC* 53:30b–31a.
[72] *YTC* 53:34b–35a.

social status of many of them, such as musicians and *tsao-hu* members, was very low. This then implies that separate jurisdiction was established for the very practical purpose of expediting judicial procedure and balancing the possible conflict of differing legal principles and customs. To this end, extensive application of the "personality principle" and the exercise of the combined court became important features of Yüan legal institutions. To be sure, there was some political, social, economic, and cultural discrimination between different groups in the Yüan, but there were also differences in treatment which were purely a reflection of a policy of separate jurisdiction rather than intentional discrimination.

LEGAL PROFESSIONALISM

For a long period of time after the establishment of the Yüan dynasty, no national examinations were held. The first such examination finally took place in 1315, and after that, the examinations were given once every three years. However, the national examinations were once again discontinued between 1333 and 1342. As a result, many officials in the Yüan dynasty were not appointed on the basis of the national examinations. As a matter of fact, many were former clerks in the government who were promoted to fill official posts without ever taking the examinations. Indeed, it seemed that the quickest way to become an official was to begin as a clerk in the central government. Normally, clerks in the central government were chosen from experienced clerks in the local government. For example, every year each Su-cheng lien-fang ssu was to select from among the local clerks two persons to serve in the central government.[73] Given these circumstances, it is not surprising that many officials were of clerkly origin. Sometimes local officials were promoted to become clerks in the central government before they were named to higher official posts. Consequently, the traditionally distinct difference between the official and clerkly backgrounds began to disappear in the Yüan period.

[73] *YS* 83:17.

Historically, officials and clerks belonged to entirely different categories in China. A clerk remained a humble clerk for his lifetime, and only in a few special cases would an outstanding clerk be promoted to become an official. By contrast, because of the new pattern of serving alternately as clerks and officials, clerks in the Yüan were given more authority and greater responsibilities.[74] On the whole, the Yüan clerks also had more prestige than those of previous dynasties. Many promising youths aspired to become clerks so as to obtain official posts eventually, and some of them even started an apprenticeship in their early teens to study closely with experienced clerks in the local government.[75] By the time they were finally appointed officials, they already had a thorough knowledge of bureaucratic affairs and had received comprehensive training in legal matters. For example, Ho Jung-tsu started his career as a clerk, and his bureaucratic training and legal knowledge were essential to the promulgation of the *Chih-yüan hsin-ko* in 1291.[76] Moreover, persons who were recommended by the Su-cheng lien-fang ssu were required to take an examination in practical affairs. The examination covered forms and questions dealing with concrete legal matters such as arrest, investigation, trial, imprisonment, confession, and evidence.[77] By comparison, officials of the previous dynasties were mostly trained in Chinese classics. As a result, except for some specialists in law, most officials of earlier dynasties were not familiar with legal matters at the time of their appointments, and some of them even strongly resented legal training. Since many Yüan officials were of clerkly origin, they were more familiar with legal matters and bureaucratic affairs than their counterparts of the earlier dynasties.[78]

The new rising interest in legal training during the Yüan dynasty resulted in the publication of numerous legal texts and commentaries. Some individuals and book stores, in their

[74] For the regulations concerning the ranks, promotion, and responsibilities of the Yuan governmental clerks, see *YS* 84:1a–27a.

[75] *YTC* 12:47a, 12:49, and 12:51b–52a.

[76] *YS* 168:17b.

[77] *YTC* 12:3a–20b.

[78] For a general discussion of the status of Yuan clerks and the significance of their service, see Abe Takeo, *Gendaishi no kenkyū*, pp. 3–52.

private capacity, even compiled legal texts containing precedents and ordinances; in previous dynasties only officials in the government had made such collections. Comparative studies of the earlier legal codes were also very popular among Yüan scholars. For instance, in addition to the reprints of the *T'ang Code*, the Yüan commentaries on T'ang law included books such as the *T'ang lü shan-yao* [*Abridgment of the T'ang Code*], *T'ang lü lei-yao* [*Classified Summary of the T'ang Code*], *T'ang lü ming-fa lei-shuo* [*Classification and Interpretation of the T'ang Code for Legal Studies*], *T'ang lü-wen ming-fa hui-yao lu* [*Summaries and Textual Interpretations of the T'ang Code for Legal Studies*], *T'ang lu shih-wen* [*Annotated Study of the T'ang Code*], and *T'ang lü tsuan-li* [*The T'ang Code with Annotated Cases*].[79] Studies on the Sung and Chin codes included the *Hsing-t'ung-fu chieh* [*Interpretations on the Unified Code in Rhyme*],[80] *Hsing-t'ung-fu shu* [*Commentaries on the Unified Code in Rhyme*],[81] *Ts'u-chieh Hsing-t'ung-fu* [*Gloss Commentaries on the Unified Code in Rhyme*],[82] *Pieh-pen Hsing-t'ung-fu* [*Supplements to the Unified Code in Rhyme*],[83] *Hsing-t'ung-fu chih-chieh* [*Straight Commentaries on the Unified Code in Rhyme*],[84] *Hsing-t'ung-fu huo-wen* [*Questions and Answers on the Unified Code in Rhyme*],[85] *Chieh Hsing-t'ung-fu* [*Annotated Unified Code in Rhyme*],[86] *Ssu-yen tsuan-chu* [*Notes on the Text in Four Letters' Rhyme*],[87] *Hsing-t'ung-fu ching-yao* [*Essential Unified Code in Rhyme*],[88] and *Hsing-t'ung-fu lüeh-chü* [*Brief Annotation on the*

---

[79] For a discussion of various studies on the *T'ang Code* in the Yuan period, see Niida Noboru, *Chūgoku hōseishi kenkyū: hō to kanshū, hō to dōtoku*, pp. 105–107.

[80] For a discussion of this text, see Shen Chia-pen, *Shen Chi-i hsien-sheng i-shu chia-pein, Wen-ts'un* [*Selected Essays*], 7:6a–7b.

[81] For a discussion of this text, see *ibid.*, 7:8.

[82] For a discussion of this text, see *ibid.*, 7:7b–8a.

[83] This text is included in the *Ts'u-chieh Hsing-t'ung-fu* [*Gloss Commentaries on the Unified Code in Rhyme*]. For a discussion of the text, see Shen Chia-pen, *Shen Chi-i hsien-sheng i-shu chia-pien, Wen-ts'un*, 7:7b–8a.

[84] This text was prepared by Ch'eng Jen-shou. For an introduction to this text, see the *Ssu-k'u ch'uan-shu tsung-mu t'i-yao*, 101:15b–16a.

[85] This text was also prepared by Ch'eng Jen-shou. For an introduction to the text, see *ibid.*, 101:15b–16a.

[86] This text is mentioned by Professor Okamoto as one of the Yuan legal publications. See Okamoto Keiji, "*Rigaku shinan no kenkyū*," p. 1.

[87] This text was prepared by Lien Tao. For an introduction to this text, see the *Ssu-k'u ch'uan-shu tsung-mu t'i-yao*, 105:15b–16a.

[88] This text was prepared by Yin Chung. For an introduction to this text, see *ibid.*

Unified Code in Rhyme].[89] Other important studies, such as the *Yung-hui fa-ching* [*The Yung-hui Code*] by Cheng Ju-i, were also made available to scholars working on the comparative aspects of the codes of the T'ang and Chin dynasties.[90]

In addition to the above legal works, there were popular handbooks on legal matters. They included books such as the *Kuan-min chün-yung* [*Standard References for Officials and Civilians*], and *Shih-min yao-lan* [*Essential References for Officials and Civilians*].[91] Many Yüan bureaucrats also wrote books on legal subjects, thus providing the public with practical knowledge for settling legal disputes. For instance, in a funeral inscription of Liu T'ai-heng, it is recorded that a reference book was edited by Liu that contained precedents established from the time of the Chung-t'ung reign to that of the Ta-te reign. It is also reported that Liu wrote books about his own legal and bureaucratic career; these books included the *Li-hsüeh ta-kang* [*Outline of the Bureaucratic Studies*] and *Che-yü p'i-shih* [*Precedents Selected from Legal Trials*].[92]

Along with the dissemination of legal knowledge through the vehicle of useful texts and popular books, comprehensive works on medical jurisprudence were also undertaken in the Yüan period. This field was originally developed by Sung officials such as Sung Tz'u whose *Hsi-yüan lu* [*On Restoration of Justice*] was the pioneer treatise on the subject. The *Hsi-yüan lu* was a famous handbook, rich in materials on forensic medicine. Its preface was dated 1247, and compared with the first European work of 1507 on the similar subject, the Sung piece was remarkably advanced and impressive.[93] This book

[89] This text was prepared by Chang Ju-chi. For an introduction to this text, see *ibid.*

[90] For an introduction to this text, see *ibid.*, 84:24a–25a.

[91] These two books are also mentioned by Professor Okamoto. See Okamoto Keiji, "*Rigaku shinan no kenkyū*," p. 1. The *Chin-yu hsin-shu* is, however, inaccurately cited by Okamoto as a Yüan work. Although this particular work is also cited as a Yüan piece in the *Ssu-k'u ch'uan-shu tsung-mu t'i-yao*, Niida has proven that it is a Sung book instead. See Niida Noboru, *Chūgoku hōseishi kenkyū: hō to kanshū, hō to dōtoku*, p. 204.

[92] Huang Chin, *Chin-hua Huang hsien-sheng wen-chi*, 34:9b–10a and 34:11b–12a.

[93] For a discussion of this achievement, see Miyashita Saburō, "Sō-Gen jidai no iryō" ("Medical Science in the Sung and Yuan Periods"), Yabuuchi

was later revised by Chao I-chai under the new title of *P'ing-yüan lu* [*On Redressing Grievances*]. During the Yüan, using these books as a basis, Wang Yü completed the famous *Wu-yüan lu* [*On Being without Grievances*] which represented a significant achievement in criminology of the Yüan dynasty.[94] Other works on anatomy were also published to supplement studies on medical jurisprudence. For example, in addition to his books on various aspects of medical sciences, Wang Hao-ku completed another text entitled *Hai-ts'ang lao-jen Yin-cheng lüeh-li* which included his writings on anatomy.[95] Because of these important works, officials and clerks began to obtain more information concerning medicine, pharmacology, and criminology. They also became more efficient in collecting evidence and in analyzing the details of criminal cases.

In practice, when a case of homicide occurred, a principal official had to lead a chief official and a *wu-tso* (coroner) to the scene to examine the corpse. The result of the examination had to be recorded on a specific form, with pictures to indicate the location of the wounds. Three copies of the form had to be signed by the examiners; one copy was for the victim's family, one was for the file, and the last was for the supervising authorities. Affidavits had to be obtained on the scene from the victim's family and witnesses. Later, the corpse had to be reexamined, and the result had to be recorded on the form in triplicate. If there was any delay or mistake in the exami-

---

Kiyoshi, ed., *Sō-Gen jidai no kagaku gijutsushi* [*History of Science and Technology in the Sung and Yuan Periods*] (Kyoto: Kyoto University Press, 1967), p. 148. The *Hsi-yuan lu* [*On Restoration of Justice*] attracted the attention of Western scholars very quickly. According to R. H. van Gulik, there appeared in 1780 an abbreviated French version of this Sung work, and in 1863 the complete text was translated and published by the Netherlands Sinologue C.F.M. de Grijs in Dutch under the title of *Geregtelijke Geneeskunde, uit het Chinees vertaald*. See R. H. van Gulik, *T'ang-Yin-Pi-Shih* (Leiden: E. J. Brill, 1956), p. 18, n. 4.

[94] For an introduction to this text, see Shen Chia-pen, *Shen Chi-i hsien-sheng i-shu chia-pien, Wen-ts'un*, 6:7a–11b.

[95] This text of Wang Hao-ku was later incorporated in the *Shih-wan-lo ts'ung-shu* (*Pai-pu ts'ung-shu chi-cheng* edition, No. 76, I-wen yin-shu-kuan, Taipei, 1968). For a brief discussion of Wang's other achievements, see Miyashita Saburō, "Sō-Gen jidai no iryō," p. 149.

nation or any inconsistency between the first and second examinations, all negligent examiners were to be punished.[96] In addition to the increasingly rigid standards for the submission of medical reports imposed by the government, the standard of medical science was also greatly improved in the Yüan at various levels. For example, to be qualified for the profession, medical doctors were required to understand books in their specialities and to pass written tests.[97] Persons who desired to practice medicine at jails were tested several times before they were appointed, and the Su-cheng lien-fang ssu and its censors were ordered to investigate any appointment of an incompetent prison doctor.[98]

While legal professionalism expanded on the level of formal trials, legal training also became available to people other than officials or clerks. Because most civil cases were disputes over land ownership or marriage, persons who were matchmakers or business brokers by profession were given some legal training so that they could help their clients avoid making improper marriage agreements or concluding illegal contracts. In general, a matchmaker had to study cases and precedents prohibiting illegal marriages and a business broker had to inform himself about cases and precedents overruling illegal transactions. In addition to this matchmakers and business brokers had to submit to the authorities affidavits committing themselves to the proper operation of their professional activities.[99]

Since matchmakers and business brokers were familiar with some legal provisions and cases, they were able to advise common people on some legal aspects of marriage or business transactions. If disputes over marriage, family property, land, house, or debt did occur, the parties involved were to ask their own she-chang (she leader, community leader) to help them settle their quarrels, provided that the disputes were not of such a serious nature as to greatly violate the law. Originally,

[96] *YTC* 43:1a–4b and 54:26a–27a.
[97] *YTC* 32:5b–7a.
[98] *YTC* 32:10.
[99] *YTC* 53:4a.

the *she* organization was designed in the Yüan to restore and
further agricultural productivity.[100] Since the primary function of a *she-chang* was to promote welfare and agricultural
activities in the village, he was not officially given authority
to intervene in a legal case. As a matter of fact, in 1294 it was
even ordered that *she* leaders, along with other functionaries
in a village, should not intervene in legal cases.[101] A *she-chang*
was, however, urged by the government to settle minor disputes for the parties involved to avoid delaying agricultural
activities or disturbing the authorities.[102] In addition to his
responsibility for mediating minor disputes, a *she-chang* could
report undesirable individuals of his village to the authorities
for punishment. To perform his task, a *she-chang* needed to
have some legal knowledge. The fact that a *she-chang* was
often consulted by village people on such legal matters as
inheritance and division of family property indicated that he
did have some practical legal experience. In the *Yüan ch'u hsüan*
there are several cases which deal with the division of family
property in which *she* leaders gave advice to the parties involved and signed documents as witnesses.[103] These plays,
therefore, illustrated the role of *she-chang* in settling disputes in
the Yüan period.

The legal professionalism of the Yüan dynasty was also
reflected in the preparation and use of legal documents. In
previous dynasties, legal documents were required for various
transactions, but during the Yüan, such documents seemed to
be used more frequently and the technique of drafting a legal
document became better known to the common people. For
example, many model forms of legal documents were printed

---

[100] For a general discussion of the *she* organization, see Matsumoto Yoshimi,
"Gendai ni okeru shasei no sōritsu" ("Foundation of the *She* System in the
Yuan Period"), *Tōhō gakuhō* (Tokyo), 11 (1940), pp. 328–337. See also Schur-
mann, *Economic Structure of the Yüan Dynasty*, pp. 43–48.

[101] *YTC* 53:5a.

[102] *YTC* 53:4a.

[103] *Yüan ch'u hsuan*, Vol. II, 1b–2a. See also Niida Noboru, "Shina kinsei no
gikyoku shōsetsu ni mietaru shihō" ("Civil Law as Reflected in Pre-Modern
Chinese Plays and Novels"), Ishii Ryōsuke, ed., *Nakada sensei kanreki shukuga
hōseishi ronshū [Collected Essays on Legal History in Honor of Mr. Nakada on the
Occasion of His 60th Birthday]* (Tokyo: Iwanami shoten, 1937), pp. 485–487.

and made known to the public. These forms included contracts for the sale of or a mortgage on land or a house, contracts for the sale of lumber, the announcement of rewards, the agreement of loans, the conclusion of adoption, the purchase of a concubine, the employment of a servant or porter, the renting of a boat, and the purchase of a house or ox.[104] Common people were also aware of the importance of completing a legal document when making a contract. It was believed that an official order required a seal, that a private agreement depended on a contract for enforcement, and that a person who had committed a breach of contract was obliged to pay the sum of damage specified in the contract. For example, in one contract for the sale of horses, the crediblity of the agreement was claimed under the slogan of *kuan-p'ing yin-hsin* (an official document requires a seal) and *ssu-p'ing yao-yüeh* (a private agreement depends on a contract), and the buyer consequently paid five taels of silver for his breach of contract.[105] The insistence on having the damage paid reflected an awareness of legal right and obligation.

Various model petitions were also printed in the Yüan period to teach the public how to submit petitions concerning legal matters to the authorities. They covered many different situations: a prisoner's petition to defend his own case, a petition on the mortgaging of a house, a petition to defend an imprisoned father, and a petition to defend a son's sexual offense.[106] That such petitions were actually used is illustrated by the two petitions recorded in the *Kuei-ch'ao kao*, one concerning the ownership of a cemetery and the other concerning false accusation.[107] These various petitions all aimed at winning

---

[104] For these various model forms, see the *Hsin-pien shih-wen lei-yao ch'i-cha ch'ing-ch'ien* (Jih-hsin shu-t'ang edition of 1324; reprinted by Koten kenkyūkai, Tokyo, 1963), pp. 747–760. See also Niida Noboru, *Chūgoku hōseishi kenkyū: tochihō, torihikihō [A Study of Chinese Legal History: Law of Land and Law of Transaction]* (Tokyo: Tokyo University Press, 1952), pp. 592–596 and 625–626.

[105] *Lao Ch'i-ta yen-chieh* (*Nogŏltae Ŏnhae*). pp. 162–163. (This book was reprinted and combined with the *P'u T'ung-shih yen-chieh* into a single text.)

[106] *Hsin-pien shih-wen lei-yao ch'i-cha ch'ing-ch'ien*, pp. 723–728.

[107] Hsieh Ying-fang, *Kuei-ch'ao kao* (*Ssu-pu ts'ung-k'an san-pien* edition, The Commercial Press, Shanghai, 1935), 16: 1a–2b and 16: 19a–20b.

legal cases, and a person who won a case was often congratulated by his friends. There was even a model form to teach one how to write a letter of congratulation on the occasion of a friend's legal triumph.[108] Owing to the publication of these materials, most people had copies of legal reference books such as the *Shih-min yao-lan* and the *Tuan-li t'iao-chang* in their houses.[109] Some people even studied law at home. For example, the impressive legal learning of Wu Yüan-kuei, a famous scholar-official, came from his early family instruction.[110]

Because legal knowledge was widely disseminated to the public at various levels, according to one account, people began to engage more often in law suits.[111] A legal document was usually drafted by a local scholar or by a business broker on behalf of an illiterate person. If it involved more complicated issues or if it was to be presented to the authorities for a legal suit, the document was often prepared by a professional *shu-hsieh-jen* (scribe). There were several names in Chinese, such as *shu-p'u*, *chuang-p'u*, *shu-chuang-jen*, and *yü-chuang-jen*, to designate the man of this profession. Normally, a man in such a profession drafted plaints for his client and received payment for his service. To perform his task, a *shu-hsieh-jen* was required to familiarize himself with some legal provisions, for it was essential that he understand and differentiate which disputes had legal grounds and which did not. He was also required to submit an affidavit to bind himself to the prevention of unwarranted suits so as to reduce the number

---

[108] *Hsin-pien shih-wen lei-yao ch'i-cha ch'ing-ch'ien*, p. 206.

[109] These books were mentioned by Cheng Chieh-fu in his memorial. See Yang Shih-ch'i, *Li-tai ming-ch'en tsou-i*, 67:25a.

[110] *YS* 117:4a.

[111] Wang Chieh, *Wen-chung chi* (*Ssu-k'u ch'uan-shu chen-pen ch'u-chi* edition, The Commercial Press, Shanghai, 1935), 6:20. Incidentally, there was another *Che-yu p'i-shih* [*Precedents Selected from Legal Trials*] by Hsü Ho-fu to record his own legal experiences. See the *Ch'iang-tung lei-kao* (*Ch'ang-chou hsien-che i-shu* edition, 1899), 9:4. This book of Hsü bears the same title as that of Liu T'ai-heng. See n. 92 above. The fact that many books were published to comment on legal cases seems to indicate the good demand for such texts and the popularity of writing them among bureaucrats of the Yüan dynasty.

of legal cases.[112] Consequently, these men helped the common people prepare presentable plaints, both in content and style. They also helped the authorities avoid cases which had no solid legal grounds.

Unavoidably, some unscrupulous members of the profession used their legal knowledge to manipulate clients in order to pursue their own personal interests. In 1301 it was stipulated that a public *shu-hsieh-jen* be established in each local government with the person selected from the waiting list of candidates who had registered to become governmental clerks. If a public *shu-hsieh-jen* performed well and made no mistakes, he eventually would be promoted to the rank of a formal clerk. At the same time, the private *shu-hsieh-jen* were placed under more strict control in order to suppress possible unlawful activities. Those who delayed the plaints, intentionally omitted the important points in the plaints, charged unreasonable fees, or incited other litigations were to be punished.[113]

Similarly, the Yüan government also developed a scheme of selection and promotion of interpreters in order to prevent them from using their influence to obtain personal profits.[114] The interpreters were originally retained to facilitate communication between parties who spoke different dialects or languages. Their service was often necessary, especially when there were legal suits between people of different ethnic backgrounds. Some interpreters, however, were unscrupulous and sought personal gain by distorting essential points of legal arguments. In order to arrest this corrupt trend, various steps were taken in the Yüan period to regulate the role and function of interpreters and to punish dishonest interpreters.[115]

The infusion of legal experience and practical knowledge at the various levels—from the formal trial to the preparation of

[112] *YTC* 12:58b and 53:4a.

[113] *YTC* 12:59a.

[114] *YTC* 12:40b–41a.

[115] For general regulations concerning the role and function of interpreters in the Yuan period as well as the procedures of their promotion, see *YTC* 12:40a–42b. See also the *T'ung-chih t'iao-ko*, 6:28a and 6.35a.

legal documents—contributed to the expansion of legal professionalism in the Yüan dynasty, thus promoting an effective administration of justice. The various legal studies and popular handbooks published in the Yüan provided officials and clerks with substantial materials to use in acquiring their legal expertise. As a matter of fact, legal texts released by Yüan publishers were so numerous that officials and clerks were unable to read all of them.[116] The interest in legal matters was so strong that it not only helped the development of a reasonable judicial system in the Yüan but also laid the foundation for the expansion of legal professionalism in the later dynasties. Therefore, the notion shared by some modern scholars that the Mongols, being barbaric, did not create a good legal system is not accurate. Actually, the Mongols, in partnership with the Chinese officials, succeeded in developing one of the most impressive and mature judicial systems that Imperial China had ever had for the administration of justice.

[116] Ou-yang Hsüan, *Kuei-chai wen-chi*, 12:7a.

PART TWO

CHIH-YÜAN HSIN-KO

PRELIMINARY REMARKS

The significance of the *Chih-yüan hsin-ko* first came to my attention in 1969 when I was asked by Professor Francis W. Cleaves if the code was identical to the *Chih-yüan hsin-fa* of Wang Yün.[1] After having studied the origin of the *Chih-yüan hsin-ko* and discovering the prominent position of the code in Yüan legal history, I also located many fragments of the code in the course of my reading and research in Yüan history. As I began to piece together these fragments, I tried to arrange them in a coherent way. The *Yüan shih* records that the code contains ten sections, but it specifies only four of them, namely, the sections of "Kung-kuei," "Chin-min," "Yü-tao," and "Li-ts'ai."[2] Although the other six sections can still be inferred from some subsections of the *Yüan tien-chang* and the *T'ung-chih t'iao-ko*, it is difficult to determine the exact titles of the six missing sections and to decide into which section a fragment might fit.

One day Professor Cleaves called my attention to a Japanese manuscript entitled *Rigaku shinan* (i.e., a Japanese edition of the *Li-hsüeh chih-nan*). I later found in this text a reference to the *ko* under which there appeared ten sections. These sections are the "Kung-kuei," "Hsüeh-ko," "Chih-min," "Li-ts'ai," "Fu-i," "K'o-ch'eng," "Ts'ang-k'u," "Tsao-tso," "Fang-tao," and "Ch'a-yü."[3] Among these ten sections, the "Kung-kuei," "Chih-min," and "Li-ts'ai" are identical to three of the four sections mentioned in the *Yüan shih*. The remaining

[1] For a detailed discussion of this issue, see Ch. I above.

[2] See Ch. I, n. 61 above.

[3] *Li-hsueh chih-nan* (*Ming, Ssu-li-chen* edition), 25b. For a detailed discussion of the Chinese and Japanese editions of the *Li-hsueh chih-nan*, see Ch. II, n. 62 above. Hereafter, unless otherwise indicated, the text refers to the *Ssu-li-chien* edition.

section of the four is "Yü-tao," which is almost identical to the "Fang-tao." While four of the ten sections listed in the *Rigaku shinan* correspond to the four sections recorded in the *Yüan shih*, the other six sections so listed also largely correspond to the titles of various subsections of the *Yüan tien-chang* and the *T'ung-chih t'iao-ko* where the fragments of the *Chih-yüan hsin-ko* appear. As the preface to the *Li-hsüeh chih-nan* was written by Hsü Yüan-jui and dated 1301, it becomes clear that its publication came no more than a decade after the promulgation of the *Chih-yüan hsin-ko*. Since in reality no other substantial code was ever established during the intervening decade, the ten sections listed in the *Li-hsüeh chin-nan* probably represent the original sections of the *Chih-yüan hsin-ko*.[4] With this discovery, I started following the framework provided in the *Li-hsüeh chih-nan* for my reconstruction of the code.

Subsequently I found a note on the *Chih-yüan hsin-ko* in an article published in 1931 by Professor Abe Takeo.[5] In this note Professor Abe has identified 56 fragments of the code from the material in the *T'ung-chih t'iao-ko*, and they are preserved in the latter text as follows:

Section	*Number of Fragments*
"Hsüan-ko" (Standard of Selection)	12
"Kuan-fang" (Prevention by Checking)	12
"Li-min" (Governing of the People)	9
"K'o-ch'a" (Imposition of Taxes)	6
"Fang-tao" (Prevention of Thefts)	6
"Tsao-tso" (Construction and Manufacturing)	11

Instead of citing specific source references to the individual fragments, Professor Abe only gives a general source reference to each section so mentioned. His source references to the

---

[4] For a discussion of the development of codes during these years, see Ch. 1 above.

[5] This article of Abe Takeo appears in the *Tōhō gakuhō* (Kyoto), 1 (1931) and is incorporated posthumously into his *Gendaishi no kenkyū* [*Historical Studies on the Yüan Period*] (Tokyo: Sōbunsha, 1972), pp. 277–318. For his note on the *Chih-yuan hsin-ko*, see the *Gendaishi no kenkyū*, pp. 313–315, n. 5.

above sections come from the *T'ung-chih t'iao-ko* and are distributed as follows:

Section	Source
"Hsüan-ko"	*Chüan* 6, "Hsüan-chü" (Selections and Recommendation)
"Kuan-fang"	*Chüan* 14, "Ts'ang-k'u" (Warehouses)
"Li-min"	*Chüan* 16, "T'ien-ling" (Land Ordinances)
"K'o-ch'a"	*Chüan* 17, "Fu-i" (Taxes and *Corvée*)
"Fang-tao"	*Chüan* 19, "Pu-wang" (Arrests and Escapes)
"Tsao-tso"	*Chüan* 30, "Ying-shan" (Construction and Restoration)

While many of these fragments are also preserved in the *Yüan tien-chang*, Professor Abe claims that there are additional thirty fragments which are recorded in the *Yüan tien-chang* but not in the *T'ung-chih t'iao-ko*. These thirty fragments are distributed as follows:

Section	Number of Fragments
"Kung-kuei" (Public Regulations)	11
"K'o-ch'eng" (Taxes and Levies)	11
"K'o-i" (Imposition of *Corvée*)	4
"Su-sung" (Complaints and Suits)	4

Without giving his source references to individual fragments, Abe just cites a general reference to each section as follows:

Section	Source
"Kung-kuei"	"Li-pu" (Board of Civil Office): 7 and 8
"K'o-ch'eng"	"Hu-pu" (Board of Revenue and Population): 8
"K'o-i"	"Hu-pu": 13
"Su-sung"	"Hsing-pu" (Board of Punishments): 15

By adding together the fragments preserved in the *Yüan tien-chang* and the *T'ung-chih t'iao-ko*, Professor Abe concludes that 86 fragments of the *Chih-yüan hsin-ko* are still in existence.

Although the ten sections arranged by him are by and large similar to those recorded in the *Li-hsüeh chih-nan*, his classification of the "K'o-ch'a" and "K'o-i" sections in reconstructing the sequence of fragments seems confusing. The "K'o-ch'a" section in the *T'ung-chih t'iao-ko* incorporates the fragments of the "Fu-i" section, which is presumably related to the "K'o-i" section. It therefore seems very unlikely that the *Chih-yüan hsin-ko* would contain both the "K'o-ch'a" and the "K'o-i" sections at the same time. Second, Abe's classification of the "K'o-ch'eng" section is also confusing. He considers the "Li-ts'ai" section as equivalent to the "K'o-ch'eng" section in the *Yüan tien-chang*. This suggestion is not in accord with the *Li-hsüeh chih-nan*, in which the "Li-ts'ai" and the "K'o-ch'eng" sections are independent of each other. Owing to these confusions, Abe Takeo's classification of the fragments of the "K'o-i" and the "Li-ts'ai" sections is very ambiguous.

In a different article published in 1932 by Professor Abe, I also discovered another note concerning the *Chih-yüan hsin-ko*.[6] Abe mentions in this note that he has received from Professors Niida Noboru and Mikino Tatsumi a joint letter calling his attention to the ten sections listed in the *Li-hsüeh chih-nan* and suggesting the idea of using these sections for the reconstruction of the code. Admitting that he has not thoroughly considered the proper sequence of the sections of the code, Abe in his reply conceives of the possibility and desirability of adopting these ten sections as a framework for the code. Abe, however, undertook no further substantial work on the text of the code after his early attempt to reconstruct it. Although he cites a few fragments of the code in a later article published in 1954, unfortunately, no systematic study of the code was prepared before his sudden death in 1959.

Several other scholars have also mentioned the *Chih-yüan hsin-ko* briefly in their works. For example, the *Azia rekishi jiten* [*Dictionary of Asian History*] has an entry written by Professor Niida on the *Chih-yüan hsin-ko*, but this entry is mainly a brief

[6] This article of Abe Takeo appears in the *Tōhō gakuhō* (Kyoto), 2 (1932) and is incorporated into the *Gendaishi no kenkyū* , pp. 253–276.

introduction to the nature and significance of the code rather than a serious study of the text.[7] In view of this gap in the scholarship of Yüan studies, I decided to write my Ph.D. thesis on the *Chih-yüan hsin-ko*. The thesis was completed and submitted to Harvard University in 1973. It includes a survey of Yüan legal institutions and a reconstructed text of the code containing 96 fragments.

After the completion of my thesis, an article published in 1972 by Uematsu Tadashi became available to me.[8] Uematsu gives a general introduction to the development of the *Chih-yüan hsin-ko* and presents a reconstructed text of the code containing 95 fragments. Although his article came too late to be consulted in the course of my thesis writing, I later found that his method of reconstruction is essentially the same as mine. His reconstructed text, aside from some differences in the classification of fragments into particular sections, is also basically similar to mine. At the same time, owing to the reproduction of the Yüan edition of *Yüan tien-chang* in 1972 by the Palace Museum in Taipei, it became possible to compare this edition with other documents. By consulting the faithful reproduction of items recorded in *Yüan tien-chang*, the textual accuracy of the *Chih-yüan hsin-ko* as reconstructed in this present study has been improved.

In accordance with the sequence of the ten sections suggested by the *Li-hsüeh chih-nan*, the 96 fragments of the *Chih-yüan hsin-ko* are arranged as follows in this study:

Section	Number of Fragments
"Kung-kuei"	12
"Hsüan-ko"	12
"Chih-min"	12
"Li-ts'ai"	8
"Fu-i"	5

[7] *Azia rekishi jiten* [*Dictionary of Asian History*] (Tokyo: Heibonsha, 1960), Vol. 4, p. 148.

[8] Uematsu Tadashi, "Ishū *Shigen shinkaku* narabini kaisetsu" ("Restoration of the *Zhi-yuan xin-ge* and Its Comment"), *Tōyōshi kenkyū*, Vol. 30, No. 4 (1972), pp. 1–29.

"K'o-ch'eng"	11
"Ts'ang-k'u"	12
"Tsao-tso"	11
"Fang-tao"	6
"Ch'a-yü"	7

It is sometimes difficult to determine the proper sequence of individual fragments of a given section. Whenever there was such uncertainty, I simply placed a fragment which appeared first in the *Yüan tien-chang* or the *T'ung-chih t'iao-ko* before one which appeared later in the same section. As a result, some fragments of a given section seem to be arranged arbitrarily. This arbitrary arrangement will have to suffice until the order of all fragments can be ascertained more accurately.

Following the translation of the reconstructed code, the Chinese text of the code as reconstructed is presented. The sources of the fragments as well as studies on the text are given in the notes. As the original text was said to be only several thousand characters in length, it might not have been much longer than what has been reconstructed and presented in this study. Although some other fragments of the code may still remain undiscovered in various Chinese sources, the reconstructed text seems to reflect clearly the essential structure of the *Chih-yüan hsin-ko*. It is hoped that in the future a more substantial analysis of the code will be made so as to provide a better perspective on Yüan legal institutions and the surrounding social, economic, and political conditions in the Yüan period.

TRANSLATION OF
CHIH-YÜAN HSIN-KO

SECTION I

"Kung-kuei" (*Public Regulations*)[1]

[Item 1.][2] All authorities shall at dawn administer [official] matters. When items scheduled for the day for deliberation are settled, then and only then may they adjourn. All authorities and the Six Boards[3] in the capital shall be dependent upon the [Chung-shu-]sheng (Secretarial Council) and the rest of them shall be dependent upon their supervising authorities. However, persons involved in urgent official matters or on night duty shall not be bound by this provision.

[Item 2.][4] With regard to all official matters, if there is any violation of the deadline or of the precedent, the responsible examiner, as matters arise, shall conduct an investigation. To him who neglects to investigate, penalties shall be also applied. The *chien-ch'a yü-shih* (investigating censors) and the Su-cheng

---

[1] The term "Kung-kuei" (Public Regulations) refers, as indicated in the *Li-hsueh chih-nan*, to the regulations to be observed constantly by the authorities. See *Li-hsüeh chih-nan*, 25b.

[2] *YTC* 13:5a. For the reference to this fragment in the Yuan edition of the text, see *Ta Yüan sheng-cheng kuo-ch'ao tien-chang* (*Yuan tien-chang*) (Yuan edition; reprinted by National Palace Museum, Taipei, 1972), 13:5a. In order to differentiate this Yuan edition of the text from that of the Shen Chia-pen edition (cited as the *YTC* in this study), the Yüan edition will be cited as the *YTC**.

Although this fragment appears without direct identification, it does have the same style as other fragments of the code. There appears in the *Yuan tien-chang* another reference containing a short citation of this fragment, which is identified as coming from the code. See *YTC* 40:5b. As a result, this particular item must be a fragment of the code. It has a subtitle, "Kuan-fu p'ing-ming chih-shih" (Authorities Shall at Dawn Administer Matters), and the fragment proper starts with the character *chu* (a). For a discussion of traditional

lien-fang ssu (Surveillance Bureau, a Branch of the Censorate)[5] shall regularly impeach [negligent officials] and shall not allow any laxity.

[Item 3.][6] Any official matter received by the authorities shall bear the imprint of a stamp indicating the date of its receipt and [the matter] shall be given attention on the same day. However, as to urgent matters, as soon as they are received, they shall be handled immediately. [For the settlement of matters], ordinary matters [shall be allowed] five days (this category refers to matters which do not require a review); matters [of] medial [importance], seven days (this category refers to matters which require a review);[7] and matters [of] major [importance], ten days (this category refers to matters

---

schedules of work and rest, especially their applications to official bodies, see Yang Lien-sheng, "Schedules of Work and Rest in Imperial China," *HJAS*, 18 (1955), pp. 301–325.

[3] The *Liu pu* (Six Boards) consisted of the *Li-pu* (Board of Civil Office), *Hu-pu* (Board of Revenue and Population), *Li-pu* (Board of Rites), *Ping-pu* (Board of War), *Hsing-pu* (Board of Punishments), and *Kung-pu* (Board of Public Works).

[4] *YTC* 13:9b and *YTC** 13:6a. This fragment, along with Items 3, 4, 5, 6, 7, and 8, appears without direct identification. Its style is, however, distinctly similar to that of other fragments of the *Chih-yuan hsin-ko*. There are in the *Yuan tien-chang* some other references which have short citations of Items 3, 4, and 5. Since these citations are identified as coming from the code, Items 3, 4, and 5 themselves must be fragments of the code. See notes 6, 9, and 10 below. Since the present fragment belongs to the same grouping as Items 3, 4, and 5 under "Kung-shih" (Official Matters)—a subsection of the "Kung-kuei" section in the *Yuan tien-chang*—and since Items 3, 4, and 5 can be identified as fragments of the code, it is most likely that this particular fragment also comes from the code. It has a subtitle, "Kung-shih sui-shih chü-wen" (Official Matters Shall be Investigated as Matters Arise), and the fragment proper starts with the character *chu*(a).

[5] The Su-cheng lien-fang ssu (Surveillance Bureau, a Branch of the Censorate) was established in 1291 to replace the T'i-hsing an-ch'a ssu. See *YS* 16:15a and 86:29a–32b.

[6] *YTC* 13:9b and *YTC** 13:6a. This fragment appears without direct identification. Its style is distinctly similar to that of other fragments of the code. Moreover, a short citation of this fragment also appears in the *Yuan tien-chang* and is identified as coming from the code. The citation further mentions parenthetically that the complete form of the cited provision is recorded in the "Kung-kuei" section of the *Yuan tien-chang*. See *YTC* 11:25a. It therefore seems clear that the present fragment also comes from the code.

which require an audit of accounts or a consultation).[8] They all shall be settled within the deadline, otherwise a violator, in proportion to the degree of importance of each matter and the number of days overdue, shall at any time be punished accordingly. Matters which are to be expedited and can be settled on the same day shall be immediately deliberated and executed. However, matters which cannot be subject to the regular deadline shall, according to circumstances, be thoroughly deliberated.

[Item 4.][9] With regard to any matter which has to be submitted to the higher authorities for decision, [officials] from below to above shall examine it carefully. If there is any falsehood or concealment, the authorities through whom the matter is to be submitted shall immediately modify or overrule it. When the examination is complete and the proposal is appropriate, then and only then may it be submitted. If the matter is not complete or the precedent [cited] is not appropriate and yet, without an immediate modification or overruling, the authorities unwarrantedly permit its submission, the responsible

---

Its subtitle is "Kung-shih liang-ch'eng liao-pi" (Official Matters Shall be Concluded According to the Appropriate Schedule), and the fragment proper starts with the character *chu*(a).

As to the short citation, the character *li*(c) in the fourth line of the *YTC* 11:25a is used to replace the character *ssu*. There appears in the *Yüan tien-chang* another short citation of this fragment. See *YTC* 14:15a. In the twelfth line of the *YTC* 14:15a the character *hsu*(a) can be deleted, and the character *tsan* is a misprint for the character *yü*(b). This misprint was not mentioned by Ch'en Yüan in his *Shen-k'o Yüan tien-chang chiao-pu* (Peking: Peking University, 1931).

[7] The first character *shih*(a) in the seventh line of the *YTC* 13:9b is a misprint for the character *ch'i*(b). This misprint was also noticed by Ch'en Yuan. See *Shen-k'o Yüan tien-chang chiao-pu*, "Cha-chi" ("Notes"), 1:44a.

[8] The character *ch'eng* in the seventh line of the *YTC* 13:9a is a misprint for the character *chang*(b). This misprint was also noticed by Ch'en Yüan. See *Shen-k'o Yüan tien-chang chiao-pu*, "Cha-chi," 1:44a.

[9] *YTC* 13:9b–10a and *YTC** 13:6a. This fragment appears without direct identification. Its style is distinctly similar to that of other fragments of the code. In addition, there appears in the *Yüan tien-chang* a short citation of this fragment, and the citation is identified as coming from the code. See *YTC* 4:5a. It therefore seems clear that the present fragment also comes from the code. It has a subtitle, "Shen-shih tzu hsia erh shang" (Submission of Matters

chief officials shall be investigated and punished. If the correction is not so effective as repeatedly and intentionally to delay matters, [they] shall also be investigated and punished.

[Item 5.]¹⁰ If an official matter is clear and, according to the precedent, shall be executed and yet the lower authorities intentionally make it ambiguous so as to apply [to the higher authorities] for review or, if a matter deserves an appeal and yet the higher authorities do not immediately apply the principle to settle it, [the responsible authorities], in accordance with each case, shall be investigated and shall also be impeached by the investigating censors and the Su-cheng lien-fang ssu.¹¹

[Item 6.]¹² With regard to any official matter which has to be deliberated, from the lower to the higher authorities, the principal officials shall select people versed in such matters to settle it impartially. If diverse opinions persist, [the dissidents]

Shall be from the Lower [Authorities] to the Higher), and the fragment proper starts with the character *chu*(a).

The character *po*(b) in both the twelfth line of the *YTC* 13:9b and the second line of the *YTC* 13:10a is a variant for the character *po*(a). As to the short citation, between the characters *shang* and *ting* in the fifth line of the *YTC* 4:5a, the character *ssu* was omitted and should be restored. This omission was also noticed by Ch'en Yuan. See *Shen-k'o Yuan tien-chang chiao-pu*, "Cha-chi," 1:10a. The character *su*(b) in both the sixth and seventh lines is a variant for the character *su*(a). The character *chao*(b) in the sixth line is a variant for the character *chao*(a).

¹⁰ *YTC* 13:10a. See also *YTC** 13:6a. This fragment appears without direct identification. Its style is distinctly similar to that of other fragments of the code. Moreover, there appears in the *Yuan tien-chang* a short citation of this fragment and it is identified as coming from the *code*. See *YTC* 4:8b. It becomes clear that the present fragment also comes from the code. It has a subtitle, "Kung-shih ming-pai ch'u-chueh" (Official Matters Shall be Clearly Settled), and the fragment proper starts with the character *chu*(a).

As to the short citation, between the characters *tso*(a) and *i*(a) in the second line of the *YTC* 4:8b, the character *yu*(a) was omitted and should be restored. This omission was not mentioned by Ch'en Yuan. Between the characters *shih*(b) and *lien* in the third line, the two characters *su-cheng* were omitted and should be restored. This last omission was also noticed by Ch'en Yuan. See *Shen-k'o Yuan tien-chang chiao-pu*, "Cha-chi," 1:11a.

¹¹ The character *ho* in the fifth line of the *YTC* 13:10a is a misprint for the character *ko*(b). Ch'en Yuan also noticed this misprint. See *Shen-k'o Yuan tien-chang chiao-pu*, "Cha-chi," 1:44a.

¹² *YTC* 13:10a. See also *YTC** 13:6a. This fragment appears without direct identification. Its style is distinctly similar to that of other fragments.

shall be permitted to explain to the supervising higher authorities. If officials of the Six Boards are of different opinions, they shall be permitted to go to the [Chung-shu-]sheng and request a deliberation. If the matter and precedent are clear, any person who changes positives into negatives or vice versa shall be separately investigated.

[Item 7.]¹³ As to the delay of an official matter, if it is readjusted earlier, correction is easier. [However,] if [adjustment] is later, [correction] is difficult to pursue. Hereafter, with regard to matters within their jurisdiction, the competent clerks of the [Chung-shu-]sheng shall once a day write matters off as settled, and the *tu-shih* (supervisor) shall once every ten days examine [the matters] and the *yüan-wai-lang* (Vice Director of a Bureau of a Board) shall once a month conduct a review. If there is any mistake, it shall be corrected according to the precedent; and, if there is any delay, it shall be immediately adjusted so as not to [let matters] accumulate by days and increase by months, lest documents shall be multitudinous and matters shall be fraudulent. In a Board, the *yüan-wai-lang* and the *chu-shih* (Secretary of a Bureau of a Board), and, in the [Yü-shih-]t'ai (Censorate) and the [Shu-mi-]yüan (Privy

---

Moreover, it belongs to the same grouping as Items 3, 4, and 5 under the same subsection in the *Yüan tien-chang*. Since Items 3, 4, and 5 are fragments of the code, it becomes clear that this fragment also comes from the code. See notes 4, 6, 9, and 10 above. It has a subtitle, "Kung-shih ts'ung-cheng yu-chueh" (Official Matters Shall be Impartially Settled), and the fragment proper starts with the character *chu*(a). The character *chu*(a) in the ninth line of the *YTC* 13:10a is a misprint for the character *ch'i*(b). Ch'en Yüan also noticed this misprint. See *Shen-k'o Yuan tien-chang chiao-pu*, "Cha-chi," 1:44a.

¹³ *YTC* 13:11b. See also *YTC** 13:6a. This fragment appears without direct identification. Its style is distinctly similar to that of other fragments. It also belongs to the same grouping as Items 3, 4, and 5 under the same subsection in the *Yuan tien-chang*. Since Items 3, 4, and 5 are fragments of the code, it becomes clear that this fragment also comes from the code. See notes 4, 6, 9, and 10 above. Its subtitle is "Ch'i-ch'ih sui-shih chu-hsing" (Delay Shall be Adjusted as Matters Arise), and the fragment proper starts with the character *chu*(a).

The character *chu*(b) in the first line of the *YTC* 13:11a is a misprint for the character *chu*(c). The character *yüan*(b) in the second line is a misprint for the character *ch'uan*, and the character *nei* in the same line is a misprint for the character *kou*(a). These three misprints were also noticed by Ch'en Yüan. See *Shen-k'o Yuan tien-chang chiao-pu*, "Cha-chi," 1:44a.

Council), the *ching-li* (registrar) shall be in charge of the reporting of matters. Elsewhere, the *ching-li* and other document-examiners shall also similarly [follow this provision].

[Item 8.][14] Authorities are so many and matters are so multiple that, [although] all faults should be totally eliminated, it is difficult to illustrate completely all situations. [Therefore,] within and without [the capital] all authorities shall carefully examine [official matters]. If there is any inconvenient matter which needs to be modified, it shall be permitted to be reported to the supervising authorities. If [the matter] is required to be reported to the [Chung-shu-]sheng, it shall be so reported.

[Item 9.][15] Officials in the *chou*, the *fu*, and the *ssu-hsien*[16] are in charge of the *corvée* duty of soldiers and civilians as well as other matters. Therefore, their responsibilities are not light. If the supervising authorities have a matter which absolutely requires the dispatching of [an official], [the authorities] shall select [a person] from an office in which officials are many and matters are simple for the mission. When [an office] has only one official, [the authorities] shall not disturb or dispatch [him]. A bureaucrat, in the event of being dispatched, when the mission shall have been completed, shall be immediately

---

[14] *YTC* 13:11a and *YTC** 13:7a. This fragment appears without direct identification. Its style is distinctly similar to that of other fragments of the code Moreover, it belongs to the same grouping as Items 3, 4, and 5 under the same subsection of the *Yuan tien-chang*. Since Items 3, 4, and 5 are fragments of the code, it becomes clear that this fragment also comes from the code. See notes 4, 6, 9, and 10 above. It has a subtitle, "Kuan-shih yung-hsin chien-chiao" (Official Matters Shall be Attentively Examined), and the fragment proper starts with the character *chu*(a).

[15] *YTC* 14:5b and *YTC** 14:4b. The present fragment has a subtitle, "Wei-ch'ien ts'ung yuan to ch'u" (Dispatching Shall be from the Place Where There are Many Officials), and the fragment proper starts with the character *chu*(a).
The character *fang*(b) in the sixth line of the *YTC* 14:5b is a misprint for the character *hsu*(b) The character *fang*(a) in the same line is a misprint for the character *fang*(c). The character *fa* in the eighth line is superfluous and should be deleted. Ch'en Yüan also noticed the misprints and the superfluous character. See *Shen-k'o Yuan tien-chang chiao-pu*, "Cha-chi," 1:45a.

[16] During the Yuan dynasty a *hsien* was the basic administrative division. In a *hsien* in which the government of a *lu* or a *fu* was located, a special district of the *hsien* was designated as the *lu-shih-ssu* and was under the direct supervision of the said *lu* or *fu* instead of the host *hsien*. The *hsien* and *lu-shih-ssu* were referred to jointly as the *ssu-hsien*. For further discussion of this term, see Ch. III above.

returned [to the original office]. The reason for the original dispatching as well as the dates of departure and return shall still be recorded in a book to close the matter. If such a dispatching is not warranted or a delay is without a proper excuse, [the matter] shall be investigated by the Su-cheng lien-fang ssu.

[Item 10.][17] All documents of settled matters shall be edited once every quarter. They shall contain subject titles and total page numbers. They shall be arranged in accordance with the sequence of year and moon and [the order] shall be recorded in a register. Persons who have examined the documents shall still inspect the editions in person. If there are no other matters which should be handled but which have not been attended to, they shall be assigned with file numbers and be sealed according to the established methods. After they have been placed in the stacks, when a consultation of references is needed, a permit shall be presented in order to look them up. When [the consultation] is completed, they shall be immediately returned [to the stacks] to write off [the borrowing].[18]

[Item 11.][19] Any bureaucrat who is to leave for an official duty or other causes, with regard to the documents and files under his custody, shall examine [them] jointly with his successor, item by item, before handing them over. If there are no mistakes, they shall jointly submit a report to the supervising authorities for a confirming inspection. Hereafter, if any item

---

[17] *YTC* 14:13a. See also *YTC** 14:9a. The character *tse* in the sixth line of the *YTC* 14:13a was suspected to be a misprint for the character *chuan* by Professor Miyazaki. See Miyazaki Ichisada, "Sō-Gen jidai no hōsei to saiban kikō" ("Law and Judicial System in the Sung-Yuan Period"), *Tōhō gakuhō* (Kyoto), 24 (1954), p. 200. Between the characters *kou*(a) and *jen*(a) in the seventh line of the *YTC* 14:13a, the character *tang* is superfluous and should be deleted. Ch'en Yüan also noticed the superfluous character. See *Shen-k'o Yüan tien-chang chiao-pu*, "Cha-chi," 1:46a.

[18] This provision regulated the procedure concerning the establishment of permanent files after they had been reviewed by the censors of the Su-cheng lien-fang ssu. For a discussion of the control of files at the various levels of the bureaucratic structure in the Yüan period, see Miyazaki Ichisada, "Sō-Gen jidai no hōsei to saiban kikō," pp. 200–202.

[19] *YTC* 14:15a. See also *YTC** 14:10a. The character *yu*(b) in the beginning of the entry is used to conjoin the preceding entry, but, for the fragment proper, this character should be deleted and the character *chu*(a) should be placed instead at the beginning of the fragment.

is missing, only the person who is currently in charge of them shall be pressed for locating it.

[Item 12.][20] With regard to any official matter which requires the dispatching of messengers and post-horses, even if there has already been an edict permitting the use of horses, it is, nevertheless, necessary to establish a register to record the issuing of each dispatching. Once every quarter [the register] shall be reported to the supervising authorities. If there is any matter for which post-horses should not have been given, the responsible person shall be investigated. The number of dispatchings ordered by the Hsing-sheng (Regional Secretarial Council)[21] shall be reported to the [Chung-shu-]sheng. If the dispatching is not given and yet the official matters can be managed without it, the subordinate authorities shall not be disturbed [by their supervising authorities].

SECTION II

"Hsüan-ko" (*Standard of Selections*)[22]

[Item 1.][23] With regard to all *chih-kuan* (appointed officials)[24]

---

[20]*YTC* 36:26a. See also *YTC** 36:18b–19a. This fragment is recorded in the "I-chan" (Postal Relay System) subsection in the *Yuan tien-chang* and, therefore, it does not in sequence exactly belong to the "Kung-kuei" section. However, since this fragment deals with official matters and would be inappropriate in other sections, it is included in the "Kung-kuei" section. A similar version of this fragment is also recorded in the "Chan-ch'ih" section of the *Yung-lo ta-tien* [*Great Institutions of the Yung-lo Reign*]. See *Chan-ch'ih* [*Jamči*] (*Kuo-hsueh wen-k'u* edition, *Pien* Nos. 28 & 30, Peking, 1936), II, 83. There also appears in the "Chan-ch'ih" a short citation of this fragment. See *Chan-ch'ih*, II, 128. Between the characters *i*(b) and *sui*(a) in the tenth line of the *YTC* 36:26a there does not exist the character *ma*, whereas the "Chan-ch'ih" version has this character. The character *li*(b) in the thirteenth line was printed as *li*(a) in the *YTC** version. Hung-li (September 25, 1711– February 7, 1799) was the fourth Emperor of the Ch'ing dynasty who ruled under the title of Ch'ien-lung (r. 1736–1796). The Shen Chia-pen edition of the *Yuan tien-chang*, published in 1908, changed the character *li*(a) to the character *li*(b) or to another form so as to observe the Ch'ing taboo. For the life of Hung-li, see Arthur W. Hummel, ed., *Eminent Chinese of the Ch'ing Period* (Washington, D.C.: United States Government Printing Office, 1943), Vol. I, pp. 369–373. The character *shih*(c) in the thirteenth line of the *YTC* 36:26a was printed as *te* in the *Chan-ch'ih* version. In the ninth line of the *YTC* 36:26a

in the capital, each term [of their appointments] shall expire in thirty moons; and [for those officials who are] outside [the capital], in three full years. For tax and grain officials, the term shall expire only when they are replaced by successors. As for clerks, when ninety moons are completed, then and only then may they leave the current posts. [However,] as for those *chih-kuan* who are transferred to become [clerks or tax and grain officials], they shall still be governed by the precedent [which stipulates the term] for the [regular] *chih-kuan*. If the term has not expired, the supervising authorities shall not abruptly bypass the precedent to begin preparing official statements for recommending [the subordinate]. If [a person's] talent is really outstanding and can be substantiated by deeds, let [him] be investigated and recommended by the Censorate. If it is a case which shall not be bound by [the procedure of] the regular selections, such as there being a sudden vacancy and a person

the 12th moon of the 28th year of the Chih-yüan reign is cited as the date of the promulgation of the *Chih-yüan hsin-ko*. The correct date should be the 6th moon of that year instead. See Ch. I above.

[21] The term *Hsing-sheng* is an abbreviation of the Hsing Chung-shu-sheng (Regional Secretarial Council). See Ch. III, n. I above.

[22] The term "Hsüan-ko" (Standard of Selections) refers, as indicated in the *Li-hsüeh chih-nan*, to the standard for the selection of talents. See *Li-hsüeh chih-nan*, 25b.

[23] *YTC* 8:10. See also *YTC** 8:7a. A similar version is also recorded in the *T'ung-chih t'iao-ko* [*Code of Comprehensive Institutions*] (Peking: Kuo-li Pei-p'ing t'u-shu-kuan, 1930) (hereafter cited as *TCTK*), 6:1. The second character *jen*(b) in the ninth line of the *YTC* 8:10a does not exist in the *TCTK* version. The character *ku*(a) in the tenth line is a variant for the character *ku*(b). The character *wei*(b) in the same line is a misprint for the character *te*. Between the characters *kuan*(a) and *pu* in the eleventh line, the character *ssu* was omitted and should be restored. Ch'en Yüan also noticed the misprint and the omission. See *Shen-ko Yuan tien-chang chiao-pu*, "Cha-chi," I : 19a. The character *sheng*(b) in the twelfth line of the *YTC* 8:10a is a variant for the character *sheng*(a). The character *ch'ueh*(b) in the thirteenth line seems to be a variant for the character *ch'üeh*(a). The character *ko*(b) in the sixth line of the *TCTK* 6:1a does not exist in the *YTC* version. There also appears a short citation of this fragment in the *Yuan tien-chang hsin-chi*. See *YTCHC* "Li-pu" (Board of Civil Office): 28a.

[24] For a discussion of the term *chih-kuan* (appointed officials), see Paul Ratchnevsky, *Un Code des Yuan* (Paris: Librairie Ernest Leroux, 1937), p. 20, n. 6.

whose talent is suitable to the post being urgently needed, [the procedure] shall be decided in accordance with the circumstances.

[Item 2.][25] With regard to any official whose term [of appointment] has expired and who is ready to be replaced, if he has borrowed to his own use any official funds or grains, the current authorities shall press him to return the items. When they are submitted to the authorities, then and only then may he be given a "certificate of discharge" and be allowed to seek an official post.[26]

[Item 3.][27] With regard to the *chieh-yu* (certificate of discharge), there has been a standard form.[28] The authorities in issuing such a certificate shall follow the form to conduct an investigation. When there is no concealment or false statement, then and only then may [the official being discharged] be guaranteed and recommended [to a new post]. If there is any false pretense or, if the investigation is not thorough, the supervising authorities who are to issue the certificate shall immediately examine [the case]. The investigating censors in reviewing documents shall pay special attention to the examination [of the certificates]. If a certificate ought not to have

---

[25] *TCTK* 6:1b and *YTC* 11:18b. See also *YTC** 11:13b. Between the characters *ko*(a) and *kuan*(a) in the first line of the *YTC* 11:18b, the character *chu*(a) was omitted and should be restored. This omission was also noticed by Ch'en Yüan. See *Shen-k'o Yüan tien-chang chiao-pu*, "Cha-chi," 1:31a.

[26] The term "certificate of discharge" translates the *chieh-yu*. For a discussion of this term see Item 3 of this section and n. 28 below.

[27] *TCTK* 6:1b-2a and *YTC* 11:18a. See also *YTC** 11:13b. A short citation of this fragment also appears in the *Yüan tien-chang*. See *YTC* 11:25a and *YTC** 11:17b-18a. The version in the *YTC* 11:18a is recorded immediately after the last character of the previous fragment. Starting with the character *chu*(a), therefore, the fragment should be recorded separately in a new paragraph. This change was also mentioned by Ch'en Yüan. See *Shen-k'o Yüan tien-chang chiao-pu*, "Cha-chi," 1:31a.

[28] With regard to the term *chieh-yu* (certificate of discharge), *chieh* refers, as indicated in the *Li-hsüeh chih-nan*, to the completion of an official term of appointment and the discharge of a post, and *yu* refers to the record of inferior or superior performance. See *Li-hsüeh chih-nan*, 20b. This term is translated by Ratchnevsky as *certificat de décharge*. See Ratchnevsky, *Un Code des Yuan*, p. 50, n. 3 and p. 98. A complete standard form of *chieh-yu* is recorded in the *Yuan tien-shang*. See *YTC* 11:14a-17a. For a French translation of this standard form, see Ratchnevsky, *Un Code des Yuan*, pp. 98-103.

been given but is abruptly given by way of personal favor or, if the case warrants the issuing of a certificate but is intentionally obstructed or delayed, the responsible officials [in either case] shall be impeached.

[Item 4.][29] With regard to any official who possesses rank and class, if he can bear complex and heavy [administrative] burdens, skillfully manage taxes and grains, intelligently comprehend bureaucratic affairs, and deeply understand the essence of statecraft or, if his talent cannot be confined to one [narrow] specialty and can [enable him to] perform well any assignment whatsoever, the Li-pu (Board of Civil Office) shall examine his merit and deeds and, furthermore, shall investigate [the details] and classify him according to the category [of his talent] in the files so as to prepare for the future selection.

[Item 5.][30] With regard to the selection of officials, as they are diverse in disposition and kind, in using them it is proper that they supplement one another. However, [among them] a person with literary qualification shall be selected to be responsible for the public records and bookkeeping and no general administrative organ shall be without such an appointment.

[Item 6.][31] With regard to the selection of officials, the candidates shall be considered by their original backgrounds

---

[29] *TCTK* 6:2a and *YTC* 8:10b. See also *YTC** 8:7a. The version in the *Yüan tien-chang* is recorded immediately after the last character of the previous fragment. Between the characters *to* and *tsai* in the first line of the *YTC* 8:10b, therefore, the character *chu*(a) should be inserted, and beginning with this character the fragment should be recorded separately in a new paragraph. Ch'en Yüan also mentioned this change. See *Shen-k'o Yüan tien-chang chiao-pu*, "Cha-chi," 1:19a.

[30] *TCTK* 6:2 and *YTC* 8:10b. See also *YTC** 8:7a. The character *t'ui* in the fourth line of the *YTC* 8:10b is a misprint for the character *wei*(a). The character *wen* in the fifth line is a misprint for the character *ch'üeh*(b). These misprints were also noticed by Ch'en Yüan. See *Shen-k'o Yuan tien-chang chiao-pu*, "Cha-chi," 1:19a.

[31] *TCTK* 6:2b and *YTC* 8:10b. See also *YTC** 8:7a. The character *li*(d) in the sixth line of the *YTC* 8:10b is a misprint for the character *yüan*(d). Ch'en Yüan also noticed this misprint. See *Shen-k'o Yüan tien-chang chiao-pu*, "Cha-chi," 1:19a. The character *yüan*(c) in the sixth line of the *YTC* 8:10b was printed as *yüan*(a) in both the *YTC** and the *TCTK* versions. This character was normally printed as *yuan*(a) during the Yüan dynasty and should, therefore,

and previous posts served by them, in conjunction with the degree of their intelligence and abilities as well as the stage of their ages and physical conditions. They shall be assigned to the suitable vacancies so as not to compel [one to serve where] one's deficiency [cannot match the post] at the expense of another's excellence.

[Item 7.][32] All merits and demerits of any official shall be together reported to the Board of Civil Office for entering into the record. When the day of selection comes, against whatever rank or class he originally deserves, the official shall be proposed in accordance with his merits and demerits and be graded accordingly. Any person who conceals demerits or exaggerates merits shall be impeached by the investigating censors.

[Item 8.][33] With regard to any ranked official, if he is dismissed or demoted because of embezzlement or, if he is promoted because of his integrity or ability and [in either case], if his deed is evident, the case shall be circulated and made known to all offices so as to let current officials all be on their guard to exert themselves.

[Item 9.][34] With regard to any official's sons and grandsons who are entitled to hereditary official rank, when having entered the civil service, they shall be made to study the governmental affairs in advance so as not to neglect in the future their duties. When the day of selection comes, if [among them] one's ability is recommended by the authorities of one's lu and, if in a test on governmental affairs, one's answers and responses are acceptable, then within the same category [of hereditary official ranks] one shall be estimated higher and be given priority.

---

be adopted as such in the fragment. Ch'en Yuan, however, did not mention this change. The character *chuang*(a) in the third line of the *TCTK* 6:2b seems to be a misprint for the character *chuang*(b).

[32] *TCTK* 6:2b and *YTC* 8:10b. See also *YTC** 8:7a.

[33] *TCTK* 6:2b–3a and *YTC* 8:10b. See also *YTC** 8:7a. The character *sheng*(b) in the twelfth line of the *YTC* 8:10b was printed as *sheng*(a) in the *TCTK* version, and the character *chieh*(a) in the thirteenth line was printed as *chieh*(b) in the *TCTK* version.

[34] *TCTK* 6:3a and *YTC* 8:11a. See also *YTC** 8:7b.

[Item 10.]³⁵ With regard to the annual *kung* (tribe) clerk,³⁶ each responsible official organ shall select them from among its current staff members, regardless of the total number, in an open fashion. [Among the candidates,] persons who are pure and attentive in nature as well as conduct and are familiar with both Confucian studies and bureaucratic affairs shall be considered superior. Persons who are bright and able in talent as well as practical matters and are skillful in the bureaucratic affairs shall be estimated next. Any person whose moons and days [in the civil service] are numerous, yet whose conduct and ability are not desirable shall not be presented for the "tribute." On the day of their arrival at the Board [of Civil Office], [the candidates] shall be examined in a public conference, and only [those who] can discuss matters intelligently and act skillfully shall be accepted. [Those who] fail in the test shall be sent back to the original official organ and the persons who have improperly recommended [the rejected candidates] shall be investigated.

[Item 11.]³⁷ In the Liang-Kuang [i.e., Kwangtung and Kwangsi] and Fukien areas, if there is any office entirely without a *cheng-kuan* (principal official),³⁸ then, before the [proper] official selected by the Imperial court can arrive at the office, it is necessary to have someone temporarily attend to affairs. Hereafter, [the candidate] shall first be selected from the officials of the neighboring areas who can be made available

---

³⁵ *TCTK* 6:3.

³⁶ The annual *kung*(tribe) of clerks was established as early as 1269 to select persons from various existing offices to serve in positions of a more responsible nature. This institution, as an effective method to recuit men for the government, became more refined and was as an important feature of the Yüan civil services system. For detailed information concerning this institution, see *YTC* 12; 1a–25b.

³⁷ *TCTK* 6:3b–4a and *YTC* 8:11a. See also *YTC** 8:7b. The character *ch'ü* in the fifth line of the *YTC* 8:11a is a misprint for the character *na*(a). Ch'en Yüan also noticed this misprint. See *Shen-k'o Yuan tien-chang chiao-pu*, "Cha-chi," 1:19a. The character *sui*(a) in the sixth line of the *TCTK* 6:3b seems to be a misprint for the character *ho*.

³⁸ For a discussion of the term *cheng-kuan* (principle officials), see Ch. III above.

for the post. If no one is available, [the candidate] shall be selected from the officials whose original terms [of appointment] have expired and are awaiting new assignments. If none of them is available either, then in the same Sheng or the Hsüan-wei-ssu (Bureau of Pacification),[39] from among the current staff members who are on the payroll [the candidate] shall be selected. [However,] a man with no official standing shall not be selected.[40]

[Item 12.][41] With regard to all officials under the jurisdiction of the Hsing-sheng, if any official for many years has not been transferred or has not arrived at the post beyond the scheduled date or has been absent from duty for a long time or has suddenly given up the position, then the authorities shall immediately investigate the case clearly and report it to the Sheng for decision. As to the arrival at or departure from the post, [the data on] the persons who, according to the precedent, have to register themselves shall be reported each moon in a circular to the immediate supervising Sheng or Board. In the *lu* and its branches the same [procedure] shall be analogously applied.

SECTION III

"Chih-min" (*Governing of the People*)[42]

[Item 1.][43] Among all matters concerning civil administra-

---

[39] For a discussion of the Hsüan-wei-ssu (Bureau of Pacification), see Ch. III, n.3, above.

[40] The term "a man with no official standing" translates *pai-shen chih jen* (plain person).

[41] *TCTK* 6:4a and *YTC* 8:11a. See also *YTC** 8:7b. The character *ch'üeh*(b) in the tenth line of the *YTC* 8:11a seems to be a variant for the character *chüeh*(a). The character *t'an* in the thirteenth line is a misprint for the character *piao*(a). This misprint was also noticed by Ch'en Yüan. See *Shen-k'o Yuan tien-chang chiao-pu*, "Cha-chi," 1:19a.

[42] The term "Chih-min" (Governing of the People) refers, as indicated in the *Li-hsüeh chih-nan*, to the pacification of and care for all people as well as the settlement of litigation. See *Li-hsüeh chih-nan*, 25b.

[43] *TCTK* 16:1a and *YTC* 60:1a. See also *YTC** 60:1a. Between the characters *min* and *ch'ih*(a) in the fourth line of the *YTC* 60:1a, the character *che* was omitted and should be restored. The character *fan*(d) in the fifth line is super-

tion, to prohibit [the officials] from disturbing the common people is the most urgent. All *li-cheng* (village-heads) and other functionaries (including the scribes), in accordance with the quota allocated by the Tsung-kuan-fu (Bureau of General Administration) of each *lu*, shall be selected by the *ssu-hsien*. Only those who are scrupulous and without negligence shall be retained, and all extra members shall be dismissed. [Moreover,] each matter shall, by establishment of rules, still be examined and checked so that [the officials] may not, as before, oppress the common people.

[Item 2.][44] With regard to the *chu-shou* (control chiefs), the *shih-tso* (assistants), and the *li-cheng* of any village, when they are urging and supervising the collection of taxes as well as the imposition of *corvée*, [they] shall not violate any law. In the village, all households and neighbors shall, in accordance with the old precedents, supervise one another and shall not commit any misdeed.

[Item 3.][45] All the *she-chang* (*she* leaders, community leaders)[46] were originally elected to encourage agricultural activities. [However,] in recent years they have often been charged with [the responsibilities of] collecting the taxes and imposing *corvée*

fluous and should be deleted. These changes were also noticed by Ch'en Yüan. See *Shen-k'o Yüan tien-chang chiao-pu*, "Cha-chi," 5:33a. The character *neng* in the sixth line of the *YTC* 60:1a was printed as *kan*(a) in the *TCTK* version.

[44] *TCTK* 16:1b and *YTC* 60:1a. See also *YTC** 60:1a. Between the characters *hsing*(a) and *ts'un* in the seventh line of the *YTC* 60:1a, the character *chu*(a) was omitted and should be restored. Beginning with this character, the fragment should be recorded separately in a new paragraph rather than under the last character of the previous fragment. The characters *ts'un-fang* at the end of the seventh line and the beginning of the eighth line were erroneously inverted and should be changed to *fang-ts'un*. The omission and the inversion were also noticed by Ch'en Yüan. See *Shen-k'o Yüan tien-chang chiao-pu*, "Cha-chi," 5:33a.

[45] *TCTK* 16:1b and *YTC* 23:7b. See also *YTC** 23.5a. Between the characters *ch'uan* and *che* in the fifth line of the *YTC* 23:7b, the character *nung* was omitted and should be restored. The omission was also noticed by Ch'en Yüan. See *Shen-k'o Yüan tien-chang chiao-pu*, "Cha-chi," 2:38b. The character *pien*(b) in the sixth line of the *TCTK* 16.1b is a misprint for the character *pan*, and between the characters *pu* and *tsun* in the eighth line the character *fu*(b) seems to be omitted.

[46] For a discussion of the authority and responsibility of a *she-chang* (*she* leader, community leader), see Ch. III above.

and, consequently, the original purpose of electing the *she* leaders has been greatly lost. Hereafter, the responsibilities of imposing *corvée* and of managing county fairs shall lie solely within the competence of the *li-cheng* and *chu-shou* and [,therefore,] the *she* leaders shall be made solely responsible for the encouragement of agriculture. Villagers who are not familiar with agricultural affairs shall be taught [by the *she* leaders], and those who are not diligent shall be pressed [by the *she* leaders] so as to assure that the agricultural labor be fully mobilized and the land be fully utilized. Any authorities who continue disobeying [the regulation] and obstructing or abolishing the encouragement of agricultural activities shall be investigated and punished by the Su-cheng lien-fang ssu.

[Item 4.][47] As for any *chou* or *hsien* official, on the day for the encouragement of agriculture, if within the *she* there are profligate and idle people who do not engage in production and do not repent despite several warnings, the *she* leaders shall have to explain [this] to the public and punish them according to the gravity of their cases. If a *she* leader is too young in age or too weak in virtue to be trusted and respected by the public, [the official] shall immediately consult with [the villagers] and select a man who is thoroughly familiar with agricultural affairs, advanced in age, and pure and attentive in conduct to replace [the *she* leader].

[Item 5.][48] With regard to using the false pretense of miracles for making up strange legends or the pretense of performing charitable activities for assembling people by night but dispersing them by day or any other matters already prohibited by the authorities, the *she* leaders once every quarter shall issue

---

[47] *TCTK* 16:2a and *YTC* 23:7a. See also *YTC** 23:5a. Between the characters *nung* and *jih* in the seventh line of the *YTC* 23:7a, the character *che* is superfluous and should be deleted. Of the two characters *yu yu* in the same line, one is superfluous and should be deleted. Ch'en Yüan also noticed these superfluous characters. See *Shen-k'o Yuan tien-chang chiao-pu*, "Cha-chi," 2:38b. The character *yeh* in the seventh line of the *YTC* 23:7b was printed as *li*(e) in the *TCTK* version. The character *hsing*(b) in the eighth line was printed as *shih*(d) in the *TCTK* version.

[48] *TCTK* 16:2a.

warnings and cause people to know how to fear [the law] so as to prevent them from suffering criminal penalties.

[Item 6.][49] In times of disaster or famine, any person who is not stingy in [sharing] his possessions [with others] and urges rich families to join in helping the poor people so as to prevent them from becoming homeless shall be recommended by the local authorities to the higher authorities to report to the Board [of Revenue and Population] for submission to the [Chung-shu-]sheng.

[Item 7.][50] With regard to any *i-ts'ang* (charity granary), [its] original [purpose] was to have common people save surplus grains in years of plenty and consume them in years of scarcity and it has proved to be a good institution. All *she* leaders shall still follow the original scheme to establish and perform [this institution]. Any authorities who dare to restrict or obstruct them shall be impeached by the Su-cheng lien-fang ssu.

[Item 8.][51] With regard to any rich family which depends on or asks for the influence of current officials to avoid taxes or *corvée*, the officials of each corresponding Su-cheng lien-fang ssu shall always attentively prohibit and investigate [the practice] so as to prevent any continuous occurrence of the old

[49] *TCTK* 16:2 and *YTC* 3:13b. See also *YTC** 3:9b. The character *ch'üeh*(c) and the character *hsieh*(b) in the fourth line of the *YTC* 3:13b were printed as *ch'üeh*(b) and *hsieh*(a), respectively, in the *TCTK* version.

[50] *TCTK* 16:2b and *YTC* 3:13b. See also *YTC** 3:9b. The character *ch'u*(a) in the first line of the *YTC* 3:13b was printed as *chu*(c) in both the *YTC** and the *TCTK* versions. I-chu (July 17, 1831–August 22, 1861) was the seventh Emperor of the Ch'ing dynasty who ruled under the reign title of Hsien-fang (r. 1851–1862). The Shen Chia-pen edition of the *Yüan tien-chang*, therefore, changed the character *chu*(c) to the character *chu*(b) or to another form such as the character *ch'u*(a) in the present fragment in order to observe the Ch'ing taboo. For the life of I-chu, see Hummel, ed., *Eminent Chinese of the Ch'ing Period*, Vol. 1, pp. 378–380. The character *hsü*(c) in the present fragment was printed as *ch'u*(b) in the *YTC** version. Between the characters *ts'ung* and *lien* in the third line of the *YTC* 3:13b, two characters *su-cheng* were omitted and should be restored. The omission was also noticed by Ch'en Yüan. See *Shen-k'o Yüan tien-chang chiao-pu*, "Cha-chi," 1:8a. The second character *nien* in the third line of the *TCTK* 16:2b was printed as *sui*(b) in both the *YTC* and the *YTC** versions.

[51] *TCTK* 16:2b–3a.

123

corrupt practice at the expense of the poor people. In any such violation, the [protecting] official and the [rich] civilian shall both be punished.

[Item 9.][52] With regard to legal disputes over marriage, family property, land, estate, or debt, if they are not grave, illegal matters, the *she* leaders shall be allowed to demonstrate reasons for reconciling the disputes so as to prevent [the parties involved] from obstructing or neglecting agricultural activities and from disturbing the authorities.

[Item 10.][53] Of all civil cases, disputes over marriage and land are most multifarious. [Therefore,] in each locality the authorities shall cause all matchmakers comprehensively to understand the precedents prohibiting cases of illegal marriage and shall cause all business brokers to understand the precedents prohibiting illegal transactions in land or estates and shall cause all professional plaint-writers to understand the precedents regulating what ought to be suitable and what ought not and [,moreover,] shall still extract [from all the persons of above professions] affidavits not to violate the commitment [to the prevention of disputes] so as to extinguish the origin of litigation.

[Item 11.][54] In any civil litigation, if evidence is beyond any

[52] *TCTK* 16:3a and *YTC* 53:4a. See also *YTC** 53:3a. While this fragment could also be put into the "Ch'a-yü" (Investigation of Cases) section, it seems more appropriate to include it in the present "Chih-min" section, because the latter section deals with the settlement of litigation and this particular fragment is also mainly concerned with litigation. See n.42 above. The character *lun* in the eleventh line of the *YTC* 53:4a is a misprint for the character *yü*(a). This misprint was also noticed by Ch'en Yüan. See *Shen-k'o Yüan tien-chang chiao-pu*, "Cha-chi," 5:1a. See also Iwamura Shinobu and Tanaka Kenji, *Gen tenshō keibu dai nisatsu* [*Board of Punishments in the Institutions of the Yuan Dynasty, Vol. Two*] (Kyoto: Kyoto University Press, 1972), p. 458. The character *hsu*(d) in the eleventh line of the *YTC* 53:4a was printed as *jao* in the *TCTK* version.

[53] *YTC* 53:4a and *YTC** 53:3a. While this fragment could also be placed in the "Ch'a-yü" section, it seems more appropriate to include it in the "Chin-min" section, because the fragment is concerned mainly with civil disputes rather than criminal matters. According to the *Li-hsueh chih-nan*, the settlement of litigation concerning civil disputes is within the category of the "Chih-min" section. See *Li-hsueh chih-nan*, 25b.

[54] *YTC* 53:4 and *YTC** 53:3a. Although this fragment could be also included in the "Ch'a-yü" section, it seems more suitable to place the fragment into

doubt and precedents are clear and yet officials or clerks in their deliberations bend the principles to make mistakes intentionally, then, even if the matter shall have been readjusted, the details of the original decision shall still be investigated.

[Item 12.]⁵⁵ With regard to all public, deserted lands, any person who desires to start cultivation shall be allowed to go before the local authorities to submit a petition for applying for the permit. Each adult shall then be given a hundred *mou* of land.⁵⁶ Officials, local magnates, and other persons who have not submitted the application to the authorities shall not lay any false claim to occupying [a piece of land]. At the end of each year the amount of land so given shall be checked and reported to the supervising authorities for collecting the documents to submit to the Board [of Revenue and Population].

SECTION IV

"Li-ts'ai" (*Management of Finances*)⁵⁷

[Item 1.]⁵⁸ With regard to any disbursement of taxes and grains to the *lu-fen* (*lu* branches) in the *fu-li* (in the metropolitan

---

the present "Chih-min" section, because the fragment is mainly concerned with civil disputes. See n.42 above. The character *hsiang* in the twelfth line of the *YTC* 53:4a is a misprint for the character *hsun*. This misprint was also noticed by Ch'en Yüan. See *Shen-k'o Yüan tien-chang chiao-pu*, "Cha-chi," 5:1a. See also Iwamura and Tanaka, *Gen tenshō keibu dai nisatsu*, p. 458. The character *yüan*(c) in the first line of the *YTC* 53:4b was printed as *yüan*(a) in the *YTC** version, but this change was not mentioned by Ch'en Yüan.

⁵⁵ *YTC* 19:9a and *YTC** 19:6a. The character *yu*(c) in the third line of the *YTC* 19:9a is a misprint for the character *wu*(a). This misprint was also noticed by Ch'en Yüan. See *Shen-k'o Yüan tien-chang chiao-pu*, "Cha-chi," 2:14b.

⁵⁶ *Mou* is a Chinese measure of land area; 6.6 *mou* = 1 acre.

⁵⁷ The term "Li-ts'ai" (Management of Finances) refers, as indicated in the *Li-hsueh chih-nan*, to the guarding of public funds and grains as well as the stabilization of prices. See *Li-hsüeh chih-nan*, 25b.

⁵⁸ *YTC* 21:14b and *YTC** 21:8b–9a. The character *tao*(a) in the seventh line of the *YTC* 21:14b is a misprint for the character *tao*(b). The character *li*(d) in the same line is also a misprint for the character *tao*(b). These misprints were also noticed by Ch'en Yüan. See *Shen-k'o Yüan tien-chang chiao-pu*, "Cha-chi," 2:23b. The character *chun*(b) in the twelfth line of the *YTC* 21:14b was printed as *chun*(a) in the *YTC** version.

area), the amount shall be subjected to the audit and examination of the Board [of Revenue and Population] of the [Chung-shu-]sheng. Among the disbursements already officially approved, if there are items, according to explicit precedents, to be reduced or readjusted, then the [original] calculated amount of disbursement for each quarter, along with necessary documents of disbursing, after a complete examination, shall be submitted no later than the second decade of the second moon of the following quarter. [Upon such submission] the relevant portion [of disbursement], after calculation, shall be subsequently reduced or readjusted. All *lu* branches under the jurisdiction of each Hsing-sheng, with regard to items to be reduced or readjusted, shall be analogously subject to the same procedure.

[Item 2.][59] With regard to taxes, grains, or other items, the Board of Revenue and Population shall establish standard forms to have [authorities of] each locality [fill out] and submit once every quarter. When the forms arrive at the Board, officials shall be appointed to examine them and, if there is any inconsistency, it shall be immediately dealt with. At the end of each year a general audit shall be conducted and it shall be thoroughly conducted so as not to become a mere formality. Each Hsing-sheng shall follow analogously the above [procedure] and report to the [Chung-shu-]sheng.

[Item 3.][60] With regard to any audit, if it is necessary to summon the functionaries, the supervising authorities shall establish a [temporary] office. Beginning with the first attendance at the office, each functionary, in proportion to the

---

[59] *YTC* 21:14b and *YTC** 21:9a. Between the characters *ch'ih*(a) and *chu*(a) in the tenth line of the *YTC* 21:14b, the character *yu*(b) was omitted and should be restored. Beginning with this character *yu*(b), the fragment should be recorded separately in a new paragraph. The omission and change were also noticed by Ch'en Yuan. See *Shen-k'o Yüan tien-chang chiao-pu*, "Cha-chi," 2:23b. Since the character here is used as a conjunction, the fragment proper should start with the character *chu*(a).

[60] *YTC* 21:15a and *YTC** 21:9a. The character *ch'ing*(a) in the first line of the *YTC* 21:15a and the *YTC** version seems to be a misprint for the character *chu*(a). The character *wan* in the third line is a misprint for the character *huan*. The latter misprint was also noticed by Ch'en Yüan. See *Shen-k'o Yüan tien-chang chiao-pu*, "Cha-chi," 2:23a.

amount of paper work, shall be given a deadline accordingly. Once every five days the sequence [of work] shall be checked and, as soon as the assignments shall have been completed, they shall be sent back [to their original offices]. If [an official organ] has submitted financial reports regularly and has established precedents for income and disbursement and [consequently] the audit can be conducted by examining the standard forms, then it is not necessary to summon [its] functionaries to the capital. All authorities, with regard to their subordinate official organs, shall follow analogously this [procedure].

[Item 4.][61] All land taxes shall be strictly guarded and the officials, magnates, and other people shall not conspire to farm the taxes.[62] If the *chin-hsia hu-chi* (lower households)[63] are far from the [official] warehouses and are willing to pay *chiao-ch'ien* (foot money)[64] to entrust the neighboring people with the

---

[61] *TCTK* 17:4a and *YTC* 24:1b. See also *YTC** 24:1b. This fragment could be included in the "Fu-i" (Taxes and *Corvée*) section. Since the fragment deals primarily with the control of taxes, however, it seems more appropiate to include it in the present "Li-ts'ai" section. See *Li-hsüeh chih-nan*, 25b. The character *huan* in the eighth line of the *YTC* 24:1b was printed as *yün* in the *TCTK* version. The character *wo* in the eleventh line is a misprint for the character *chih*(a). The last misprint was also noticed by Ch'en Yüan. See *Shen-k'o Yüan tien-chang chiao-pu*, "Cha-chi," 2:41a.

[62] The term "farming the taxes" translates the term *chieh-lan* which refers, as indicated in the *Li-hsüeh chih-nan*, to the solicitation and collection of taxes and grains for submission collectively to the authorities. See *Li-hsüeh chih-nan*, 62a. See also Schurmann, *Economic Structure of the Yüan Dynasty*, p. 85, n. 36.

[63] The category of *chin-hsia hu-chi* (lower households) refers to the poor and humble households. According to a document released shortly after the promulgation of the *Chih-yüan hsin-ko* and dated 1294, a household upon which were imposed only four taels of *pao-yin* (taxes in silver) for taxes was classified as a lower household. See *Chan-ch'ih*, II, 172. The *pao-yin* was a form of household tax and was literally translated by Schurmann as "farming the silver [tax]." See Schurmann, *Economic Structure of the Yüan Dynasty*, pp. 103–104, n.3. For a detailed discussion of this form of tax, see Abe Takeo, *Gendaishi no kenkyū*, pp. 75–232. However, in 1291 or 1294, households in South China were not required to pay taxes in the form of *pao-yin*. According to another document dated 1296, a household in South China upon which were imposed only three *tan* (one Chinese *tan* = 133⅓ lb.) of grain was then classified as a lower household. See *TCTK* 17:14a. This document of 1296, with some changes, is also recorded in the *Yüan tien-chang*. See *YTC* 60:2a. It therefore becomes clear that at the time of the *Chih-yüan hsin-ko* a lower household in North China was taxed four taels of *pao-yin* and in South China was taxed three *tan* of grain.

[64] The term *chiao-ch'ien* (foot money) refers to freight expenses.

delivery of their taxes to the warehouses, they shall be permitted to do so. The tax officials at the headquarters shall consider the distance of each locality to arrange the sequence of the shipping schedule accordingly and [then] designate the place of focus [to collect] all shippings. If no *ch'ing-chi* (commutation goods) or other tax-farming profits are involved,[65] the tax officials [at the headquarters] shall then order the branch officials to supervise the delivery [of taxes] into the warehouses. When the exact amount of taxes has been submitted and the *chu-ch'ao* (receipt bearing the vermilion seal) has been issued, [the branch officials] on the same day shall be sent back [to the original offices]. However, as to officials of the headquarters, when [the taxes of] each *chou* and *hsien* shall have been fully submitted, then and only then may they return to their offices.

[Item 5.][66] With regard to items for annual, regular disbursement and maintenance, they may be consumed either slowly or rapidly, and for preparation they may be either difficult or easy to obtain. The responsible officials and clerks, with regard to the necessary amount of each item, shall check and examine in season and shall prepare and apply to obtain [the item] in advance lest in the case of sudden shortage the public and the private shall both be inconvenienced.

[Item 6.][67] With regard to all items in the *ho-mai* (harmonious purchase)[68] practice, [the authorities] shall check the place of

---

[65] The term *ch'ing-chi* (commutation goods) refers, as indicated in the *Li-hsüeh chih-nan*, to the submission of paper currency to the authorities in commutation for the tax to be originally paid in grain. See *Li-hsüeh chih-nan*, 62b. For a discussion of this term, see Schurmann, *Economic Structure of the Yüan Dynasty*, p. 83, n.18.

[66] *YTC* 26:4b and *YTC** 26:3a.

[67] *YTC* 26:4b and *YTC** 26:3a. This fragment is recorded in the *Yuan tien-chang* immediately under the last character of the previous fragment. Beginning with the character *chu*(a), therefore, the fragment should be recorded separately in a new paragraph. This change was also noticed by Ch'en Yüan. See *Shen-k'o Yüan tien-chang chiao-pu*, "Cha-chi," 2:44b. The character *neng* in the seventh line of the *YTC* 26:4b is a misprint for the character *te*, but this misprint was not mentioned by Ch'en Yüan.

[68] The practice of *ho-mai* (harmonious purchase) was already in existence in the late T'ang and the Sung periods. Although this practice, in principle, was supposed to be a harmonious transaction, it was not unusual for many

their production and storage and shall purchase them proportionately and fairly. The official or clerks shall not pay [unfairly] low prices to collect them by force and [later] press the civilian households to pay additional, higher prices for buying and submitting them to the office, otherwise violators shall be severely punished and the additional profits shall be calculated and returned in the exact amount [to the victims].

[Item 7.][69] In each "harmonious purchase" [the authorities] shall make at each place for receiving goods a public notification to announce the nature of items currently purchased as well as the price of each item. Upon the delivery of these items to the office, the cash payment shall be immediately made. The principal officials shall supervise the original record. With regard to any receipt of goods and the payment, it shall be registered in the record who has submitted what kind of goods at what amount and how much price has been paid. The original owner shall draw his mark on the entry of the record and the supervising officials shall still impress the official seal and tally to check and guard the record so as to prepare it for future examination.

[Item 8.][70] With regard to the merchandise in the streets or markets, [the authorities] shall order the *hang-jen* (business

---

common people to be exploited by the local authorities by being forced to sell their goods for extremely low prices. For a discussion of this practice, see Yang Lien-sheng, *Excursions in Sinology* (Cambridge, Mass.: Harvard University Press, 1969), pp. 226 and 234. See also Sudō Yoshiyuki, *Tō-So shakai keizaishi kenkyū* [*Studies in the Social and Economic History of the T'ang and Sung Dynasties*] (Tokyo: Tokyo University Press, 1965), pp. 415–446. See also Abe Takeo, *Gendaishi no kenkyū*, pp. 182–191.

[69] *YTC* 26:4b and *YTC** 26:3b. This fragment is recorded in the *Yuan tien-chang* immediately under the last character of the previous fragment. Beginning with the character *chu*(a) in the eighth line of the *YTC* 26:4b, therefore, the fragment should be recorded separately in a new paragraph. The first character *ch'ao* in the ninth line is a misprint for the character *ch'ien*(a), and the character *shih*(d) in the same line is a misprint for the character *chu*(d). Between the characters *tzu*(a) and *chien*(a) in the eleventh line, the character *ch'i*(a) was omitted and should be restored. These misprints and the omission were also noticed by Ch'en Yüan. See *Shen-k'o Yüan tien-chang chiao-pu*, "Cha-chi," 2:44b.

[70] *YTC* 26:15 and *YTC** 26:6a.

brokers) each moon to evaluate the price. If any price is significantly higher or lower than what was previously reported, [the proprietor] shall explain the reason for such an increase or decrease and the detail shall be reported from the *ssu-hsien* to the *fu* or *chou* which in turn shall report it to the supervising *lu* for transfer to the Board of Revenue and Population. The report shall be first confirmed to be true and [later], along with the affidavit [of confirmation], be submitted. With regard to items which, according to the annual practice, shall be bought from the native place through the "harmonious purchase," if they happen to become more in production and cheaper in price and it is worth taking advantage of the cheaper price to collect and buy them, the price shall be immediately specified in a separate report which is to be submitted as soon as possible.

SECTION V

"Fu-i" (*Taxes and* Corvée) [71]

[Item 1.][72] With regard to the imposition of taxes and *corvée*, the principal officials of the *ssu-hsien* shall supervise the functionaries in establishing a bureau and the imposition shall be even and fair lest it shall be unbalanced. In accordance with the imposed amount, following the precedent, [the authorities] shall issue [to each taxpayer] a [tax]form bearing the official signature and seal and shall still set up in each village a *fen-pi* (pastewall) to have people widely notified. If the [current] amount, in comparison with that of the previous year, is more, less, or different, then [the authorities], in accordance with the detail, shall clearly establish the files to prepare for future examination.

[71] The term "Fu-i" (Taxes and *Corvée*) refers, as indicated in the *Li-hsueh chih-nan*, to the imposition of taxes and grains as well as to the fair imposition of *corvée*. See *Li-hsueh chih-nan*, 25b.

[72] *TCTK* 17:3 and *YTC* 3:1b–2a. See also *YTC** 3·1b. A short citation of fragment is also recorded in the *Yuan shih*. See *YS* 93:13b. The characters *ch'en yuan-yin* in the first line of the *YTC* 3:2a were printed as *chu yuan-yu* in the *TCTK* version. The character *chun*(b) and the character *chao*(b) in the second line were printed as *i*(c) and *chao*(a), respectively, in the *TCTK* version.

130

[Item 2.][73] With regard to the imposition of *corvée*, [the authorities] shall first [call upon] the rich and the strong and then the poor and the weak. If [two households] are equally poor or rich, [the one] with more male adults shall be first [called upon] and then [the one] with fewer male adults. The names of all households shall be registered from the top [priority] to the low [priority] in the record to await [their] turn. When there is a call for the *corvée*, the principal officials shall in person select the necessary number of people [from the record] and issue the permit bearing the official seal and check the number of people for the implementation of the *corvée* so as to prevent the governmental clerks, village heads, and other people from exempting the rich but drafting the poor or from shifting the priority and making corruption. The record of *corvée* shall, moreover, be kept and sealed by the *chang-kuan* (leading official)[74] and, if the *chang-kuan* is on leave, it shall be kept and sealed by the assistant official.

[Item 3.][75] Disasters from floods or drought shall all be investigated and, when the facts are obtained, they shall be promptly reported to the Board [of Revenue and Population]. If the damage amounts to eight-tenths or more of a field, the taxes shall be totally exempted. If the damage amounts to seven-tenths or less, only the damaged portion shall be exempted from the taxes. When the harvest has achieved six-tenths [of the total amount], the full amount of taxes has to

[73] *TCTK* 17:3b–4a and *YTC* 3:2a. See also *YTC** 3:1b. A short citation of this fragment is also recorded in the *Yüan shih*. See *YS* 93:13b. The character *hu* in the third line of the *YTC* 3:2a was printed as *fu*(c) in the *TCTK* version.

[74] In the local government of the Yüan dynasty both the *ta-lu-hua-ch'ih* (*daruyači*) and the *hsien-yin* (magistrate) were normally referred to as the *chang-kuan* (leading officials). In the *lu* government the *ta-lu-hua-ch'ih* (*daruyači*) and the *tsung-kuan* (chief administrator) were referred to as the *chang-kuan*. See Ch. III above. See also Miyazaki Ichisada, "Sō-Gen jidai no hōsei to saiban kikō," pp. 159–160.

[75] *TCTK* 17:4b and *YTC** 23:15b. The fragment in the *YTC** version was omitted in the Shen Chia-pen edition of the text. The omission was also noticed by Ch'en Yüan. The missing fragment is recorded by Ch'en Yüan in the *Shen-k'o Yüan tien-chang chiao-pu*, "Ch'üeh-wen" ("Omitted Entries"), 1:41. The character *shih*(e) in the first line of the *TCTK* 17:4b was misprinted as *t'i*(b) in the *YTC** and as *t'i*(a) in the missing entry, as recorded by Ch'en Yüan, of the *YTC*.

be imposed in any case. Thus it is not necessary to apply for an investigation. Even if the damage has reached the standard of [full or partial] tax-exemption, yet, if the season permits a new plantation, then, having preserved convincing and obvious indications [of the damage], [the owner] shall immediately start the new planting so as not to lose time.

[Item 4.][76] With regard to any imposition of *corvée*, an official document bearing the seal and signature shall be used. Any oral transmission of message for the imposition shall not be honored, otherwise any violator, even if the imposition is to the public benefit, shall be punished.

[Item 5.][77] With regard to any *ho-ku* (harmonious hiring)[78] of porters, it shall be first applied to households of carters. If these households are inadequate, [the authorities] shall be permitted to hire among the rest of *chin-shang* [*hu-chi*] (upper [households])[79] which own carts. [The authorities] shall, more-

[76] *TCTK* 17:4b and *YTC* 3:2a. See also *YTC** 3:1b. The characters *k'o-ch'ai* in the sixth line of the *TCTK* 17:4b were printed as *ch'ai-k'o* in both the *YTC* 3:2a and the *YTC** 3:1b. In Item 2 of this section the word *ch'ai-k'o* is used as a verb, whereas in the present Item 4 the word *k'o-ch'ai* as a noun is more suitable to the context. The word *k'o-ch'ai* as used in the *TCTK* therefore seems more reliable. The character *fu*(d) in the eighth line of the *YTC* 3:2a was printed as *fu*(e) in the *TCTK* version.

[77] *TCTK* 17:4b–5a and *YTC* 26:11b. See also *YTC** 26:8b. The character *ku*(d) in the *TCTK* and the *YTC** versions was printed as *ku*(c) in the *YTC* 26:11b. Although these two characters may have been used interchangeably, this possible misprint was not mentioned by Ch'en Yüan. The character *yü*(c) in the third line of the *YTC* 26:11b is a misprint for the character *yü*(b), and the characters *fen-ssu* in the sixth line are misprints for the characters *kung-shih*(a). These misprints were also noticed by Ch'en Yüan. See *Shen-k'o Yüan tien-chang chiao-pu*, "Cha-chi," 2:45b. The character *yu*(a) in the ninth line of the *TCTK* 17:4b was printed as *li*(f) in both the *YTC* and the *YTC** versions.

[78] The practice of *ho-ku* (harmonious hiring), in principle, was supposed to be fair and harmonious. The common people, however, were frequently underpaid and exploited by the local authorities, despite the good intentions of the practice. See n. 68 above.

[79] The category of *chin-shang hu-chi* (upper households) refers to households of the upper division of a three-category classification, the other two being *cho-chung hu-chi* (middle households) and *chin-hsia hu-chi* (lower households). See n. 63 above. See also Kobayashi Takashirō and Okamoto Keiji, eds. *Tsūsei jōkaku no kenkyū yakuchū dai issatsu [An Annotated Translation of the Code of Comprehensive Institutions, Vol. One]* (Tokyo: Chūgoku keihōshi kenkyūkai, 1964), p. 268, n. 2.

over, prepare a record for the rotation [of harmonious hiring] and shall establish the regulation so as to prevent clerks, village-heads, and other functionaries from shifting the priority and engaging in corrupt practices.

Section VI

"K'o-ch'eng" (*Taxes and Levies*)[80]

[Item 1.][81] With regard to any calculation of taxes and grains of various localities, each Hsing-sheng annually shall conduct an investigation. If any method for the management of finances has not been fully developed or any corrupt practice of abusing public funds has not been extinguished or any way for the increase of treasure has not been performed, [each item] shall be deliberated one by one and be proposed to the [Chung-shu-]sheng. As to places under the jurisdiction of the Board of Revenue and Population, this [procedure] shall be analogously applied.

[Item 2.][82] With regard to the levies [administered] by the [tax-collecting] courts and bureaus, the supervising authorities shall often establish methods to prevent [violation] by checking and shall once every moon conduct a review. If levies are light and unencumbered and yet the amount of increase [of production] does not match the quota, [the authorities] shall immediately investigate [the matter] thoroughly and shall, moreover, appoint a scrupulous and able principal official to supervise the administration. The Board of Revenue and Population of the Hsing-sheng, with regard to all subordinate *lu* branches, once every quarter shall conduct a general comparison and shall have [the levies] submitted completely and truthfully to the office so as to prevent any cheating or concealment.

---

[80] The term "K'o-ch'eng" (Taxes and Levies) refers, as indicated in the *Li-hsüeh chih-nan*, to regulations and impositions of taxes on salt, wine, and other monopolized items. See *Li-hsüeh chih-nan*, 25b.

[81] *YTC* 22:10b and *YTC** 22:7b.

[82] *YTC* 22:10b and *YTC** 22:7b.

[Item 3.][83] As there already exists a standard system governing the monopoly of tea and salt, the Board of Revenue and Population of the Hsing-sheng shall examine and consult the established precedents and articles. If any officials in recent years have violated the prohibition to pursue personal profits, to embezzle the public levies, or to obstruct merchants, the Board shall announce their names one by one in public so as to enforce the prohibition strictly. Moreover, it shall dispatch scrupulous and able officials to regularly conduct secret investigations so as to maintain the circulation of tea and salt and the convenience of things public and private.

[Item 4.][84] The salt bags at each [salt]yard shall all be packed under the supervision of a *p'an-kuan* (commissary of records) and the utensil for measuring shall weigh evenly and fairly so as to have no surplus or deficiency.[85] The *yün-shih* (commissary of salt transportation) and assistant officials shall rotate and examine [the salt bags]. For each bag there shall, moreover, be written down the title and name of the official who has supervised the packing and the official who has examined it. It shall be, by adopting [the sequence in] the *Ch'ien tzu wen* [*The Thousand Character Essay*],[86] given a mark and arranged [under the mark] and stored in order. Whenever

---

[83] *YTC* 22:10b–11a and *YTC** 22:7b. The characters *li-t'iao* in the thirteenth line of the *YTC* 22:10b were erroneously inverted and should be changed to *t'iao-li*. The character *ai*(a) in the first line of the *YTC* 22:11a was printed as *ai*(b) in the *YTC** version. The inversion and the misprint were not mentioned by Ch'en Yüan. The characters *ch'ai-hsüan* in the second line of the *YTC* 22:11a were also erroneously inverted and should be changed to *hsüan-ch'ai*. This last inversion was also noticed by Ch'en Yuan. See *Shen-k'o Yüan tien-chang chiao-pu,* "Cha-chi," 2:27a.

[84] *YTC* 22:11a and *YTC** 22:7b–8a. Below the character *yun* in the fourth line of the *YTC* 22:11a, the character *shih*(c) was omitted and should be restored. This omission was also noticed by Ch'en Yüan. See *Shen-k'o Yüan tien-chang chiao-pu,* "Cha-chi," 2:27a. The character *ta* in the second line of the *YTC** 22:8a and in the seventh line of the *YTC* 22:11a seems to be a misprint for the character *chia*(a).

[85] During the Yuan dynasty, the unit amount of salt obtainable for one *yin* (license) was fixed at 400 catties. See *YTC* 22:51b–52a. See also Schurmann, *Economic Structure of the Yüan Dynasty*, p. 183, n. 3.

[86] The *Ch'ien tzu wen* [*The Thousand Character Essay*] was a primer by which children learned the Chinese language. The text consisted of 1,000 characters, none of which was alike.

a merchant applies and requests [a salt bag], [the authorities] shall check the sequence and give [him] the one from the top. The Board of Revenue and Population of the Hsing-sheng shall dispatch officials to investigate without any notice. If there is any smuggling of surplus salt or deduction on the weight of the measurement or violation of the sequence of giving away a bag or obstruction of a salt merchant, [the authorities] shall immediately press an investigation. And, if [the case] proves to be true, each [violator], in proportion to the gravity of the offense, shall be punished accordingly and shall, moreover, be impeached by the investigating censors.

[Item 5.][87] When any delivery by the *tsao-hu* (salt-refining households) of *chung-yen* (salt of harmonious purchase)[88] arrives at the [salt]yard, it shall be immediately weighed fairly and be received without any delay or imposition of obstruction. [The amount of] *kung-pen* (labor and capital money)[89] owed [to the salt-refining households] shall be reimbursed under the personal supervision of a [salt]transportation official. Any official or clerk of the Salt Bureau who takes this occasion to deduct or substitute something else for the reimbursement, in proportion to the amount [abused],

[87] *YTC* 22:11a and *YTC** 22:8a. The character *pe'i*(b) in the twelfth line of the *YTC* 22:11a was normally printed as *pe'i*(a) during the Yüan dynasty and was indeed so printed in the *YTC** version of this fragment. This variant was not mentioned by Ch'en Yüan.

[88] In the Sung period, owing to military needs, merchants were ordered to exchange their grains for salt in lieu of payment by the government. This practice became a standard form of exchange between merchants and the government under the name of *chung-yen* (salt of harmonious purchase) and was later observed in the Yüan period. According to the *Yüan shih*, *k'o-yen* (kernel salt), *mo-yen* (powder salt), and *ching-yen* (well salt) were the three major types of salt in use during the Yuan period. There were also several sizes of salt such as *hsiao-yen* (small salt) and *ta-yen* (large salt), the former being produced in the T'ai-yüan region of Shensi and the latter in Manchuria. See *YS* 94:9a–14a. See also Schurmann, *Economic Structure of the Yuan Dynasty*, p. 166.

[89] The term *kung-pen* (labor and capital money) refers to wages. During the Yüan dynasty, the wages for the *tsao-hu* (salt-refining households) varied from time to time and place to place. According to the *Yüan shih*, the wages for the salt-refining households in the Ta-tu area in 1291, the same year that the *Chih-yüan hsin-ko* was promulgated, amounted to eight *liang* (taels) of *Chung-t'ung ch'ao* (Chung-t'ung note). See *YS* 94:10a.

shall be punished accordingly and shall, moreover, be pressed for repayment. On each occasion of paying "labor and capital money," the Su-cheng lien-fang ssu shall dispatch persons to investigate secretly.

[Item 6.][90] Any [salt]yard, in accumulating and storing the amount of unrefined salt, shall keep it in order on a high hill where the tidewater cannot encroach. [The authorities] shall, moreover, appoint [salt]transportation officials to visit often on the spot and investigate. If the storage has not been in compliance with the proper methods or the preservation has been so unthorough as to result in damage, the negligent person shall be pressed for compensation.

[Item 7.][91] With regard to [the number of] officials at a [tax collecting] court or bureau, a large one shall have no more than three members. [The posts of] assistants and other functionaries shall be preserved or established in accordance with *the amount of levies to be collected and the excess persons* shall be dismissed so as to prevent [them] from overflowing [the court or bureau], oppressing the common people, and illegally consuming public funds.

[Item 8.][92] Any [commissioner of] the Chuan-yün-ssu (Bureau of Salt Transportation) or its intendant official or clerk who takes away or borrows from the [tax collecting] court or bureau of his own jurisdiction funds or goods shall be treated as a thief and the accomplice shall be subjected to the same punishment. With regard to any taxable item, any person who, without following the precedent of imposing the *ch'ou-fen* (per-

---

[90] *YTC* 22:11b and *YTC** 22:8a. The character *yen* in the second line of the *YTC* 22:11b is a misprint for the character *chien*(b). The character *pe'i*(b) in the third line is a variant for the character *pe'i*(a); between the preceding character *ping*(a) and this character *pe'i*(a), the character *le* was omitted and should be restored. Ch'en Yüan also noticed these changes. See *Shen-k'o Yüan tien-chang chiao-pu*, "Cha-chi," 2:27a.

[91] *YTC* 22:11b and *YTC** 22:8a. The character *ch'ien*(b) in the fourth line of the *YTC* 22:11b is a misprint for the character *kan*(b). This misprint was not mentioned by Ch'en Yüan. Below the character *kuan*(a) in the sixth line, the character *ch'ien*(a) was omitted and should be restored. This omission was also noticed by Ch'en Yüan. See *Shen-k'o Yuan tien-chang chiao-pu*, "Cha-chi," 2:27a.

[92] *YTC* 22:11b and *YTC** 22:8a.

centage levy),[93] impresses the "tax stamp" [on the item] shall be also so punished.

[Item 9.][94] Any Salt Bureau, upon receiving a report of salt smuggling, shall specify the site of evaporation and storage [of illegal salt] to investigate thoroughly and clearly and shall then plan and act with the authorities of the locality where the site is located jointly to search for and arrest [the offenders]. Without being informed of [salt smuggling], a salt patrolman shall only be permitted to follow the precedent of patrolling attentively and shall not be allowed to enter abruptly into any house to search for or arrest [any person].

[Item 10.][95] With regard to any seizure of smuggled salt or distilled grain, if the interrogation proves [the offense] to be true, [the seized item] shall be, in accordance with the article, confiscated. The detail of such offense as well as the confiscated cash and goods shall be specified by establishing a case and then be examined. [The authorities] shall, moreover, attach [each case] to a separate file and submit [them] once every moon to the supervising authorities.

[Item 11.][96] With regard to the salt system, all salt licenses shall be paid for in cash.[97] When the notes for the price [of salt] shall have entered the treasury and the salt bags shall have left the [salt]yard, then and only then may [the operation of] the imposition of levy be completed. Any [salt]transportation

---

[93] For a discussion of the *ch'ou-fen* (precentage levy), see Schurmann, *Economic Structure of the Yüan Dynasty*, p. 225. See also Ratchnevsky, *Un Code des Yuan*, pp. 142–143.

[94] *YTC* 22:11b and *YTC** 22:8a.

[95] *YTC* 22:11b–12a and *YTC** 22:8a. The character *h*(b) in the first line of the *YTC* 22:12a is a taboo form for the character *h*(a). See n. 20 above.

[96] *YTC* 22:12a and *YTC** 22:8b.

[97] During the Yüan period, the price for each *yin* (license) weighing 400 catties of salt changed several times. When the salt system was first established in the year 1230/1231, the price was fixed at ten taels of silver. It was reduced to seven taels in the year 1261/1262. It was changed to nine *kuan* (string) of Chung-t'ung notes in the year 1276/1277 and was increased to 65 strings in the year 1296/1297. During the years between 1309 and 1315/1316, it was increased to 150 strings. See *YS* 94:9a. See also Schurmann, *Economic Structure of the Yüan Dynasty*, p. 175. In the document cited by Schurmann in the above reference, however, the 26th year of the Chih-yuan reign [January 23, 1289–February 10, 1290] was wrongly converted to the year 1286/1287 by him.

official who is so attentive to each matter as to cause the salt quota to have a surplus, to make officials and clerks observe the law, to suit the convenience of merchants, and to increase the levies, upon the hearing of the memorial, shall be promoted and rewarded.

SECTION VII

"*Ts'ang-k'u*" (*Warehouses*)[98]

[Item 1.][99] With regard to the system of all expenditures and receipts, the officials of warehouses shall inspect in person the measuring of the weight and the counting of the amount [of goods]. From the *t'i-chü* (intendant) and the *chien chih-na* (supervising cashier) down to the *tsuan-tien* (accountant)[100] and other functionaries, they shall mutually keep an eye on one another. He who reports a case of theft, fraud, or violation of law to the authorities shall be rewarded in accordance with the nature of each case. If there is any embezzlement of funds or grains or any pretense of an undesirable or false item and yet the offender has [either] escaped or, even though still about, has no property

[98] The term "Ts'ang-k'u" (Warehouses) refers, as indicated in the *Li-hsüeh chih-nan*, to regulations concerning careful disbursement and receipt of wares as well as storage and preservation in compliance with proper methods. See *Li-hsüeh chih-nan*, 25b.

[99] *TCTK* 14:1a and *YTC* 21:1a. See also *YTC** 22:1a. A citation of this fragment is also recorded in the *Yüan shih*. See *YS* 103:3b. The character *ch'ien*(b) in the fourth line of the *YTC* 21:1a is a misprint for the character *kan*(b). Between the character *chieh*(c) and *hu* in the fourth line, the character *te* was omitted and should be restored. The misprint and the omission were also noticed by Ch'en Yüan. See *Shen-k'o Yüan tien-chang chiao-pu*, "Cha-chi," 2:22a. The character *mu* in the fourth line of the *TCTK* 14:1a is a misprint for the character *tzu*(b). This fragment was also discovered and translated into French by Ratchnevsky. See Ratchnevsky, *Un Code des Yuan*, p. 253.

[100] For a discussion of the *t'i-chu* (intendant), the *chien chih-na* (supervising cashier), and the *ts'uan-tien* (accountant), see Ratchnevsky, *Un Code des Yuan*, pp. 250–252. Ratchnevsky defines the *ts'uan-tien* as an *employé de grenier*, a definition that was later adopted by Schurmann who translated the *ts'uan-tien* as "employee." See Schurmann, *Economic Structure of the Yuan Dynasty*, p. 77. To be sure, the *ts'uan-tien* worked at a warehouse as an employee. Since the *ts'uan-tien* was primarily a clerk who calculated and dealt with figures and accounts, however, the term can be more closely and specifically translated as "accountant." For a definition of this term, see *Li-hsüeh chih-nan*, 12.

to be exacted, [the authorities] shall press the *kuan-tien* (official and accountant),[101] the *ssu-k'u* (treasurer), the *ssu-ts'ang* (warehouse-keeper), and other [responsible] persons of the same jurisdiction to compensate evenly.[102]

[Item 2.][103] With regard to all expenditures and receipts of

[101] In this fragment the term *kuan-tien* (official and accountant) stands for the *ts'ang-k'u-kuan* (warehouse official) and the *ts'uan-tien* (accountant). Ratchnevsky wrongly translates "ping le t'ung-chieh kuan-tien ssu-k'u ssu-ts'ang jen teng i-t'i chün-pe'i" as "on obligera également les mandarins du même service [ainsi que] les officiers préposés à la garde (*tien-sseu*), le préposé au trésor (*k'ou-sseu*), les individus employés dans le grenier et autres, à contribuer uniformément à parte égales au comblement [du déficit]." Because he punctuated the original Chinese document incorrectly, Ratchnevsky, in this translation of the text, regards the *tien-ssu*, the *k'u-ssu*, and the *ts'ang-ssu* as individual terms. When the text is properly punctuated, however, we have *kuan-tien* (official and accountant), *ssu-k'u* (treasurer), and *ssu-ts'ang* (warehouse-keeper) as the terms in question. In a reference recorded in the *T'ung-chih t'iao-ko* relative to preventing public grains from being embezzled, we further read: "If the offender has escaped or has no [property] to be exacted, [the authorities] shall press jointly the *kuan-tien* and others of the same jurisdiction, by establishing a deadline, to compensate evenly (ping le t'ung-chieh kuan-tien jen teng li-hsien chun-pe'i)." See *TCTK* 14:9a. The structure of this particular reference is similar to that of the present fragment of the *Chih-yüan hsin-ko*, and the word *kuan-tien* is also used as a term in itself in the *T'ung-chih t'iao-ko* version. Thus, this particular sentence of the fragment was not translated correctly by Ratchnevsky. The *ssu-k'u* refers to the person who was in charge of the treasure of a warehouse. Although Ratchnevsky mistakes *k'u-ssu* for *ssu-k'u* in this fragment because he punctuated the text incorrectly, in another fragment he regards *ssu-k'u* as a term used to designate "un fonctionnaire spécial de l'administration d'un trésor." See Ratchnevsky, *Un Code des Yuan*, p. 254, n. 3. For the function of a *ssu-k'u*, see *TCTK* 14:26b–27a.

[102] In addition to the security measures taken by members of the warehouse staff to exercise surveillance over one another, according to the *Yüan shih* and the *T'ung-chih t'iao-ko*, the security of warehouses in the capital and some other places was further maintained by groups of officers and soldiers who were stationed around the warehouses to prevent the officials, clerks, and other functionaries from embezzling or stealing the official goods and to prevent outsiders from coming unnecessarily to the doorways of warehouses. See *YS* 99:15 and *YTC* 7:13a–14a.

[103] *TCTK* 14:1b and *YTC* 21:1a. See also *YTC** 21:1a. From the character *kuan*(a) to the character *i*(d) in the eighth line of the *YTC* 21:1a, nine characters —*kuan-ssu sui-chi li-hui ch'i wu i*—were misplaced and should be removed and reinserted between the characters *ho* and *tao*(a) in the tenth line. The character *tao*(a) in the ninth line is superfluous and should be deleted. Between the characters *na*(b) and *ching* in the same line, the character *che* was omitted and should be restored. These changes were also noticed by Ch'en Yüan. See *Shen-k'o Yuan tien-chang chiao-pu*, "Cha-chi," 2:22a.

funds and grains, if all certified vouchers of official items have already arrived at the warehouses and yet the items to be received have not been received within ten days or the items to be disbursed have not been disbursed within a month, the matter shall be reported to the official organ, which has originally issued the certified vouchers, so as to attend to it immediately. If the items have already arrived at the warehouses and yet the [corresponding] certified vouchers have not been obtained, [the same procedure] shall also be followed.

[Item 3.][104] With regard to the disbursement of official items, [the authorities] shall first pay out and exhaust items which have been stored from earlier years. As to items which are currently numerous in stock and yet the occasions of use are rare and which are unfit for long preservation, [the authorities] shall report [the matter] immediately to the supervising authorities to disburse urgently so as to prevent them from being damaged or spoiled. Any violator [of this provision] shall be investigated and punished.

[Item 4.][105] At any Hsing-yung-k'u (Treasury for Note Circulation),[106] when any person comes to exchange the *hun-*

---

[104] *TCTK* 14:1b and *YTC* 21:1. See also *YTC** 21:1a. The characters *hsien-tsai*(b) in the eleventh line of the *YTC* 21:1b were printed as *hsien-tsai*(a) in both the *YTC** and the *TCTK* versions. During the Yuan dynasty, they were normally printed as *hsien-tsai*(a) instead of *hsien-tsai*(b). The character *chu*(b) in the same line is a taboo form for the character *chu*(c). See n. 50 above. These variants in the *YTC* 21:1b were not mentioned by Ch'en Yuan.

[105] *TCTK* 14:1b-2a and *YTC* 20:11a. See also *YTC** 20:8a. There also appears in the *Yuan tien-chang hsin-chi* a short citation of this fragment. See *YTCHC* "Hu-pu": 6b. Between the characters *wei*(c) and *chu* in the fifth line of the *YTC* 20:11a, the character *che* was omitted and should be restored. This omission was also noticed by Ch'en Yuan. See *Shen-k'o Yuan tien-chang chiao-pu*, "Cha-chi," 2:19a. Between the characters *yü*(d) and *jen*(a) in the eighth line of the *TCTK* 14:1b, the character *chu*(a) does not exist in the *YTC* or the *YTC** version. This fragment was also discovered and translated into French by Ratchnevsky. See Ratchnevsky, *Un Code des Yuan*, p. 254.

[106] The Hsing-yung-k'u (Treasury for Note Circulation) was established in the Yuan period to facilitate the exchange of damaged paper currency for new notes. Various localities had Hsing-yung-k'u for the convenience of the people. In the year 1289/1290, for example, there were six such Hsing-yung-k'u in the capital. See *YS* 85:12a. For a discussion of the structure of this institution, see Ratchnevsky, *Un Code des Yuan*, p. 254, n. 1.

ch'ao (shady note)[107] for the *liao-ch'ao* (raw note),[108] the *k'u-kuan* (official of the Treasury) shall oversee the *ssu-k'u*, in the presence of the person [coming to] exchange the notes, to view and examine [the note] and count the amount. If there is no jointed, patched, picked out, gouged, or counterfeited note, [the *k'u-kuan*] shall then and there in person apply [to the notes] the stamp of "[Note] being Exchanged" and shall have the *hun-ch'ao* put into the treasury and the *liao-ch'ao* handed over to the owner. The supervising authorities shall dispatch officials to come often to inspect [the operation]. Any violator [of this provision] shall be investigated and punished.

[Item 5.][109] With regard to the receipts of taxes at each *lu*, starting from the day on which the warehouses open, the principal officials of the *lu* shall rotate and have one member to inspect [the operation]. When the exact amount to be submitted has been received, [the official] shall immediately issue to the [taxpaying-]*kuan-hu* (official households) the *chu-ch'ao* and shall not obstruct, delay, or detain any person. Any *chou* where warehouses have been established shall also [follow] similarly [this procedure].

[Item 6.][110] All warehouses in receiving rice and grain shall have it dry, round, and clear. The supervising authorities shall take a sample of each to examine, identify, and seal with a mark and shall have one [sample] kept at the original warehouse and one preserved at their office. A principal official, moreover, shall come often [to the warehouses] to inspect. If what has

---

[107] The *hun-ch'ao* (shady note) refers to the damaged or deteriorated note. For various regulations concerning the control of the *hun-ch'ao*, see *YTC* 20: 11a–17a.

[108] The *liao-ch'ao* (raw note) refers to the new note.

[109] *TCTK* 14:2a and *YTC* 21:1b. See also *YTC** 21:1a. The character *chu*(f) in the third line of the *YTC* 21:1b is a variant for the character *chu*(e). Between the characters *wu*(b) and *tiao* in the same line, the character *shih*(c) was omitted and should be restored. This omission was also noticed by Ch'en Yüan. See *Shen-k'o Yuan tien-chang chiao-pu*, "Cha-chi," 2:22a.

[110] *TCTK* 14:2 and *YTC* 21:1b. See also *YTC** 21:1a. The character *yuan*(c) in the seventh line of the *YTC* 21:1b was printed as *yuan*(a) in both the *YTC** and the *TCTK* versions. During the Yüan dynasty, this character was normally printed as *yuan*(a). This change was not mentioned by Ch'en Yuan.

been received or disbursed is different from the original sample, [the violator] shall be immediately investigated and punished. (Items to be freighted shall be checked against the original sample. If the items are identical with the sample, they shall then be packed and dispatched. When they are to be unloaded, they shall also be checked against the sample and, if they are identical with it, be received.)

[Item 7.][111] With regard to goods stored at any warehouse or collected by the Pa-tso ssu (Bureau of Eight Manufacturings), if there are items which bear only names and amounts, but have no use, [the authorities] shall list and report the items in question. When they are inspected and proved to be truly [useless], an official shall be dispatched to estimate and sell [them]. If no one buys, in accordance with the circumstance, [the items] shall be disposed of lest they become damaged or spoiled.

[Item 8.][112] With regard to the funds and goods of any warehouse, any supervising official or clerk who takes, borrows, embezzles, or misappropriates them shall be treated as a thief and his accomplice shall also be so punished. If goods have not been submitted to the authorities and yet the *chu-ch'ao* is furnished groundlessly, [the violator of law] shall be similarly [punished]. [The authorities] shall, moreover, have a public notification posted at the doorway of the warehouse to enforce uninterruptedly the prohibition and rule.

[Item 9.][113] With regard to the *ch'ih-li* (red-seal register) and voucher of any warehouse, the supervising authorities once every moon shall examine and review them. If any statement is unclear or any balance is incorrect, an investigation shall be conducted as matters arise.

---

[111] *TCTK* 14:2b and *YTC* 21:1b. See also *YTC** 21:1b. The character *yü*(b) in the tenth line of the *YTC* 21:1b is a misprint for the character *kan*(b). This misprint was also noticed by Ch'en Yüan. See *Shen-k'o Yuan tien-chang chiao-pu*, "Cha-chi," 2:22a.

[112] *TCTK* 14:2b–3a and *YTC* 21:1b–2a. See also *YTC** 21:1b. The character *chu*(f) in the thirteenth line of the *YTC* 21:1b is a variant for the character *chu*(e). This change was not mentioned by Ch'en Yuan.

[113] *TCTK* 14:3a and *YTC* 21:2a. See also *YTC** 21:1b. The character *li*(b) in the second line of the *YTC* 21:2a is a taboo form for the character *li*(a). See n. 23 above.

[Item 10.][114] With regard to any warehouse, court, or bureau, if it is deteriorating, [the matter] shall be immediately reported to apply for repairs. When a rain keeps pouring, [the authorities] shall inspect [the place] often and, in accordance with the circumstance, prepare methods to withstand difficulties so as to prevent official goods from being damaged. If the storage and preservation have not been done in compliance with the proper methods or preventive measures have not been thoroughly taken or exposure to the sunshine and removal of moisture have not been conducted in the proper seasons so as to cause goods to be damaged or spoiled, [the negligent person,] in proportion to the gravity of the matter, shall be punished accordingly and shall, moreover, be pressed for compensation.

[Item 11.][115] At any warehouse, court, or bureau, with regard to the prevention [of violation], guarding, searching, inspecting, patrolling, overnight-stationing, and matters concerning the enforcement of prohibitions, the supervising authorities shall have a principal official once every moon rotate and inspect [the operation] and [it] shall always be serious and strict so as to prevent any laxity or negligence.

[Item 12.][116] With regard to officials of any warehouse, when a new official is to replace an old one, in the capital the supervising authorities shall dispatch an official to oversee [the replacement]. Outside [the capital] the principal official of each

[114] *TCTK* 14:3a and *YTC* 21:2a. See also *YTC** 21:1b. The character *su*(a) in the fourth line of the *YTC* 21:2a is a variant for the character *su*(b). This change was not mentioned by Ch'en Yüan. The first character *ju* in the fifth line is a misprint for the character *jo*, and the character *chu*(b) in the same line is a taboo form for the character *chu*(c). The character *pe'i*(b) in the sixth line was normally printed as *pe'i*(a) during the Yüan dynasty and was so printed in the *YTC** version of the present fragment. These changes were also noticed by Ch'en Yüan. See *Shen-k'o Yüan tien-chang chiao-pu*, "Cha-chi," 2:22a.

[115] *TCTK* 14:3 and *YTC* 21:2a. See also *YTC** 21:1b. The character *wu*(c) in the second line of the *TCTK* 14:3a was printed as *wu*(b) in both the *YTC* and *YTC** versions.

[116] *TCTK* 14:3b–4a and *YTC* 21:2. See also *YTC** 21:1b. Between the character *shou* in the tenth line and the character *wen* in the eleventh line of the *YTC* 21:2a, the character *chih*(b) was omitted and should be restored. Between the characters *hsü*(a) and *chao*(a) in the eleventh line, the character *tien* is superfluous and should be deleted. The omission and the superfluous character were also noticed by Ch'en Yuan. See *Shen-k'o Yuan tien-chang chiao-pu*, "Cha-chi," 2:22a. The characters *shou-chih* in the thirteenth line of the *YTC** 21:1b were erroneously inverted as *chih-shou* in the *TCTK* version.

lu shall oversee [it]. (This also applies to the *lu* or *fu* which is directly subordinate to the Board of Revenue and Population of the [Chung-shu-]sheng). As to the branch warehouses along the River,[117] an official of the Ts'ao-yün ssu (Bureau of Maritime Transportation) shall oversee [it]. All relevant documents of [previous] receipts and expenditures as well as currently existing goods shall be counted and examined clearly. If none of the amount is short, abused, or false, the old official shall itemize and present the exact amount and the new official shall then examine the amount and keep it in his management. Both officials shall, moreover, submit a joint petition to the supervising authorities to report [the detail]. After everything has been handed over, if there is any item missing or there is any undesirable or false item, then under the name of the new official [the matter] shall be pressed and dealt with.

<h2 style="text-align:center">Section VIII</h2>

"Tsao-tso" (Construction and Manufacturing)[118]

[Item 1.][119] With regard to any construction, [the authorities] shall, by estimating the [necessary working] hours and days, calculate the task of construction and shall check daily and review monthly so as to prevent any laxity. However, [any delay owing to] illness of the craftsmen or obstruction by rain or snow shall be excluded [from the schedule]. The inspecting official shall, moreover, prepare a register and constantly examine [the operation]. The supervising authorities shall come often to check and inspect so as to prevent any false delay of days and moons for the lengthy use of labor.

---

[117] The River in this fragment refers to the Huang Ho (Yellow River).

[118] The term "Tsao-tso" (Construction and Manufacturing) refers, as indicated in the *Li-hsueh chih-nan*, to the supervision of construction and the appropriation of materials. See *Li-hsueh chih-nan*, 25b.

[119] *TCTK* 30:1a and *YTC* 58:1a. See also *YTC** 58:1a. The characters *kung-fu* in the seventh line of the *YTC* 58:1a were erroneously inverted and should be changed to *fu-kung*. This inversion was also noticed by Ch'en Yuan. See *Shen-k'o Yuan tien-chang chiao-pu*, "Cha-chi," 5:26a. The characters *chi-ping* in the fifth line of the *YTC* 58:1a were printed as *ping-chi* in the *TCTK* version.

[Item 2.][120] With regard to the materials for any construction or production, it is necessary to select a person who is reliable and thoroughly familiar with the construction or production to examine [the need]. When [the need] shall have been ascertained, then and only then may [the applicant] be permitted to apply for and request [the materials]. The authorities in reviewing such an application shall also follow this [procedure]. Any person who has applied inaccurately or falsely shall, in proportion to the misrepresented amount, be punished accordingly and, by calculating the exact amount which has been put into his personal possession, shall be pressed for compensation.

[Item 3.][121] With regard to the construction or production of any official item, when the task is completed, if among the originally appropriated materials which have already been approved and sustained there is any surplus, then within the limit of ten days the surplus shall be submitted and delivered for return to the authorities. If the deadline has expired and yet [the surplus] has not been submitted, [the violator] shall be subject to the provision concerning the concealment and stealing of official funds and be punished by law.

[Item 4.][122] With regard to various kinds of materials appropriated for any construction or production by the *chü-fen* (branch bureau) [of the Board of Public Works], they shall not be abruptly changed or removed. When there is any Imperial disposition or reconstruction, having calculated comparatively the expenses of the current construction or production, if the originally appropriated materials are not enough, [the balance]

[120] *TCTK* 30:1b and *YTC* 58:1a. See also *YTC** 58:1a. The characters *pi-jan* in the tenth line of the *YTC* 58:1a are superfluous and should be deleted. Ch'en Yuan also noticed these superfluous characters. See *Shen-k'o Yuan tien-chang chiao-pu*, "Cha-chi," 5.26a. The character *chiao*(b) in the eighth line of the *YTC* 58:1a was printed as *chiao*(a) in the *TCTK* version.

[121] *TCTK* 30:1b and *YTC* 58:1b. See also *YTC** 58:1a. The character *na*(b) in the second line of the *YTC* 58:1b was printed as *huan* in the *TCTK* version.

[122] *TCTK* 30:1b–2a and *YTC* 58:1b. See also *YTC* 58:1a. The character *ling* in the fourth line of the *YTC* 58:1b is a misprint for the character *ho*. Between the characters *i*(e) and *shang* in the same line, the character *yü*(a) was omitted and should be restored. The misprint and the omission were also noticed by Ch'en Yuan. See *Shen-k'o Yuan tien-chang chiao-pu*, "Cha-chi," 5:26a.

shall be exactly appropriated and supplied and, [on the other hand,] if the materials are excessive, the exact surplus shall be returned to the authorities.

[Item 5.]¹²³ With regard to any construction or production by a branch bureau [of the Board of Public Works], its official shall every day personally circulate and inspect [the operation] and the Kung-pu [Board of Public Works] each moon shall dispatch an official to examine. It is essential that the construction or production comply with the proper methods and the operation be without any deficit, otherwise any violator shall be immediately investigated and punished. As to a branch bureau [of the Board of Public Works] outside [the capital], a principal official of the respective *lu* shall follow the above [procedure] to conduct an examination and shall once a quarter itemize the sequence of each operation and submit it to the Hsüan-wei-ssu to transfer in a notification to the Board of Public Works. The Board of Public Works shall widely compare [all operations] and shall once a quarter submit a report to the [Chung-shu-]sheng. By the end of each year [any construction or production] shall be concluded and any deficit or debt shall be avoided. A branch bureau [of the Board of Public Works] under the jurisdiction of the Hsing-sheng shall also follow this [procedure].

[Item 6.]¹²⁴ With regard to the construction of any official residence, the person appointed to supervise the construction shall personally command and delineate [the operation]. It is essential that each matter comply with the proper methods and everything be thorough and solid. If [, after the completion of the construction,] the years or moons [which have passed] are

---

¹²³ *TCTK* 30:2a and *YTC* 58:1b. See also *YTC** 58:1. Between the characters *kuan*(b) and *tsao* in the tenth line of the *YTC* 58:1b, the two characters *kung-pu* were omitted and should be restored. The two characters *shang-shu*, the character *mei*, and the character *hsing*(b) in the same line are all superfluous and should be deleted. The two characters *i-ch'ieh* in the eleventh line are superfluous and should also be deleted. The omission and the superfluous characters were also noticed by Ch'en Yüan. See *Shen-k'o Yuan tien-chang chiao-pu,* "Cha-chi," 5:26a.

¹²⁴ *TCTK* 30:2 and *YTC* 58:1b–2a. See also *YTC** 58:1b. Below the character *chiu* in the first line of the *YTC* 58:2a, the character *chih*(c) was omitted and should be restored. This omission was also noticed by Ch'en Yüan. See *Shen-k'o Yuan tien-chang chiao-pu,* "Cha-chi," 5:26a.

not many and yet in what ought not to deteriorate there is deterioration, then the supervising person, along with the craftsmen, shall be apprehended, investigated, and punished.

[Item 7.][125] With regard to any equipment or supply at an official organ, if it is so damaged as to be incapable of repair, when the official appointed to examine it shall have confirmed the case, then and only then may it be replaced. If the new item has been furnished, the old one shall be returned within ten days to the authorities so as to dispatch it to the subordinate organ for the utilization in the future of whatever can still be of use. If the old one cannot be considered as an item [owing to its severe damage], it shall be presented to the authorities for inspection and there is no need to list it as an item [so as to preclude] its wasteful registration in the file. (Vessels of brass or iron shall be collected for [making] brass or iron. Vessels of bamboo or wood shall be used for firewood.)

[Item 8.][126] With regard to funds and materials appropriated for any construction or production, on the day when the operation is completed, the chief inspector who has personally supervised [it] shall summon all responsible officials and clerks to audit [all expenditures] one by one thoroughly. When the governing authorities review and find no mistakes, then, if an expenditure warrants a readjustment, [the amount] shall, in accordance with precedent, be listed for application for readjustment. If [, on the other hand,] there is any [surplus] to be returned to the official treasury, [it] shall be exactly delivered and submitted for return to the official treasury. [The readjustment] shall not be delayed beyond the year or season lest the conduct of the audit be made difficult.

[Item 9.][127] With regard to all necessary materials for any

---

[125] *TCTK* 30:2b and *YTC* 58:2a. See also *YTC** 58:1b. The character *chi*(a) in the fourth line of the *YTC* 58:2a is a misprint for the character *kua*. This misprint was also noticed by Ch'en Yuan. The character *i*(c) in the fifth line was printed as *ch'ai* in the *TCTK* version. The character *chieh*(d) in the same line is a misprint for the character *hsin*. The last misprint was also noticed by Ch'en Yuan. See *Shen-k'o Yüan tien-chang chiao-pu,* "Cha-chi," 5:26a.

[126] *TCTK* 30:2b–3a and *YTC* 58:2a. See also *YTC** 58:1b.

[127] *TCTK* 30:3a and *YTC* 58:2a. See also *YTC** 58:1b. The character *pao* in the tenth line of the *YTC* 58:2a is a misprint for the character *chin*(a). This misprint was also noticed by Ch'en Yuan. See *Shen-k'o Yüan tien-chang chiao-pu,* "Cha-chi," 5:26a.

construction, they shall first be supplied exclusively from whatever the official treasury has. If [the official materials] are
currently not sufficient and the inadequate amount can be
supplemented [from other sources] and its price will not cause
the official treasury to suffer any loss, then [the amount] shall
be reported for application for reimbursement.

[Item 10.][128] With regard to any *lu*, when it is to impose
additional *corvée* to produce military weapons or other items,[129]
concerning all necessary materials, it is necessary to establish
clearly files for future examination. [The authorities] shall
select a man of good character to prepare the register and take
charge of [the operation]. On the day when the production is
completed, an audit shall be immediately conducted to calculate the amount being received, expended, and currently in
existence. When a principal official of the governing *lu* has
reviewed and confirmed [the audit], the relevant parts shall be
reported for notification.

[Item 11.][130] With regard to any *lu*, if there is any annual
encounter with flood damage, whatever place can be possibly
dredged, closed up, or repaired, the supervising authorities
shall, during the slack season for agriculture, dispatch officials
to visit and inspect in advance so as to evaluate the condition of
the places and prepare the labor and materials. If the operation
does not require the drafting of many workers or the use of
official funds, then it shall be permitted that neighboring

---

[128] *TCTK* 30:3 and *YTC* 58:2. See also *YTC** 58:1b. The character *kou*(b)
in the second line of the *YTC* 58:2a is a misprint for the character *heng*. The
term *heng-tsao* refers, as indicated in the *Li-hsueh chih-nan*, to the additional
imposition of *corvée* over and above the originally appropriated quota. See
Li-hsueh chih-nan, 62b. This misprint was not mentioned by Ch'en Yüan.

[129] The original Chinese term for the additional imposition of *corvée* to
produce military weapons is *heng-tsao chun-ch'i*. For a definition of the term
heng-tsao, see n. 128 above.

[130] *TCTK* 30:3b and *YTC* 58:2b. See also *YTC** 58:1b–2a. The character
k'o in the third line of the *YTC* 58:2b is a misprint for the character *liao*(a).
Between the characters *chi*(b) and *pu* in the sixth line, the character *hsu*(a) was
omitted and should be restored. The character *t'iao* in the same line is superfluous and should be deleted. The misprint, the omission, and the superfluous
characters were also noticed by Ch'en Yuan. See *Shen-k'o Yuan tien-chang chiao-
pu*, "Cha-chi," 5:26a. The character *yü*(e) in the eighth line of the *TCTK*
30:3b does not exist in either the *YTC* or the *YTC** version.

civilians be dispatched to repair immediately. If [the operation] certainly requires the disbursement of funds and mobilization of the public, [the official] shall promptly report to the governing, supervising authorities. By the beginning of the spring farming season of the following year, all constructions shall be concluded. Any other repair operation which requires the mobilization of civilian labor shall also follow this [procedure]. [However,] a matter requiring the urgent dispatch of labor shall not be bound by this provision.

SECTION IX

"*Fang-tao*" (*Prevention of Thefts*)[131]

[Item 1.][132] With regard to military officers, [their] duty is to maintain order and it is essential that no robber or thief emerge. [As to] civilian officials, [their] duty is to pacify and govern [the people] and it is essential that [the administration] be peaceful and quiet with no trouble. Hereafter, any Hsing-sheng or Hsing-yüan (Branch Bureau) [of the Shu-mi-yüan], with regard to any [negligent] subordinate such as a civilian official who pacifies or governs so unthoroughly as to cause the common people to run away or a military officer who maintains order so unstrictly as to induce robbers and thieves to sprout and flourish, shall examine the details and follow the principle to investigate and punish [the person].

[Item 2.][133] With regard to any Hsing-yüan [of the Shu-mi-

---

[131] The term "Fang-tao" (Prevention of Thefts) refers, as indicated in the *Li-hsueh chih-nan*, to the prohibition and suppression of evil deeds. See *Li-hsueh chih-nan*, 25b.

[132] *TCTK* 19:1a and *YTC* 51:3a. See also *YTC** 51:2a. The character *min* in the third line of the *YTC* 51:3a is a misprint for the character *kuan*(a). This misprint was also noticed by Ch'en Yüan. See *Shen-k'o Yüan tien-chang chiao-pu*, "Cha-chi," 4:39a. See also Iwamura Shinobu and Tanaka Kenji, *Gen tenshō keibu dai nisatsu*, p. 407.

[133] *TCTK* 19:1b and *YTC* 51:3a. See also *YTC** 51:2. The character *fang*(a) in the seventh line of the *YTC* 51:3a is a misprint for the character *fen*. The character *fu*(b) in the ninth line is a misprint for the character *hou*. The four characters *pien-hsing ch'in-ch'ih* in the tenth line are not part of the fragment proper and should be deleted. These misprints and superfluous characters were also noticed by Ch'en Yuan. See *Shen-k'o Yüan tien-chang chiao-pu*, "Cha-

yüan], [an officer] upon arrival at his post shall take notice of
the current number of occurrences of *ts'ao-tsei* (grass thieves)[134]
in the area and shall evaluate the condition of the situation
and strictly instruct the [subordinate] officers of various localities *to guard and defend with proper methods and to attract*
[them] to surrender or arrest in compliance with propriety,
aiming at bringing all robberies to an end. [Meanwhile,] the
current number of occurrences shall, moreover, be first reported
to the [Shu-mi-]yüan. Hereafter, [the officer] each quarter
shall report specifically the number [of robbers] being already
or not yet summoned or arrested as well as whether there is
any reemergence of *tsei-jen* (evil persons)[135] to the [Shu-mi-]
yüan to submit to the [Chung-shu-]sheng.

[Item 3.][136] As the robbers or thieves were initially not of
the same heart, but were either coerced into following or
deceived and seduced to act together, each Hsing-sheng and
Hsing-yüan [of the Shu-mi-yüan] shall often post a public
notification to permit [them] mutually to turn themselves in
to the authorities and arrest one another. If, before a conspiracy
shall have been committed, [a person] shall immediately report
it to the authorities or, if [the robbers or thieves] shall have
already organized and gathered themselves and yet [a person]
himself manages to arrest [any of them], [the authorities]

---

chi," 4:39a. See also Iwamura Shinobu and Tanaka Kenji, *Gen tenshō keibu dai
nisatsu*, p. 408. The character *yu*(a) in the second line of the *TCTK* 19:1b was
printed as *lun* in both the *YTC* and the *YTC** versions, and the *TCTK* version
seems more appropriate.

[134] The term *ts'ao-tsei* (grass thief) stands for *ts'ao-mang chih tsei* (grass-and-
plant thief, i.e., thief in the field) and refers broadly to a rebel or a robber.
For instance, in a reference dated 876, Wang Hsien-chih is recorded and
considered as a *ts'ao-tsei* in the *Chiu T'ang shu*, because he invaded and robbed
fifteen *chou* of Honan. See *Chiu T'ang shu* (*Po-na-pen*, Sung edition; reprinted
by The Commercial Press, Shanghai, 1936), 19b:5a. See also *Tz'u-hai* (Taipei:
Chung-hua shu-chü, 1959), II, 2,451. The *ts'ao-tsei*, in a narrow sense, refers
to someone who commits highway robbery.

[135] The term *tsei-jen* (evil person) refers broadly to any person of evil nature
and more specifically to a robber or a thief.

[136] *TCTK* 19:1b and *YTC* 51:9b. See also *YTC** 51:6a. The characters
huo-pu in the eighth line of the *YTC* 51:9b were erroneously inverted and should
be changed to *pu-huo*. This inversion was also noticed by Ch'en Yüan. See
Shen-k'o Yüan tien-chang chiao-pu, "Cha-chi," 4:40a. See also Iwamura Shinobu
and Tanaka Kenji, *Gen tenshō keibu dai nisatsu*, p. 416.

shall assess the matter and merit and reward [the person] accordingly.

[Item 4.]¹³⁷ With regard to any emergence of robbers or thieves, the residents of the area in question shall promptly report [it] to the authorities who are in charge of arresting such people; they will then immediately pursue and capture the wrongdoers. If it is absolutely necessary to muster up [forces of] the neighboring areas, the authorities who have received such a request shall come in compliance with the appointed schedule and join forces in arresting and pursuing [the robbers and thieves] and shall not confine themselves to the distinction of that territory or this boundary. Any violator [of this provision] shall be investigated and punished.¹³⁸

[Item 5.]¹³⁹ With regard to all *ts'ao-tsei*, after they shall have been suppressed through summoning and arresting, [the authorities] shall, nevertheless, properly administer, carefully guard, and strictly instruct the auxiliary authorities to be attentive so as to prevent any laxity.

[Item 6.]¹⁴⁰ Of all officers who are responsible for arresting

¹³⁷ *TCTK* 19:2a and *YTC* 51:9b. See also *YTC** 51:6a. The character *tso*(b) in the eleventh line of the *YTC** 51:6a is a misprint for the character *chih*(d). The character *ping*(c) in the twelfth line of the *YTC* 51:9b is a misprint for the character *ping*(b). The latter misprint was also noticed by Ch'en Yuan. See *Shen-k'o Yüan tien-chang chiao-pu*, "Cha-chi," 4:40a. See also Iwamura Shinobu and Tanaka Kenji, *Gen tenshō keibu dai nisatsu*, p. 416.

¹³⁸ It is recorded in the *Yüan shih* that any official who shall have insisted on the difference of jurisdiction over that territory and this boundary and failed to join forces in arresting and pursuing robbers or thieves was to be punished by a beating of 47 blows with a light stick and was, moreover, to be dismissed from his current office. See *YS* 105:26b.

¹³⁹ *TCTK* 19:2a and *YTC* 51:3a. See also *YTC** 51:2b. The character *yü*(b) in the twelfth line of the *YTC* 51:3a is a misprint for the character *kan*(b). This misprint was also noticed by Ch'en Yuan. See *Shen-k'o Yüan tien-chang chiao-pu*, "Cha-chi," 4:39a. See also Iwamura Shinobu and Tanaka Kenji, *Gen tenshō keibu dai nisatsu*, p. 408. The character *man* in the seventh line of the *TCTK* 19:2a was printed as *shih*(f) in both the *YTC* and the *YTC** versions.

¹⁴⁰ *TCTK* 19:2b and *YTC* 11:19a and 51:20b. See also *YTC** 11:13b and 51:14a. The character *i*(c) in the second line, the character *tao*(c) in the third line, and the character *pieh* in the fourth line of the *TCTK* 19:2b were printed as *ch'i*(a), *ts'ao*, and *ling*(a), respectively, in both the *YTC* and the *YTC** versions. The characters *kuo-shih* in the eighth line of the *YTC* 11:19a were erroneously inverted and should be changed to *shih-kuo*. Between the character *an* and *ling*(a) in the eleventh line, the character *che* was omitted and should

robbers, those who shall have patrolled so attentively as to bring all robberies in the area to an end shall be estimated superior. Those who, despite failure and negligence [to prevent] some robberies from occurring, nevertheless, within the deadline shall have arrested all robbers shall be considered secondary. Those officers who, owing to the failure [to prevent] robberies, have been repeatedly disciplined, if the number [of robbers] not yet arrested is still many, shall be considered inferior. When the day of selection comes, [each officer] shall be examined in light of his performance to decide accordingly his promotion or demotion. As to the South, in the places where there currently are *ts'ao-tsei*, if any person can so evenly govern with methods as to have robberies cleared up and people pacified, the person shall be discussed separately and upon the hearing of the [recommending] memorial be promoted.

Section X

"Ch'a-yü" (Investigation of cases)[141]

[Item 1.][142] Any offense punishable by beating with 57 blows or less of the stick shall be decided by the *ssu-hsien*; 87

---

be restored. Both the inversion and the omission were also noticed by Ch'en Yuan. See *Shen-k'o Yuan tien-chang chiao-pu*, "Cha-chi," 1:31a. The character *mu* in the tenth line of the *YTC* 11:19a is superfluous and should be deleted. The same character *mu* in the fourteenth line of *YTC** 11:14a should also be deleted.

In this reference as recorded in the *YTC* 51:20b, the two characters *shih-kuo* were not erroneously inverted. Neither is there any superfluous character such as the character *mu*. Comparing this reference with the one in *YTC* 11:19a, we find that there is an inconsistency concerning the existence of the character *mu*. Iwamura and Tanaka suggest that the character *mu*, or perhaps the character *chin*(b), may have been omitted between the character *chi*(c) in the seventh line and the character *nan* in the eighth line of the *YTC* 51:20b. See Iwamura Shinobu and Tanaka Kenji, *Gen tenshō keibu dai nsatsu*, p. 423. Given the context of the fragment and the fact that the *TCTK* version does not have the character *mu*, it seems reasonable to assume that the character *mu* is unnecessary in this fragment. Between the character *an* and *ling*(a) in the eighth line of the *YTC* 51:20b, the character *che* was omitted and should be restored. Similarly, the same character *che* should be restored between the characters *an* and *ling*(a) in the sixth line of the *YTC** 51:14a.

[141] The term "Ch'a-yu" (Investigation of Cases) refers, as indicated in the *Li-hsüeh chih-nan*, to the investigation and trial of imprisoned persons. See *Li-hsueh chih-nan*, 25b.

152

blows or less, by the *san-fu*,[143] the *chou*, or the *chün*; 107 blows or less, by the Hsüan-wei-ssu or Tsung-kuan-fu.[144] Any offense punishable by exile or death shall, in accordance with precedent, be fully investigated and reviewed and be submitted to the Board of Punishments to await a review. Offenses to be reported to the *cha-lu-huo-ch'ih* (*Jaryuči*)[145] shall also [follow] this same [procedure].

[Item 2.][146] With regard to the interrogation of any criminal

---

[142] *YTC* 39:2a and *YTC** 39:1a. A similar short version of this fragment and a short citation are also recorded in the *Yüan tien-chang*. See *YTC* 4:5a and 40:1b. See also *YTC** 4:3b and 40:1b. The first character *hsia* in the sixth line of the *YTC* 39:2a is superfluous and should be deleted. Similarly, the same character *hsia* between the characters *ch'i*(b) and *i*(c) in the sixteenth line of the *YTC** 39:1b should also be deleted. Between the characters *ch'i*(b) and *i*(c) in the fourth line of the *YTC* 4:5a, the character *shih*(a) is superfluous and should be deleted. This superfluous character was also noticed by Ch'en Yüan. See *Shen-k'o Yüan tien-chang chiao-pu*, "Cha-chi," 1:10a.

[143] During the Yuan dynasty, the *lu* normally controlled the *chou*. Certain *chou* were changed to *fu* and given special status. The post of a *fu-yin* (prefect) was often held concurrently by the *tsung-kuan* (chief administrator) of the governing *lu*. When a post of a *fu-yin* was not held by the *tsung-kuan* of the *lu*, this particular type of *fu* was called a *san-fu* (losse *fu*).

[144] The Tsung-kuan-fu (Bureau of General Administration) was established in the early period of the Chih-yüan reign to administer each *lu*. In the year 1283/1284 it was further stipulated that a *lu* of 100,000 households or more be designated as an upper *lu*, and a *lu* of fewer than 100,000 households be designated as a lower *lu*. A *lu* of strategic importance was to be classified as an upper *lu*, even if it had fewer than 100,000 households. The *ta-lu-hua-ch'ih* (*daruyači*) and the *tsung-kuan* of an upper *lu* were both of the *cheng san-p'in* (third rank), whereas those of a lower *lu* were of the *ts'ung san-p'in* (subthird rank). See *YS* 91:13b.

[145] The office of *cha-lu-huo-ch'ih* (*Jaryuči*) (judge) was first established in 1206 to administer judicial and other matters. The head judge was known as *Yeke Jaryuči* (Grand Judge). During the Yüan dynasty, the office of *Jaryuči* was placed under the control of the Ta Tsung-cheng-fu (Grand Bureau for the Affairs of the Imperial Clan) which later changed its name to the Tsung-cheng-fu (Bureau for the Affairs of the Imperial Clan) in the time of Jen-tsung (Buyantu Qaγan). The *Jaryuči* primarily administered the judicial matters of Mongols. The total number of the *Jaryuči* varied from ten persons in the year 1261/1262 to 42 persons in the year 1324/1325. The court rank for a *Jaryuči* was *ts'ung i-p'in* (subfirst rank). See *YS* 87:1a–2a. See also Tamura Jitsuzō, *Chūgoku seihuku ōchō no kenkyū: chū* [*Dynasties of Conquest in China: Part Two*] (Kyoto: Kyoto University Press, 1971), pp. 444–463.

[146] *YTC* 40:17 and *YTC** 40:13a. A short citation of this fragment also appears in the *Yüan tien-chang*. See *YTC* 40:7a and *YTC** 40:5a. The character *fu*(f) in the eleventh line of the *YTC* 40:17a is a misprint for the character *chang*(a). This misprint was also noticed by Ch'en Yuan. See *Shen-k'o Yüan tien-chang chiao-pu*, "Cha-chi," 4:5a. See also Iwamura Shinobu and Tanaka

offender, [the official] shall look into the original details of the offense and review thoroughly the statement and argument of the offender and examine exhaustively all appropriate evidence and investigate carefully [other] reliable, distinctive traces. If a case is reasonably suspicious and [, moreover,] evidence and other indications are clear and yet [the offender], nevertheless, conceals and does not confess, then [the official] shall establish with other participating officials [of the joint conference] a case to confer together and, in accordance with law, impose torture for eliciting a confession. If neither an accusation is clear nor evidence is reliable [the official] shall first use reason to analyze and surmise and shall not impose abruptly any torture.

[Item 3.][147] With regard to any official organ's quarterly report on the imprisoned offenders, the supervising authorities shall examine thoroughly [each report]. If any case has been suppressed or delayed, it shall immediately be dealt with. As to each *lu*, since a *t'ui-kuan* (judge) has specifically been entrusted with the administration of punishment and imprisonment, therefore, if any subordinate office is not fair in investigating a criminal case or is not proper in imprisoning [an offender], [the *t'ui-kuan*] shall be allowed to investigate clearly and report to the governing *lu* to follow the principle for restoring justice. If an investigation has been completed [by the *t'ui-kuan*] and yet other authorities in reviewing and dealing with the case discover any concealment or falsehood, then the statement of the *t'ui-kuan* shall be taken for the deliberation of discipline.

[Item 4.][148] With regard to a serious offense in any locality,

---

Kenji, *Gen tenshō keibu dai issatsu* [*Board of Punishments in the Institutions of the Yüan Dynasty, Vol. One*] (Kyoto: Kyoto University Press, 1964), p. 46. The character *chü*(e) in the tenth line of the *YTC* 40:17a was originally printed as *chu*(d) in the *YTC** version. This change was not mentioned by Ch'en Yüan.

[147] *YTC* 40:9a and *YTC** 40:7a. The character *chuang*(a) in the sixth line of the *YTC* 40:9b is a misprint for the character *fu*(f). This misprint was also noticed by Ch'en Yüan. See *Shen-k'o Yüan tien-chang chiao-pu*, "Cha-chi," 4:4a. See also Iwamura Shinobu and Tanaka Kenji, *Gen tenshō keibu dai issatsu*, p. 33.

[148] *YTC* 40:9a and *YTC** 40:7a. The character *tso*(c) in the seventh line of *YTC* 40:9a is a misprint for the character *tso*(b). The character *fan*(b) in the eighth line is a misprint for the character *fan*(c). These two misprints were also noticed by Ch'en Yüan. See *Shen-k'o Yüan tien-chang chiao-pu*, "Cha-chi," 4:4a. The character *pien*(b) in the eighth line is a variant for the character

the governing authorities shall hold at the public office a joint conference to decide the case. When the affidavit of accepting the decision shall have been obtained [from the offender], the case shall be transferred to the Su-cheng lien-fang ssu for review. If no grievance is found, the case shall be concluded to await a [routine] report. [On the other hand,] if the offender shall retract his statement or his family shall plead a grievance, the case shall be permitted to be transferred to the governing *lu* for rehearing. However, if evidence shall have been clear and the family cannot indicate in argument the details of their grievance, [the case] shall not be within [the scope of] the provision concerning transferring and rehearing.

[Item 5.][149] With regard to all offenders currently imprisoned, in each locality a principal official once every moon shall rotate to conduct the inspection. If any imprisonment is not proper or any hindrance is not obviated or any disease [of an inmate] is not treated, or if any appropriated ration for inmates is not given in accordance with the schedule, [the official] shall, as matters arise, conduct an investigation. The officials of each Su-cheng lien-fang ssu, with regard to localities under its jurisdiction, shall follow the above [procedure] to review and investigate. As to the offenders imprisoned in the capital, the Board of Punishments of the Chung-shu-[sheng], the Censorate, and the *cha-lu-huo-ch'ih* (*Jaryuči*) shall appoint respectively an official once a quarter to review and deal with [their cases] so that the grievance may be clarified and the delay may be pressed for action and trivial matters may be [immediately] decided and discharged so as to prevent any grievance or hindrance.

---

pien (a). The *Li-hsueh chih-nan* uses the expression *fu-pien* (a) instead of *fu-pien* (b). For a discussion of this expression, see Yang Lien-sheng, *Excursion in Sinology*, pp. 78–80. The character *tsei* in the ninth line of the *YTC* 40:9a and the *YTC** 40:7a seems to be a misprint for the character *tsang* (a). This possible misprint was also noticed by Iwamura and Tanaka, although it was not mentioned by Ch'en Yüan. See Iwamura Shinobu and Tanaka Kenji, *Gen tenshō keibu dai issatsu*, p. 33.

[149] *YTC* 40:9 and *YTC** 40:7a. The character *li* (g) in the second line of the *YTC* 40:9a is a misprint for the character *chi* (d). This misprint was also noticed by Ch'en Yüan. See *Shen-k'o Yüan tien-chang chiao-pu*, "Cha-chi," 4:4a. See also Iwamura Shinobu and Tanaka Kenji, *Gen tenshō keibu dai issatsu*, p. 33.

[Item 6.][150] With regard to any offense or litigation, if the original accusation is clearly stated, and it is easy to administer [the case] thoroughly, then the governing authorities upon receiving the plaint of litigation shall at once carefully examine it in detail. If the statement of accusation is not clear and there is no supporting evidence, [the authorities] shall order submission of another substantial statement so as to depend on it for summoning and investigating [the offender]. However, if the accused offense is so grave that an arrest should be urgently made, then it shall not be bound by this provision.

[Item 7.][151] With regard to the hearing and other judicial matters concerning all imprisoned offenders, the governing authorities shall, from the initial summons and investigation through the process in the middle period to the final conclusion of the case, prepare separately a register to clear up [each step] with a vermilion seal. The Su-cheng lien-fang ssu shall specially review it so as to prevent any hindrance.

[150] *YTC* 53:4a and *YTC** 53:3a. The character *yüan*(c) in the second line of the *YTC* 53:4a is a variant for the character *yüan*(a). This variant was not mentioned by Ch'en Yüan.

[151] *YTC* 53:4b and *YTC** 53:4a. The character *hsi*(b) in the second line of the *YTC* 53:4b is a variant for the character *hsi*(a). This variant was also noticed by Ch'en Yüan. See *Shen-k'o Yüan tien-chang chiao-pu*, "Cha-chi," 5:1a. See also Iwamura Shinobu and Tanaka Kenji, *Gen tenshō keibu dai nisatsu*, p. 458.

CHINESE TEXT OF
CHIH-YÜAN HSIN-KO
AS RECONSTRUCTED

I. 公規

1. 諸官府皆須平明治事凡當日合行商議發遣之事了則方散其在都官府六部視省餘視所屬上司若公務急速及應直宿人員不拘此例

2. 諸公事違限違例者皆當該檢校人員隨事舉問失舉問者罪亦及之其監察御史肅政廉訪司常務糾彈毋容弛慢

3. 諸官司所受之事各用日印於當日付絕事關急速隨至即付常事五日程（謂不須檢覆者）中事七日程（謂須檢覆者）大事十日程（謂須計算簿帳或諮詢者）並要限內發遣了事違者量事大小計日遠近隨時決罰其事應速行當日可了者即議須行若必非常限所拘臨時詳酌

4. 諸應申上司定奪之事皆自下而上用心檢校但有不實不盡其所由官司即須疏駁必要照勘完備議擬相應方許申呈若事未完例或不當不即疏駁而輒准申呈者各將當該首領官吏究治駁而不益至於再三故延其事者亦如之

5. 諸公事明白例應處決而在下官司故作有疑申審若事合申稟而在上官司不即依理與決者各隨其事究治仍從監察御史並肅政廉訪司糾彈

6. 諸公事應議者皆由下而上長官擇其所長從正與決若執見不同許申合屬上司六部官所見有異者赴省稟議其事例明白變易是非者別行究問

7. 諸公事稽遲速則易改久則難追今後凡各掌行之事當該省掾每日一勾銷都事每旬一檢舉員外郎每月一審校錯者依例改正遲者隨事舉行毋使日積月增文繁事弊部員外郎主事臺院經歷報事其餘經歷檢勾文字人員並同

8. 諸官府之眾事務之繁弊欲盡除事難備舉凡內外官司各須用心檢校若事有不便理當更張者聽申合屬上司應呈省者呈省

9. 諸州府司縣官掌管軍民差役一切事務責任非輕當該上司事有必當委遣者須從員多事簡去處撝差或止獨員不許妨占其司吏人等若遇須合勾攝之事責限了畢即須發還仍將元勾緣由來回月日置簿銷附有不應勾攝或無故停留者從肅政廉訪司究治

10. 諸已絕經刷文卷每季一擇各具事目首尾張數皆以年月編次注籍仍須當該檢勾人員躬親照過別無合行不盡事理依例送庫立號封題如法架閣後遇照用判付檢取了則隨即發還勾銷

159

11. 諸吏員差除事故其元管簿籍文卷須與應代之人一一交點無差連署呈報本屬官司照驗後有失落止著見管之人追尋

12. 諸事應差人給驛雖有元降起馬聖旨皆須置曆開附每季申報合屬上司有不應給驛而給者隨即究問行省差過起數咨省雖不給驛其不須差人可辦之事凡於所屬官司毋使因而煩擾

II. 選格

1. 諸職官隨朝以三十箇月日爲任滿在外以叁週歲爲任滿錢穀之官以得代爲滿吏員須以九十箇月方得出職由職官轉補者同職官例若未及任滿本管官司不得輒動公文越例保申果才幹不凡有事跡可考者從御史臺察舉其非常選所拘若急闕擇人才識相應者臨時定奪

2. 諸官員雖已任滿得代本身若有侵借係官錢糧見任官司直須追納到官方許給由聽其求仕

3. 諸官員解由已有定式凡當該給由官司並須依式勘會別無不盡不實事理方得保申有詐冒不實並勘當未盡者所由上司隨即究問察官刷卷日更須加意檢校但不應給由而循情濫給并理應出給而刁蹬留難者並聽糾彈

4. 諸在流品人員凡能任繁劇善理錢穀明達吏事深識治體或器非一用無施不可者吏部考其功狀加之訪察以類注籍時備選擇之用

5. 諸銓注官員品類不一用宜相叅惟文資壹員任其簿書計數之責凡於總管官司不許有闕

6. 諸官員入選視其元係是何出身歷過是何職任叅以才器大小年齒衰壯宜於何等闕內銓注不可強其所短因廢人之所長

7. 諸官員功罪並送吏部標注到選之日於應得資品上視其功罪斟酌議擬有蔽匿其罪增飾其功者從監察御史糾彈

8. 諸品官若犯贓黜降或廉能升遷事迹昭著者皆下隨處照會其使在官之人共知勸誡

9. 諸官員子孫應合承廕之人比及入仕以來預使學習政事不致將來曠廢其職到選之日如本路官司保其才能及問以政事應對可取者本等人內量與從優

10. 諸歲貢吏員皆當該官司於見役人內不限名次公同選舉以性行純謹儒吏兼通者爲上才識明敏吏事熟閑者次之若月日雖多行能無取者不許呈貢到部之日公座試驗必說事明白行遣閑熟者爲中如或不應並擬發元役官司其當該濫貢人員仍須究問

11. 諸兩廣福建地面或有全闕正官去處比及朝廷選官到任合須使人權攝其事今後先於側近可以摘那見任官內選差無則許

於任滿得代聽除官內選差又無聽於本省或宣慰司見役請俸
人內選差白身之人不許委用

12. 諸行省管轄官員若有多歲不經遷過時不到任及久曠未注或
緊急闕官即須照勘明白咨省定奪其到任下任例合標附人員
每月通行類咨直隸省部路分准此

III. 治民

1. 諸理民之務禁其擾民者此爲最先凡里正公使人等（貼書亦
同）從各路總管府擬定合設人數其令司縣選留廉幹無過之
人多者罷去仍須每事設法關防毋致似前侵害百姓

2. 諸村主首使佐里正催督差稅禁止違法其坊村人戶鄉居之家
照依舊例以相檢察勿造非違

3. 諸社長本爲勸農而設近年以來多以差科干擾大失元立社長
之意今後凡催差辦集自有里正主首其社長使專勸課凡農事
未喻者敎之人力不勤者督之必使農盡其功地盡其利官司有
不復遵守妨廢勸農者從肅政廉訪司究治

4. 諸州縣官勸農日社內有游蕩好閑不務生理累勸不改者社長
須得對衆舉明量示懲戒其社長若年小德薄不爲衆人信服即
聽詢學深知農事年高純謹之人易換

5. 諸假托靈異妄造妖言佯修善事夜聚明散并凡官司已行禁治
事理社長每季須一誡諭使民知恐毋陷刑憲

6. 諸遇災傷闕食或能不恡己物勸率富有之家協同周濟困窮不
致失所者從本處官司保申上司申部呈省

7. 諸義倉本使百姓豐年貯蓄歉歲食用此已驗良法其社長照依
元行當復修舉官司敢有拘檢煩擾者從肅政廉訪司糾彈

8. 諸富戶依托見任官員影避差役者所在肅政廉訪司官常須用
心禁察毋使循習舊弊靠損貧民違者其官與民並行治罪

9. 諸論訴婚姻家財田宅債負若不係違法重事並聽社長以理諭
解免使妨廢農務煩擾官司

10. 諸民訟之繁婚田爲甚其各處官司凡媒人各使通曉不應成婚
之例牙人使知買賣田宅違法之例寫詞狀人使知應告不應告
言之例仍取管不違甘結文狀以塞起訟之源

11. 諸詞訟若證驗無疑斷例明白而官吏看循故有枉錯者雖事已
改正其元斷情由仍須究治

12. 諸應係官荒地貧民欲願開種者許赴所在官司入狀請射每丁
給田百畝官豪勢要人等不請官司无得冒占年終照勘已給數
目開申合屬上司類册申部

IV. 理財

1. 諸應支錢糧腹裏路分皆憑省部勘合理算其有申准諸支明文

例應倒除者每季照勘所支數目抄連合用文憑檢校一切完備
須要不過次季仲月中旬開申合干部分照勘相應隨即除破各
處行省所轄路分應申倒除者准此

2. 諸錢糧等物戶部立式其使諸處每季一報到部委官檢較但有
不應隨即追理年終通行照算務要實行毋爲文具行省准上咨
省

3. 諸照算須勾人吏者皆當官置局自入局爲始各以文字大小斟
酌立限每五日考其次第了則隨即發還其攢報有常收支有例
可以立式取勘者不須勾攝人吏赴都諸司於所屬亦准此

4. 諸稅石嚴禁官吏勢要人等不得結攬若近下戶計去倉地遠願
出脚錢就令近民帶納者聽其總部稅官斟酌各處地里定立先
後運次約以點集處所覷得別無輕賫攬納之數令分部官管押
入倉依數交納得訖朱鈔即日發還惟總部官直須州縣納盡方
許還職

5. 諸年例支持物件用時有緩急備時有難易其當該官吏凡合置
備之數各須以時點校預爲擧呈毋得急闕公私不便

6. 諸和買物須驗出産停蓄去處分俵均買其官吏不得先以賤直
拘收揹勒人戶多添價錢轉買送納違者痛行斷罪計其餘價依
數追還

7. 諸和買須於收物處榜示見買物色各該價錢物既到官鈔即給
主仍須正官監臨置簿凡收物支價開寫某人納到某物多少支
訖價錢若干就令物主於上畫字其監臨之官仍以印牌關防以
備檢勘

8. 諸街市貨物皆令行人每月一平其直其比前申有甚增減者各
須稱說增減緣由自司縣申府州由本路申戶部並要體度是實
保結申報凡年例必於本處和買之物如遇物多價少可以趁賤
收買者即具其直另狀飛申

V. 賦役

1. 諸科差稅皆司縣正官監視人吏置局科攤務要均平不致偏重
據科定數目依例出給花名印押由帖仍於村坊各置粉壁使民
通知其比上年元科分數有增損不同者須據緣由明立案驗以
備照勘

2. 諸差科夫役先富强後貧弱貧富等者先多丁後少丁開具花戶
姓名自上而下置簿挨次遇有差役皆須正官當面點定該當人
數出給印押文引驗數勾差無致公吏里正人等放富差貧那移
作弊其差科簿仍須長官封收長官差故次官封收

3. 諸水旱災傷皆隨時檢覆得實作急申部拾分損捌以上其稅全

162

免損柒以下止免所損分數收及陸分者稅既全徵不須申檢雖
及合免分數而時可改種者但存堪信顯跡隨宜改種毋失其時

4. 諸科差皆用印押公文其口傳言語科斂者不得應付違者所取
雖公並須治罪

5. 諸和雇腳力皆儘行車之家少則聽於其餘近上有車戶內和雇
仍須置簿輪轉有法無致司吏里正公使人等那攢作弊

VI. 課程

1. 諸錢穀之計其各處行省每歲須一檢較凡理財之法或有未盡
蠹財之弊或有未去生財之道或有未行逐一議擬咨省戶部該
管去處准此

2. 諸院務課程當該上司常須設法關防每月體度若課額輕省而
所增分數不及者隨即窮問仍委廉幹正官監辦行省戶部凡在
所屬路分每季通行比較須要盡實到官不致欺隱

3. 諸茶鹽課程已有成法其行省戶部檢會元降條例凡近年官吏
違犯禁條營謀私利侵損官課阻碍商人者逐一出榜嚴行禁治
仍須選差廉幹人員不時暗行體察務要茶鹽通行公私便利

4. 諸場鹽袋皆判官監裝須要斤重均平無有餘欠運使以下分轉
檢較仍於袋上書寫監裝檢較職位姓名以千字文爲號如法編
垛凡遇商客支請驗其先後從上給付行省戶部差官不測體驗
但有夾帶餘鹽或尅除斤重及支給失次刁蹬鹽商者隨即追問
是實各依所犯輕重理罪仍聽察官糾彈

5. 諸竈戶中鹽到場皆須隨時兩平收納不得留難其合給工本運
官一員監臨給付若鹽司官吏因而有所尅減或以他物移易准
折者計其多少論罪仍勒陪償每給工本時肅政廉訪司差人暗
行體察

6. 諸場積垛未椿鹽數須於高阜水潦不能侵犯去處如法安置仍
委運官時至點檢若積垛不如法防備不盡心以致損敗者並勒
陪償

7. 諸院務官大者不過三員其攢攔合干人等依驗所辦課額斟酌
存設多者罷去無使冗濫侵削百姓盜食官錢

8. 諸轉運司幷提點官吏凡於管下院務取借錢物者以盜論與者
其罪同即應稅之物不經依例抽分使訖稅印者亦如之

9. 諸鹽司凡承告報私鹽皆須指定煎藏處所詳審明白計會所在
官司同共搜捉非承告報其巡鹽人員止許依例用心巡捕不得
妄入人家搜捉

10. 諸捉獲私鹽酒麵取問是實依條追沒其所犯情由幷追到錢物
皆須明立案驗另附文曆每月開申合屬上司

11. 諸鹽法並須見錢賣引必價鈔入庫鹽袋出場方始結課其運司
官如每事盡心能使鹽額有餘官吏守法商賈通便課程增多者
聞奏陞賞

VII. 倉庫

1. 諸出納之法皆須倉庫官面視稱量檢數自提舉監支納以下攢
典合干人以上皆得互相覺察有盜詐違法者陳首到官量事理
賞其有侵盜錢粮幷濫僞之物若犯人逃亡及雖在無財可追者
並勒同界官典司庫司倉人等一體均陪

2. 諸支納錢粮一切官物勘合已到倉庫應納者經拾日不納應支
者經壹月不支並須申報元發勘合官司隨即理會其物已到倉
庫未得勘合者亦如之

3. 諸官物出給先儘遠年其見在數多用處數少不堪久貯者速申
當該上司作急支發毋致損敗違者究治

4. 諸行用庫凡遇人以昏鈔易換料鈔皆須庫官監視司庫對倒鈔
人眼同辨驗檢數如不係接補挑剜僞鈔當面用訖退印昏鈔入
庫料鈔付主當該上司委官時至檢校違者究治

5. 諸路收受差發自開庫日爲始本路正官壹員輪番檢察並要兩
平收受隨時出給官戶朱鈔無使刁蹬停留人難諸州置庫去處
並同

6. 諸倉收受米糧並要乾圓潔淨當該上司各取其樣驗同封記壹
付本倉收掌壹爲當司存留仍須正官時至檢校其收支但與元
樣不同隨即究治（應攢運者比驗樣料相同裝發其至下卸亦
驗樣料相同交收）

7. 諸庫藏幷八作司所收物內其有名數而無用者開申合干部分
勘驗是實委官檢估出賣無人買者量宜支遣不致損敗

8. 諸倉庫錢物監臨官吏取借侵使者以盜論與者其罪同若物不
到官而虛給朱鈔者亦如之仍於倉庫門首出榜常川禁治

9. 諸倉庫赤曆單狀當該上司月一查照但開附不明收支有差隨
事究問

10. 諸倉庫局院踈漏速申修理霖雨不止常須檢視隨宜備禦不致
官物損壞若收貯不如法防備不盡心曝曬不以時致有損敗者
各以其事輕重論罪所壞之物仍勒陪償

11. 諸倉庫局院凡關防搜檢巡宿禁治事理其當該上司正官每月
分輪點視常須謹嚴毋致弛廢

12. 諸倉庫官新舊交代在都本管上司委官監視在外各路正官監
視（直屬省部州府亦同）沿河倉分漕運司官監視凡應干收
支文憑合有見在官物皆須照算交點明白別無短少濫僞之數
舊官具數關發新官驗數收管仍須同署申報合屬上司照會旣
給交關之後若有短少濫僞之物並於新官名下追理

VIII. 造作

1. 諸營造皆須視其時月計其工程日驗月考毋使有廢惟夫匠疾
病雨雪妨工者除之其監造官仍須置簿常切拘檢當該上司時
至點校不致虛延日月久占夫工

2. 諸造作物料須選信實通曉造作人員審較相應方許申索當該
官司體覆者亦如之有冒破不實計其多少爲罪已入己者驗數
追償

3. 諸造作官物工畢之日其元給物料雖經覆實而但有所餘者須
限拾日呈解還官限外不納者從隱盜官錢法科

4. 諸局分課定合造物色不許輒自變移有上位處分改造者即以
見造生活比算元關物料少則從實關撥多則依數還官

5. 諸局分造作局官每日躬親遍歷巡視工部每月委官點檢務要
造作如法工程不虧違者隨即究治其在外局分本路正官依上
提點每季各具工程次第申宣慰司移關工部照會工部通行比
較季一呈省比及年終俱要了畢毋致虧欠行省管下局分准此

6. 諸營建官舍其所委監造人員皆須躬親指畫必要每事如法一
切完牢若歲月不多未應損壞而有損壞者並將監造人員當該
工匠檢舉究治

7. 諸官司器物損壞不堪修理者差官相驗是實方許易換若已給
新物其故物拾日以裏即須還官發下合屬隨宜備用不堪作數
者赴官呈驗不須開寫名色虛掛文籍（銅鐵之器作銅鐵收竹
木之器作柴薪用）

8. 諸造作支破錢物工畢之日其親臨總司即須拘集當該官吏一
一照算完備本司檢勘無差合除破者依例開申除破合還官者
從實解納還官毋使隔越歲時致難理算

9. 諸營造合用諸物先儘官有見在其不足之數有可代支而價不
虧官者申稟折支

10. 諸隨路如遇橫造軍器諸物其一切所須必要明立案驗選差好
人置簿掌管工畢之日隨即照算元收已支見在數目本路正官
體校是實開申合干部分照會

11. 諸隨路每年該值水害凡可疏通閉塞修完去處當該上司須於
農隙之時委官預爲踏視相其地宜料其工物若役人數少不動
官錢聽差近民隨即修理必支錢動衆者速申合屬上司比至來
年春作之前併工須要了畢其餘修作應動民力者准此其事須
急差不拘此例

IX. 防盜

1. 諸管軍官職當鎮守其要盜賊不生管民官職當撫治其要安靜
不擾今後行省行院凡於所屬若管民官撫治不到以致百姓逃
亡管軍官鎮守不嚴以致盜賊滋盛即須審其所由依理究治

165

2. 諸行院到任取會所管地分見有草賊起數相其事宜嚴諭諸處軍官各使鎮守有法招捕得宜期於盜息而已仍將見有起數先行報院今後每季具已未招捕起數并有無續生賊人咨院呈省

3. 諸盜賊相聚初非同心或被嚇從或爲誑誘其行省行院常須多出文榜許令自相首捕若始謀未行隨即告發或已相結聚能自捕獲者量其事功理賞

4. 諸盜賊生發當該地分人等速報應捕官司隨即追捕如必當會合隣境者承報官司即須應期而至并力捕逐勿以彼疆此界爲限違者究治

5. 諸草賊招捕既平之後仍須區處得宜防備周密嚴責合干官司常令用心無致疎慢

6. 諸捕盜官如能巡警盡心使境內盜息者爲上雖有失過起數而限內全獲者爲次其因失盜累經責罰未獲數多者爲下到選之日考其實跡定其陞降即南方見有草賊去處若平治有法使盜清民安者另議聞奏陞擢

X. 察獄

1. 諸杖罪五十七以下司縣斷決八十七以下散府州軍斷決一百七以下宣慰司總管府斷決配流死罪依例勘審完備申關刑部待報申札魯火赤者亦同

2. 諸鞫問罪囚必先參照元發事頭詳審本人詞理研窮合用證佐追究可信顯迹若或事情疑似贓仗已明而隱諱不招須與連職官員立案同署依法拷問其告指不明無證驗可據者先須以理推尋不得輒加拷掠

3. 諸隨處季報罪囚當該上司皆須詳視但有淹滯隨即舉行其各路推官既使專理刑獄凡所屬去處察獄有不平繫獄有不當即聽推問明白咨申本路依理改正若推問已成他司審理或有不盡不實却取推官招伏議罪

4. 諸所在重刑皆當該官司公廳圓坐取訖服辯移牒肅政廉訪司審復無冤結案待報若犯人翻異家屬稱冤聽牒本路移推其贓驗已明及不能指論抑屈情由者不在移推之例

5. 諸見禁罪囚各處正官每月分輪檢視凡禁繫不廉淹滯不決病患不治并合給囚糧依時不給者並須隨事究問肅政廉訪司官所在之處依上審察其在都罪囚中書刑部御史臺札魯火赤各須委官季一審理冤者辨明遲者催問輕者斷遣不致冤滯

6. 諸獄訟元告明白易爲窮治其當該官司凡受詞狀即須仔細詳審若指陳不明及無證驗者省會別具的實文狀以憑勾問其所告事重急應掩捕者不拘此例

7. 諸繫囚聽訟事理當該官司自始初勾問及中間施行至末後歸結另置簿朱銷其肅政廉訪司專以照刷無致淹滯

GLOSSARY

(In this glossary, the English translations for the titles of articles are given in parentheses; those for books are given in brackets. No distinction has been made between the original translations and mine.)

A-ho-ma (Aḥmad) 阿合馬
Abe Takeo 安部健夫
ai (a) 礙
ai (b) 碍
Akai Setsu 赤井節
an 安
ao-lu (a'uruγ) (camp) 奧魯
Asami Rintarō 浅見倫太郎
Azia rekishi jiten [Dictionary of Asian History]
　アジア歴史事典

Baikeikai 楳溪會

Cha-chi [Notes] 札記
Cha-lu-huo-ch'ih (jarγuči) (judge) 札魯火赤
Cha-sa (Jasaγ) 札撒
Cha-wei (Deceptions and Frauds) 詐偽
Ch'a-yü (Investigation of Cases) 察獄
ch'ai 柴
ch'ai-hsüan 差選
ch'ai-k'o 差科
chan (decapitation) 斬
Chan-ch'ih [Jamči] [On the Postal Relay System] 站赤
chan-hu (households of the postal relay system) 站戶
chang (beating with a heavy stick) 杖
chang (a) 仗
chang (b) 帳
Chang Ju-chi 張汝楫
chang-kuan (leading official) 長官
Chang-tsung 章宗
Chang Yang-hao 張養浩
Ch'ang-chou hsien-che i-shu 常州先哲遺書
chao (a) 照
chao (b) 炤
Chao I 趙翼
Chao I-chai 趙逸齋
Chao Liang-pi 趙良弼
Chao Shih-yen 趙世延
ch'ao 鈔
Ch'ao-kang (Court Principles) 朝綱
che 者
Che-chiang shu-chü 浙江書局
Che-yü p'i-shih [Precedents Selected from Legal Trials] 折獄比事
Chen-pi-lo ts'ung-shu 枕碧樓叢書
Ch'en Ssu-ch'ien 陳思謙
Ch'en Yüan 陳垣

ch'en yuan-yin 稱元因

cheng (government) 政

Cheng Chieh-fu 鄭介夫

Cheng-chung shu-chü 正中書局

Cheng Ju-i 鄭汝翼

cheng-kuan (principal official) 正官

cheng san-p'in (third rank) 正三品

Cheng-tung Hsing-sheng (Regional Secretarial Council for Eastern Expedition) 征東行省

ch'eng 賑

Ch'eng-chi-ssu (Činggis) 成吉思

Ch'eng-chi-ssu huang-ti cha-sa [The Code of the Emperor Činggis Qan] 成吉思皇帝札撒

Ch'eng-hsien kang-yao [Essential Outlines of Established Principles] 成憲綱要

Ch'eng Jen-shou 程仁壽

Ch'eng-tsung (Temur Qaγan) 成宗

chi (a) 籍

chi (b) 急

chi (c) 即

chi (d) 季

Chi-ling (Ordinances of Sacrifice) 祭令

chi-ping 疾病

ch'i (a) 其

ch'i (b) 七

Ch'i-ch'ih sui-shih chü-hsing (Delay Shall be Adjusted as Matters Arise) 稽遲隨事舉行

chia (wooden cangue, collar) 枷

chia (a) 夾

ch'iang ch'ieh-tao i-tu (robbery

or theft once) 強竊盜一度

ch'iang-tao (robbery) 強盜

Ch'iang-tung lei-kao 牆東類稿

chiao (strangulation) 絞

chiao (a) 校

chiao (b) 較

chiao-ch'ien (foot money) 脚錢

chieh (a) 戒

chieh (b) 誡

chieh (c) 皆

chieh (d) 節

Chieh Hsing-t'ung fu [Annotated Unified Code in Rhyme] 解刑統賦

chieh-lan (farming the taxes) 結攬

chieh-yu (certificate of discharge) 解由

chien (a) 監

chien (b) 檢

chien-ch'a yu-shih (investigating censor) 監察御史

chien chih-na (supervising cashier) 監支納

Chien-fei (Evilness and Misdeeds) 姦非

ch'ien (a) 錢

ch'ien (b) 千

ch'ien-hsi (forced removal from one's residence) 遷徙

Ch'ien-lung 乾隆

Ch'ien tzu wen [The Thousand Character Essay] 千字文

Chih (Treatise) 志

chih (a) 職

chih (b) 支

chih (c) 治

chih (d) 至

Chih-chih (Administrative Regulations) 職制

Chih-cheng 至正

Chih-cheng t'iao-ko [Chih-cheng Code] 至正條格

Chih-cheng t'iao-ko hsu (Preface to the Chih-cheng Code) 至正條格序

Chih-chih 至治

chih-chung (assistant prefect) 治中

chih-kuan (appointed officials) 職官

Chih-min (Governing of the People) 治民

chih-shou 支收

Chih-shun 至順

Chih-yüan 至元

Chih-yüan ch'ao (Chih-yüan note) 至元鈔

Chih-yüan hsin-fa [Chih-yüan New Code] 至元新法

Chih-yüan hsin-ko [Chih-yüan New Code] 至元新格

Chih-yüan hsin-lü [Chih-yuan New Statutes] 至元新律

Chih-yüan t'ung-hsing pao-ch'ao (circulating precious note of the Chih-yüan reign) 至元通行寶鈔

ch'ih (decrees) 敕

ch'ih (beating with a light stick) 笞

ch'ih (a) 此

ch'ih-li (red-seal register) 赤曆

Chikuma shobō 筑摩書房

Chin 金

chin (a) 儘

chin (b) 今

Chin Ching-shih ta-tien piao (Dedication of The Great Institutions of Statecraft to the Emperor) 進經世大典表

chin-hsia hu-chi (lower house-holds) 近下戶計

Chin-hua Huang hsien-sheng wen-chi 金華黃先生文集

Chin-ling (Ordinances of Prohibitions) 禁令

Chin-lü chih yen-chih [A Study of the Statutes of the Chin Dynasty] 金律之研究

chin-shang hu-chi (upper households) 近上戶計

Chin shih [Chin History] 金史

chin-tzu (jailers) 禁子

Chin-yü hsin-shu 金玉新書

Ch'in-ting Hsü Wen-hsien t'ung-k'ao 欽定續文獻通考

ching 經

ching-chi-jen (person on alert, auxiliary police) 警迹人，景迹人，景蹟人.

ching-li (registrar) 經歷

Ching-shih ta-tien [The Great Institutions of Statecraft] 經世大典

Ching-shih ta-tien hsü-lu (Preface to The Great Institutions of Statecraft) 經世大典序錄

ching-yen (well salt) 井鹽

Ch'ing 清

ch'ing 清

ch'ing (a) 請

ch'ing-chi (commutation goods) 輕賷

Ch'ing-ya chi 青崖集

chiu 究

Chiu-k'u (Stables and Treasures) 廄庫

Chiu T'ang shu 舊唐書

Ch'iu-chien hsien-sheng ta-ch'üan wen-chi 秋澗先生大全文集

cho-chung hu-chi (middle

households) 酌中戶計

Cho-keng lu 輟耕錄

Chou 周

chou 州

Chou-li 周禮

Chou-li chu-shu 周禮注疏

Chou lü [Chou Code] 周律

ch'ou-fen (percentage levy) 抽分

chu (a) 諸

chu (b) 貯

chu (c) 貯

chu (d) 主

chu (e) 朱

chu (f) 硃

chu-ch'ao (receipt bearing the vermilion seal) 朱鈔

chu-pu (record-keeper) 主簿

chu-shih (secretary of a Bureau of a Board) 主事

chu-shou (control chiefs) 主首

ch'u (a) 儲

ch'u (b) 畜

ch'u-chun (banishment to serve in the army) 出軍

chuan 撰

chuan-fa yüan-chi (dispatch back to one's native place) 轉發原籍

Chuan-yün-ssu (Bureau of Salt Transportation) 轉運司

ch'uan 掾

chuang (a) 狀

chuang (b) 壯

chuang-p'u (scribe) 狀舖

Chūgoku hōseishi kenkyū: hō to kanshū, hō to dōtoku [A Study of Chinese Legal History: Law and Customs, Law and Morality] 中国法制史研究：法と慣習・法と道徳

Chūgoku hōseishi kenkyū: keihō [A Study of Chinese Legal History: Criminal Law] 中国法制史研究：刑法

Chūgoku hōseishi kenkyū: tochihō, torihikihō [A Study of Chinese Legal History: Law of Land and Law of Transaction] 中国法制史研究：土地法・取引法

Chūgoku keihōshi kenkyūkai 中国刑法志研究会

Chūgoku no nōson kazoku [Chinese Peasant Families and Clans] 中国の農村家族

Chūgoku ritsuryōshi no kenkyū [A Study of the History of Statutes and Ordinances in China] 中国律令史の研究

Chūgoku seihuku ōchō no kenkyū: chū [Dynasties of Conquest in China: Part Two] 中国征服王朝の研究：中

chun (a) 準

chun (b) 准

Ch'un-ming meng-yü lu 春明夢餘錄

Chung-chou ming-hsien wen-piao nei-chi 中州名賢文表內集

Chung-hua shu-chü 中華書局

Chung-kuo huo-pi-shih [History of Chinese Money and Credit] 中國貨幣史

Chung-shu-sheng (Secretarial Council) 中書省

Chung-shu yu-ch'eng (Right Vice Minister of the Secretarial Council) 中書右丞

Chung-t'ung 中統

Chung-t'ung ch'ao (Chung-t'ung note) 中統鈔

chung-yen (salt of harmonious
　purchase) 中鹽
ch'ung-chün (banishment to
　serve in the army) 充軍
Ch'ung-chün k'ao [Studies on
　Military Exile] 充軍考
chü (a) 具
chu (b) 據
chü (c) 舉
chu (d) 鞫
chü (e) 鞠
Chu-chia pi-yung shih-lei
　ch'uan-chi hsin-chi
　居家必用事類全集辛集
chu-fen (branch bureau) 局分
chü yuan-yu 據緣由
ch'u 取
chuan 卷
Chuan-shou (Prologue) 卷首
ch'üan 勸
ch'üeh (a) 闋
ch'üeh (b) 闕
ch'üeh (c) 缺
Ch'üeh-wen [Omitted Entries]
　闕文
chün (army) 軍
Chün-lü (Statutes of Army)
　軍律

Erh-shih-erh shih cha-chi [Notes
　on the Twenty-Two Histories]
　二十二史劄記

fa 罰
Fa Ching [Cannon of Law] 法經
Fa-ssu (Bureau of Law) 法司
fan (a) 反
fan (b) 番
fan (c) 翻
fan (d) 凡
fang (a) 方

fang (b) 訪
fang (c) 妨
Fang Hsuan-ling 房玄齡
Fang Kuo-chen 方國珍
Fang-tao (Prevention of Thefts)
　防盜
fang-ts'un 坊村
fen 分
Fen-k'ao [Separate Studies] 分考
fen-pi (paste wall) 粉壁
fen-ssu 分司
Feng-hsien hung-kang [Exten-
　sive Principles of Disciplines]
　風憲宏綱
Feng-hsien hung-kang hsü
　(Preface to The Extensive
　Principles of Disciplines)
　風憲宏綱序
fu (a) 府
fu (b) 復
fu (c) 夫
fu (d) 副
fu (e) 付
fu (f) 伏
Fu-i (Taxes and *Corvée*) 賦役
Fu-keng-t'ang 復耕堂
fu-kung 夫工
fu-li (in the metropolitan area)
　腹裏
Fu-lu (Appendix) 附錄
fu-pien (a) 服緋
fu-pien (b) 服辨
fu-yin (prefect) 府尹

Gen no Keisei daiten narabini
　Genritsu (The Great Institu-
　tions of Statecraft of the Yuan
　Dynasty and the Yüan Code)
　元ノ経世大典並二元律
Gen-tenshō keibu dai issatsu
　[Board of Punishments in the

171

Institutions of the Yuan
Dynasty, Volume One]
元典章刑部第一冊
Gen tenshō keibu dai nisatsu
[Board of Punishments in the
Institutions of the Yuan
Dynasty, Volume Two]
元典章刑部第二冊
Gen tenshō keibu no kenkyū
(Criminal Procedure under
the Yuan Dynasty)
元典章刑部の研究
Gen tenshō no buntai (The
Style of Documentary Chinese
in the Yuan tien-chang)
元典章の文体
Gen tenshō no ryūden (Biblio-
graphical Notes on the Yüan
tien-chang) 元典章の流傳
Gendai hōseishi zakkō (Some
Remarks on the Codes of the
Yuan Dynasty)
元代法制史雑考
Gendai keizaishi jō no ichi shin
shiryō (A New Historical
Document Concerning the
Economic History of the Yuan
Dynasty)
元代経済史上の一新史料
Gendai ni okeru shasei no
sōritsu (Foundation of the *She*
System in the Yuan Period)
元代に於ける社制の創立
Gendai toshi seido to sono kigen
(L'état et l'origine du système
municipal dans la Chine sous
les Mongols)
元代都市制度と其の起源
Gendaishi no kenkyū [Historical
Studies on the Yüan Period]
元代史の研究

Genshi keihōshi no kenkyū
yakuchū [An Annotated
Translation of the "Treatise
on Punishment and Law" in
the Yuan shih]
元史刑法志の研究譯註

Hai-ts'ang lao-jen Yin-cheng
lüeh-li 海藏老人陰証略例
Han 漢
Han-jen (Northern Chinese)
漢人
Han-lin hsüeh-shih (Han-lin
academician) 翰林學士
Haneda hakushi shigaku ronbunshū jōkan rekishihen
[Historical Essays of Dr.
Haneda, Volume One: On
History] 羽田博士史学
論文集上巻：歴史篇
Haneda Tōru 羽田亨
hang-jen (business brokers) 行人
Hao-han ch'u-pan she
浩瀚出版社
Harada Keikichi 原田慶吉
Heburaihō ni okeru dōgai
hōhuku no keibatsu nı tsuite
(Lex Talionis in the
Pentateuch)
ヘブライ法における同害報復
の刑罰に就いて
Heibonsha 平凡社
heng 横
heng-tsao 横造
heng-tsao chün-ch'i 横造軍器
Higashigawa Tokuji 東川德治
ho 合
Ho Jung-tsu 何榮祖
ho-ku (harmonious hiring) 和雇
ho-mai (harmonious purchase)
和買

GLOSSARY

Ho-nan kuan-shu-chü
河南官書局
Hōgaku kyōkai zasshi
法学協会雑誌
Hōseishigaku no shomondai
[Various Problems Con-
cerning the Scholarship of
Legal History]
法制史学の諸問題
Hōseishi kenkyū 法制史研究
Hōseishi ronshū dai ikkan
[Collected Studies of Legal
History, Volume One]
法制史論集第一巻
hou 後
hsi (a) 繋
hsi (b) 系
Hsi-yuan lu [On Restoration of
Justice] 洗冤錄
Hsi-pao-hsien i-shu 惜抱軒遺書
Hsi-pao-hsien shu-lu 惜抱軒書錄
Hsia 夏
hsia 下
hsiang 詳
hsiao-yen (small salt) 小鹽
hsieh (a) 叶
hsieh (b) 協
Hsieh Jang 謝讓
Hsieh Ying-fang 謝應芳
hsien 縣
hsien-ch'eng (assistant magistrate) 縣丞
Hsien-feng 咸豐
Hsien-tien (Judicial Institutions) 憲典
Hsien-tien tsung-hsü (General
Preface to the "Judicial
Institutions") 憲典總序
hsien-tsai (a) 見在
hsien-tsai (b) 現在
hsien-wei (police commissioner)

縣尉
hsien-yin (magistrate) 縣尹
hsin 薪
Hsin-fa [New Code] 新法
Hsin-pien shih-wen lei-yao ch'i-
cha ch'ing-ch'ien
新編事文類要啓劄青錢
Hsin-ting ch'ih-t'iao [New
Codified Decrees] 新定敕條
Hsin Yüan shih [New Yuan
History] 新元史
hsing (punishment) 刑
hsing (a) 姓
hsing (b) 行
Hsing Chung-shu-sheng
(Regional Secretarial Council)
行中書省
Hsing-fa chih (Treatise on
Punishment and Law) 刑法志
Hsing-pu (Board of Punish-
ments) 刑部
Hsing T'ung [Unified Code]
刑統
Hsing-t'ung-fu chieh [Inter-
pretations on the Unified
Code in Rhyme] 刑統賦解
Hsing-t'ung-fu chih-chieh
[Straight Commentaries on
the Unified Code in Rhyme]
刑統賦直解
Hsing-t'ung-fu ching-yao
[Essential Unified Code in
Rhyme] 刑統賦精要
Hsing-t'ung-fu huo-wen
[Questions and Answers on
the Unified Code in Rhyme]
刑統賦或問
Hsing-t'ung-fu lueh-chu [Brief
Annotation on the Unified
Code in Rhyme] 刑統賦略注
Hsing-t'ung-fu shu [Commenta-

173

ries on the Unified Code in Rhyme] 刑統賦疏

Hsing-yung-k'u (Treasury for Note Circulation) 行用庫

Hsing-yüan (Regional Bureau of the Shu-mi-yüan) 行院

hsü (a) 須

hsü (b) 許

hsu (c) 蓄

hsü (d) 紊

Hsu Chin-hua ts'ung-shu 續金華叢書

Hsu Heng 許衡

Hsü-hsing (Leniency of Punishments) 恤刑

Hsü Ho-fu 徐和父

Hsü Shou-hui 徐壽輝

Hsü T'ien-lin 徐天麟

Hsü Yu-jen 許有壬

Hsü Yuan-jui 徐元瑞

hsuan-ch'ai 選差

Hsüan-chü (Selections and Recommendation) 選舉

Hsüan-k'o (Standard of Selections) 選格

Hsüan-wei-ssu (Bureau of Pacification) 宣慰司

Hsüan-wen-ko (The Academy of the Hsüan-wen Pavilion) 宣文閣

Hsueh-kuei (Regulations of Studies) 學規

Hsüeh Yün-sheng 薛允升

hsün 循

hsun-chang (interrogation stick) 訊杖

Hu Chih-yü 胡祗遹

hu 戶

Hu-hun (Families and Marriages) 戶婚

Hu-Kuang 湖廣

Hu-pu (Board of Revenue and Population) 戶部

hua-wai-jen (person outside the culture, foreigner) 化外人

huan 還

Huang Chin 黃溍

Huang Ho (Yellow River) 黃河

Hui-yao [Summaries] 會要

hun-ch'ao (shady note) 昏鈔

Hung-li 弘曆

Hung-wu 洪武

huo-pu 獲捕

i (a) 疑

i (b) 驛

i (c) 以

i (d) 已

i (e) 移

I-chan (Postal Relay System) 驛站

i-ch'ieh 一切

I Ching [Book of Changes] 易經

I-chu 奕貯

i-hai 乙亥

i-hsiang (removal from one's village) 移鄉

i-ts'ang (charity granary) 義倉

I-tu-hu (Iduqut) 易都護

I-wen yin-shu-kuan 藝文印書館

Ichimura Sanjirō 市村瓚次郎

Ishii Ryōsuke 石井良助

Ishū Shigen shinkaku narabini kaisetsu (Restoration of the Zhi-yuan xin-ge and Its Comment) 彙輯「至元新格」並びに解説

Iwai Hirosato 岩井大慧

Iwamura Shinobu 岩村忍

Iwanami shoten 岩波書店

jao 擾

jen (a) 人
jen (b) 任
Jen-min ch'u-pan she
　人民出版社
Jen-tsung (Buyantu Qaγan) 仁宗
jih 日
Jih-hsin shu-t'ang 日新書堂
Jimbun Kagaku Kenkyūjo
　人文科学研究所
jo 若
ju 如

Kai-p'ing 開平
kan (a) 幹
kan (b) 干
Kanagawa Kenritsu Gaigo
　Tankidaigaku kiyō: Jinbun
　shakai hen [Humanities and
　Social Science, Bulletin of the
　College of Foreign Studies,
　Yokohama] 神奈川県立外語
　短期大学紀要：人文社会篇
Kang-mu (Outlines) 綱目
Kinritsu no kenkyū [A Study of
　the Chin Statutes] 金律之研究
Kiyomizu kōbundō shobō
　清水弘文堂書房
ko (code) 格
ko (a) 格
ko (b) 各
ko-shih (codes and regulations)
　格式
k'o 科
K'o-ch'ai (Imposition of Taxes)
　科差
k'o-ch'ai 科差
K'o-ch'eng (Taxes and Levies)
　課程
K'o-i (Imposition of *Corvée*) 科役
K'o Shao-min 柯劭忞
k'o-yen (kernel salt) 顆鹽

Kobayashi Takashirō
　小林高四郎
Kokusho kankōkai 国書刊行会
Kōraishi (Koryŏsa) [Korean
　History] 高麗史
Kotake Fumio 小竹文夫
Koten kenkyūkai 古典研究会
kou (a) 勾
kou (b) 構
ku (a) 谷
ku (b) 穀
ku (c) 顧
ku (d) 雇
Ku-hsiang-chai hsiu-chen shih-
　chung 古香齋袖珍十種
k'u-chu (victim, victim's
　family) 苦主
k'u-kuan (official of the
　Treasury) 庫官
k'u-ssu 庫司
kua 掛
kuan (string) 貫
kuan (a) 官
kuan (b) 關
Kuan-fu p'ing-ming chih-shih
　(Authorities Shall at Dawn
　Administer Matters)
　官府平明治事
Kuan-fang (Prevention by
　Checking) 關防
kuan-hu (official households)
　官戶
Kuan-min chün-yung [Standard
　References for Officials and
　Civilians] 官民準用
kuan-p'ing yin-hsin (an official
　document requires a seal)
　官憑印信
Kuan-shih yung-hsin chien-
　chiao (Official Matters Shall
　be Attentively Examined)

官事用心檢校
kuan-ssu sui-chi li-hui ch'i wu i
官司隨即理會其物已
kuan-tien (official and ac-
　countant) 官典
Kuang-p'ing 廣平
Kuei-chai wen-chi 圭齋文集
Kuei-chang-ko (The Academy
　of the Kuei-chang Pavilion)
　奎章閣
Kuei-chang-ko ts'ung-shu
　奎章閣叢書
Kuei-ch'ao kao 龜巢稾
kung (tribute) 貢
kung-fu 工夫
Kung-kuei (Public Regulations)
　公規
kung-pen (labor and capital
　money) 工本
Kung-pu (Board of Public
　Works) 工部
Kung-shih (Official Matters)
　公事
kung-shih (a) 公使
Kung-shih liang-ch'eng liao-pi
　(Official Matters Shall be
　Concluded According to the
　Appropriate Schedule)
　公事量程了畢
Kung-shih ming-pai ch'u-chüeh
　(Official Matters Shall be
　Clearly Settled) 公事明白處決
Kung-shih sui-shih chü-wen
　(Official Matters Shall be
　Investigated as Matters Arise)
　公事隨事舉問
Kung-shih ts'ung-cheng yü-
　chueh (Official Matters Shall
　be Impartially Settled)
　公事從正與決
kung-shou (archers, police) 弓手

Kuo-ch'ao wen-lei [Specimens
　of Our Dynastic Literature]
　國朝文類
Kuo-hsüeh wen-k'u 國學文庫
Kuo-li Pei-p'ing t'u-shu-kuan
　國立北平圖書館
Kuo Pao-yü 郭寶玉
kuo-shih 過失
Kurata Junnosuke 倉田淳之助
Kusabigata moji hō no kenkyū
　[Study of Cuneiform Law]
　楔形文字法の研究
Kuwabara Jitsuzō 桑原隲藏
Kuwabara Jitsuzō zenshū dai
　go kan [Collected Works of
　Kuwabara Jitsuzō, Volume
　Five] 桑原隲藏全集第五卷
Kyōiku shoseki 教育書籍

Lao Ch'i-ta yen-chieh (Nogŏltae
　Ŏnhae) 老乞大諺解
lao-tzu (jailers) 牢子
le 勒
li (rites) 禮
li (a) 曆
li (b) 歷
li (c) 吏
li (d) 例
li (e) 理
li (f) 立
li (g) 李
li-cheng (village-heads) 里正
Li-hsüeh chih-nan [Guidance to
　the Bureaucratic Studies]
　吏學指南
Li-hsüeh ta-kang [Outline of the
　Bureaucratic Studies]
　吏學大綱
Li Meng 李孟
Li-pu (Board of Rites) 禮部
Li-pu (Board of Civil Office)

吏部
Li-ta ming-ch'eng tsou-i
[Memorials Submitted by
Eminent Ministers in Various
Dynasties] 歷代名臣奏議
li-t'iao 例條
Li-ts'ai (Management of
Finances) 理財
Li Tuan 李端
Li Yuan-pi 李元弼
Li-yün shu-wu ts'ung-k'o
勵耘書屋叢刻
liang (taels) 兩
Liang Chen 良楨
Liang-Kuang 兩廣
Liao 遼
liao (fetters) 鐐
liao (a) 料
liao-ch'ao (raw note) 料鈔
Liao shih [Liao History] 遼史
Liao-yang 遼陽
lien 廉
Lien Tao 練道
ling (ordinances) 令
ling (a) 另
ling-ch'ih (death by slow
slicing) 淩遲
ling-lei (miscellaneous ordi-
nances) 令類
liu (life exile) 流
Liu Chi 劉濟
Liu Fu-t'ung 劉福通
Liu Ping-chung 劉秉忠
Liu pu (Six Boards) 六部
Liu T'ai-heng 劉泰亨
lu 路
lu-fen (lu branches) 路分
lu-shih-ssu 錄事司
lü (statutes) 律
Lü-ling [Statutes and Ordi-
nances] 律令

lun 論

ma 馬
Ma Tsu-ch'ang 馬祖常
Ma Tuan-lin 馬端臨
mai-tsang-ch'ien (cash for
burying expenses) 埋葬錢
Makino Tatsumi 牧野巽
man 慢
Matsumoto Yoshimi 松本善海
mei 每
Meng Ssu-meng 蒙思明
Meng-Yüan shih-tai ti fa-tien
pien-tsuan (The Codification
during the Mongol-Yuan
Period) 蒙元時代的法典編纂
min 民
Mindai Mōko no hōkanshū
(Legal Customs of the
Mongols in the Ming
Dynasty) 明代蒙古の法慣習
Ming-li (Terms and General
Principles) 名例
Miyashita Saburō 宮下三郎
Miyazaki Ichisada 宮崎市定
Mōko hōten no kenkyū [Study
of Mongolian Codes]
蒙古法典の研究
Mōkoshi kenkyū [Studies of
Mongolian History]
蒙古史研究
mo-yen (powder salt) 末鹽
Mongoru shakai keizaishi no
kenkyū [Studies in the Social
and Economic History of the
Mongols]
モンゴル社会経済史の研究
mou 畝
mu 目
Mu-an chi 牧庵集
Mu-lu (Contents) 目錄

Mu Wan 慕完

na (a) 那
na (b) 納
Naitō Kenkichi 內藤乾吉
Nakada Kaoru 中田薰
Nakada sensei kanreki shukuga
  hōseishi ronshū [Collected
  Essays on Legal History in
  Honor of Mr. Nakada on the
  Occasion of His 6oth Birth-
  day] 中田先生還曆祝賀法
  制史論集
nan 南
Nan-jen (Southern Chinese) 南人
nei 內
Nei-fu 內府
neng 能
nien 年
Nihon daigaku hōgakkai
  日本大学法学会
Nihon gakujutsu shınkōkai
  日本学術振興会
Niida Noboru 仁井田陞
niu (wooden handcuffs) 杻
nung 農

Okamoto Keiji 岡本敬二
Otagi Matsuo 愛宕松男
Ou-yang Hsuan 歐陽玄

Pa 跋
Pa-tso-ssu (Bureau of Eight
  Manufacturings) 八作司
Pai-chu (Baijù) 拜住
pai-shen chih jen 白身之人
pan 辦
p'an-kuan (commissary of
  record) 判官
pao 保
pao-yin (taxes in silver) 包銀

pei-tsang (twofold repayment)
  倍臟
pe'i (a) 陪
pe'i (b) 賠
P'eng Hsin-wei 彭信威
pi-jan 必然
Piao (Tables) 表
piao (a) 標
pieh 別
Pieh-pen Hsing-t'ung-fu [Sup-
  plements to the Unified Code
  in Rhyme] 別本刑統賦
Pien 編
pien (a) 辯
pien (b) 辨
pien-hsing ch'in-ch'ih 遍行欽此
ping (a) 并
ping (b) 併
ping (c) 並
ping-chi 病疾
ping le t'ung-chieh kuan-tien jen
  teng li-hsien chun-pe'i 並勒同
  界官典人等立限均陪
ping le t'ung-chieh kuan-tien
  ssu-k'u ssu-ts'ang jen teng i-t'i
  chün-pe'i 並勒同界官典司庫
  司倉人等一體均陪
Ping-pu (Board of War) 兵部
P'ing-fang (Redressment of
  Wrong Decisions) 平反
P'ing-yüan lu [On Redressing
  Grievances] 平冤錄
po (a) 駁
po (b) 駮
Po-na-pen 百衲本
Po-chu-lu Chung 孛朮魯翀
pu 不
pu-huo 捕獲
pu-mu (discord in families) 不睦
Pu-wang (Arrests and Escapes)
  捕亡

pu-ying-tsou (need not be
memorialized) 不應奏
P'u T'ung-shih yen-chieh (Pak
T'ongsa Ŏnhae) 朴通事諺解

Rigaku shinan (Li-hsüeh chih-
nan) 吏學指南
Rigaku shinan no kenkyū
(Study of Li-hsüeh chih-nan:
The Historical Significance of
Law in the Yüan Dynasty)
吏学指南の研究
Rinji Taiwan kyūkan chōsakai
臨時台湾旧慣調査会
Rokumeikan 六盟館

san-fu (loose *fu*) 散府
Sang-ko (Sengge) 桑哥
Se-mu-jen (Miscellaneous
Aliens) 色目人
Sha-shan (Homicides and
Injuries) 殺傷
Shan-hsing (Unauthorized
Corvée Levies) 擅興
Shang 商
shang 上
shang-shu 尙書
Shang-shu-sheng (Presidential
Council) 尙書省
Shang-shu yu-ch'eng (Right
Vice Minister of the Pre-
sidential Council) 尙書右丞
Shang-tu 上都
shao-chih (decretal regulations)
詔制
Shao-ling (Decrees) 詔令
shao-mai-yin (silver for the
burning and burying ex-
penses) 燒埋銀
shao-she (decrees and amnesties)
詔赦

she 社
she-chang (*she* leader, community leader) 社長
She-yu (Amnesties) 赦宥
Shen Chi-i hsien-sheng i-shu
chia-pien [Bequested
Writings of Mr. Shen Chi-i,
First Series]
沈寄簃先生遺書甲編
Shen Chia-pen 沈家本
Shen Chung-wei 沈仲緯
Shen-k'o Yüan tien-chang chiao-
pu 沈刻元典章校補
Shen-shih tzu hsia erh shang
(Submission of Matters Shall
be from the Lower [Authori-
ties] to the Higher)
申事自下而上
sheng (a) 升
sheng (b) 陞
Sheng-cheng (Holy Govern-
ment) 聖政
shih (a) 十
shih (b) 史
shih (c) 使
shih (d) 示
shih (e) 拾
shih (f) 失
Shih-chieh shu-chü 世界書局
Shih-huo (Food and Goods)
食貨
shih-kuo 失過
Shih-min yao-lan [*Essential
References for Officials and
Civilians*] 仕民要覽
shih-o (ten abominations) 十惡
Shih T'ien-tse 史天澤
shih-tso (assistants) 使佐
Shih-tsu (Qabilai Qaγan) 世祖
Shih-wan-lo ts'ung-shu
十萬樓叢書

179

su-cheng 肅政

Su-cheng lien-fang ssu (Surveillance Bureau, a Branch of the Censorate) 肅政廉訪司

Su-sung (Complaints and Suits) 訴訟

Su T'ien-chüeh 蘇天爵

Sudō Yoshiyuki 周藤吉之

sui (a) 雖

sui (b) 歲

Sun Ch'eng-tse 孫承澤

Sung 宋

Sung-fen-shih ts'ung-k'an 誦芬室叢刊

Sung Tz'u 宋慈

suo (chain) 鎖

ta 答

Ta cha-sa (Yeke Ĵasaɣ) 大扎撒

Ta fa-ling (Great Code) 大法令

Ta hua yin-shu-kuan 大華印書館

Ta-li-shih (Grand Court of Revision) 大理寺

ta-lu-hua-ch'ih (daruɣači) 達魯花赤

Ta-ming-hsien 大名縣

Ta Ming hui-tien [Institutions of the Great Ming Dynasty] 大明會典

Ta-o (Great Abominations) 大惡

Ta-te 大德

Ta-te lü-ling [Statutes and Ordinances of the Ta-te Reign] 大德律令

Ta-te tien-chang [Institutions of the Ta-te Reign] 大德典章

Ta-tu 大都

Ta Tsung-cheng-fu (Grand Bureau for the Affairs of the Imperial Clan) 大宗正府

ta-yen (large salt) 大鹽

Ta Yüan (The Great Yüan Dynasty) 大元

Ta Yüan hsin-lü [New Code of the Great Yüan] 大元新律

Ta Yüan ma-cheng chi [On the Administration of Imperial Stud of the Great Yüan] 大元馬政記

Ta Yüan sheng-cheng kuo-ch'ao tien-chang (Yüan tien-chang) [Institutions of the Great Yüan] 大元聖政國朝典章

Ta Yüan sheng-cheng kuo-ch'ao tien-chang hsin-chi (Yüan tien-chang hsin-chi) [New Supplements to the Yüan tien-chang] 大元聖政國朝典章新集

Ta Yüan t'ung-chih [Comprehensive Institutions of the Great Yüan] 大元通制

Ta Yüan t'ung-chih hsü (Preface to The Comprehensive Institutions of the Great Yüan) 大元通制序

Tai En-fui (Tai Yen-hui) 戴炎輝

Tai Yen-hui 戴炎輝

T'ai-ho lü [T'ai-ho Statutes] 泰和律

T'ai-kang (Censorate Principles) 臺綱

T'ai-ting Ti (Yesun Temür Qaɣan) 泰定帝

T'ai-tsu (Činggis Qan) 太祖

T'ai-tsung (Ögedei Qaɣan) 太宗

T'ai-yüan 太原

Tamura Jitsuzō 田村實造

tan 石

t'an 探

Tanaka Kenji 田中謙二

tang 當

T'ang 唐

T'ang lü lei-yao [Classified Summary of the T'ang Code] 唐律類要

T'ang lu ming-fa lei-shou [Classification and Interpretation of the T'ang Code for Legal Studies] 唐律明法類説

T'ang lü shan-yao [Abridgment of the T'ang Code] 唐律删要

T'ang lü shih-wen [Annotated Study of the T'ang Code] 唐律釋文

T'ang lü tsuan-li [The T'ang Code with Annotated Cases] 唐律纂例

T'ang lü t'ung-lun [On the General Principles of the T'ang Code] 唐律通論

T'ang lü wen ming-fa hui-yao lu [Summaries and Textual Interpretations of the T'ang Code for Legal Studies] 唐律文明法會要錄

T'ang Ming lü ho-pien [A Combined Text of the T'ang and Ming Codes] 唐明律合篇

tao (a) 到

tao (b) 倒

tao (c) 盜

Tao-tsei (Thefts and Violence) 盜賊

Tao-yüan hsüeh-ku lu 道園學古錄

T'ao Tsung-i 陶宗儀

Tayama Shigeru 田山茂

te 得

t'i (a) 體

t'i (b) 体

t'i-chü (intendant) 提舉

T'i-hsing an-ch'a ssu (Surveillance Bureau, a Branch of the Censorate) 提刑按察司

t'i-k'ung lao-yü kuan (prison intendant) 提控牢獄官

tiao 刁

t'iao 條

T'iao-hua [Rules] 條畫

t'iao-ko (articles and codes) 條格

t'iao-li 條例

T'ieh-mu-tieh-erh (Temüder) 鐵木迭兒

tien 點

tien-shih (record officials) 典史

tien-ssu 典司

T'ien-ling (Land Ordinances) 田令

ting (ingots) 錠

ting 定

to 奪

Tōhō gakuhō 東方学報

Tōkō shoin 刀江書院

Tōkyō kyōiku daigaku bunga-kubu kiyō [The Bulletin of the Tokyo Kyoiku University Literature Department] 東京教育大学文学部紀要

Tōritsu ni okeru jomen tōzokuhō (The Provision for the Expulsion-Dismissal and Atonement in T'ang Law) 唐律に於ける除免當贖法

Tōryō shūi [Remnants of the T'ang Ordinances] 唐令拾遺

Tō-Sō hōritsu bunsho no kenkyū [The Critical Study

on Legal Documents of the
T'ang and Sung Eras]
唐宋法律文書の研究
Tō-Sō shakai keizaishi kenkyū
[Studies in the Social and
Economic History of the
T'ang and Sung Dynasties]
唐宋社會經済史研究
Tou Erh 竇娥
Tou-o (Conflict and Battery)
鬭毆
Tou-sung (Conflicts and Suits)
鬭訟
Tōyōshi kenkyū 東洋史研究
Tsa-lü (Miscellaneous Statutes)
雜律
Tsa-fan (Miscellaneous Offenses)
雜犯
tsai 在
tsan 參
tsang (a) 臟
tsang (b) 賍
Ts'ang-k'u (Warehouses) 倉庫
ts'ang-k'u-kuan (warehouse
official) 倉庫官
Ts'ang Pi-te 昌彼得
ts'ang-ssu 倉司
tsao 造
tsao-hu (salt-refining households) 竈戶
Tsao-tso (Construction and
Manufacturing) 造作
ts'ao 草
ts'ao-mang chih tsei (grass-and-
plant thief, thief in the field)
草莽之賊
ts'ao-tsei (grass thief, thief in
the field) 草賊
Ts'ao-yun ssu (Bureau of
Maritime Transportation)
漕運司

Ts'ao mu tzu 草木子
tse 擇
ts'e 冊
tsei 賊
tsei-jen (evil persons) 賊人
Tsei-tao (Thefts and Violence)
賊盗
tso (a) 作
tso (b) 坐
tso (c) 座
Tso-i tzu-chen 作邑自箴
Ts'u-chieh Hsing-t'ung-fu
[Gloss Commentaries on the
Unified Code in Rhyme]
粗解刑統賦
ts'uan-tien (accountant) 攅典
Ts'ui Yü 崔彧
Tsūsei jōkaku no kenkyū
yakuchū dai issatsu [An
Annotated Translation of the
Code of Comprehensive
Institutions, Volume One]
通制條格の研究譯註第一冊
tsun 遵
ts'un 村
ts'un-fang 村坊
Tsung-cheng-fu (Bureau for the
Affairs of the Imperial Clan)
宗正府
tsung-kuan (chief administrator)
總管
Tsung-kuan-fu (Bureau of
General Administration)
總管府
ts'ung 從
ts'ung i-p'in (subfirst rank)
從一品
ts'ung san-p'in (subthird rank)
從三品
Tu Ju-hui 杜如晦
Tu-hu-fu (Bureau of Guardian-

ship) 都護府

Tu-sheng (capital *Sheng*, the
Chung-shu-sheng or Shang-
shu-sheng) 都省

tu-shih (supervisor) 都事

t'u (penal servitude) 徒

tuan-li (decided precedents)
斷例

Tuan-li t'iao-chang 斷例條章

Tuan-yü (Trial and Im-
prisonment) 斷獄

t'ui 推

t'ui-kuan (judge) 推官

T'ung-chih [Comprehensive
Institutions] 通制

t'ung-chih (associate prefect)
同知

T'ung-chih t'iao-ko [Code of
Comprehensive Institutions]
通制條格

tzu (a) 字

tzu (b) 自

Tzu-shan ta-ch'üan chi
紫山大全集

Tz'u-hai 辭海

Tz'u-hsi wen-kao 滋溪文稿

tz'u-tzu (writing with a stylus,
branding a criminal by
tattooing) 刺字

Uematsu Tadashi 植松正

wan 完

Wan-yu wen-k'u 萬有文章

Wang Chieh 王結

Wang Hao-ku 王好古

Wang Hsien-chih 王仙芝

Wang Yu 王與

Wang Yüeh 王約

Wang Yun 王惲

wei (a) 惟

wei (b) 爲

wei (c) 違

Wei-ch'ien ts'ung yüan to ch'u
(Dispatching Shall be from
the Place Where There are
Many Officials)
委遣從員多處

Wei-chin (Imperial Guards and
Prohibitions) 衞禁

Wei Ch'u 魏初

wen 文

Wen-chung chi 文忠集

Wen-hsien t'ung-k'ao 文獻通考

Wen-tsung (Tuγ Temür Qaγan)
文宗

Wen-ts'un [Selected Essays]
文存

Weng Tu-chien 翁獨健

wo 我

wu (a) 无

wu (b) 無

wu (c) 毋

Wu Ch'eng 吳澄

wu-fu (five degrees of mourning) 五服

wu-hsing (five punishments)
五刑

Wu Li-pu chi 吳禮部集

Wu Shih-tao 吳師道

wu-tso (coroner) 仵作

Wu-tsung (Külüg Qaγan) 武宗

Wu Wen-cheng kung wen-chi
吳文正公文集

Wu Yüan-kuei 吳元珪

Wu-yüan lu [On Being without
Grievances] 無寃錄

Yabuuchi Kiyoshi 藪内清

Yamashita sensei kanreki
tōyōshi ronshū [Collected
Essays on Oriental History

in Honor of Mr. Yamashita
on the Occasion of His 60th
Birthday] 山下先生還暦記念
東洋史論文集
Yanai Watari 箭內亙
Yang P'ei-kuei 楊培桂
Yang Shih-ch'i 楊士奇
Yao Nai 姚鼐
Yao Shu 姚樞
Yao Sui 姚燧
yeh 業
Yeh Ch'ien-chao 葉潛昭
Yeh-lü Chu 耶律鑄
Yeh-lü ch'u-ts'ai 耶律楚材
Yeh Tzu-ch'i 葉子奇
yen 驗
Yen-ching she-hui k'o-hsüeh
燕京社會科學
Yen-fa k'ao [Studies on the
Salt System] 鹽法考
Yen-yu 延祐
Yin 殷
yin (license) 引
Yin Chung 尹忠
Ying-shan (Construction and
Restoration) 營繕
ying-tsou (should be memori-
alized) 應奏
Ying-tsung (Gegen Qaγan) 英宗
Yō Sen-sho (Yeh Ch'ien-chao)
葉潛昭
Yoshikawa kōbunkan
吉川弘文館
Yoshikawa Kōjirō 吉川幸次郎
Yoshikawa Kōjirō zenshū dai
jūgo kan [Collected Works of
Yoshikawa Kōjirō, Volume
Fifteen]
吉川幸次郎全集第十五卷
Yoshikawa Kōjirō zenshū dai
jūyon kan [Collected Works

of Yoshikawa Kōjirō,
Volume Fourteen]
吉川幸次郎全集第十四卷
yu (a) 有
yu (b) 又
yu (c) 尤
yu yu 有有
yü (a) 諭
yü (b) 於
yü (c) 餘
yü (d) 遇
yü (e) 亦
Yü Chi 虞集
yü-chung-jen (scribe) 鬻狀人
Yü-k'ung (Empty Prisons) 獄空
Yü-shih chung-ch'eng (Vice
Censor-in-Chief) 御史中丞
Yü-shih-t'ai (Censorate) 御史臺
Yü-tao (Prevention of Thefts)
禦盜
yü-tien (prison clerk) 獄典
Yüan 元
yüan (a) 元
yüan (b) 緣
yüan (c) 原
yüan (d) 員
Yüan Chang Wen-cheng kung
Kuei-t'ien lei-kao
元張文正公歸田類稿
Yüan ch'ü hsüan [Selection of
Yüan Dramas] 元曲選
Yüan Hsi-yü-jen hua-hua k'ao
[Studies on the Sinicization of
Central Asians of the Yüan
Dynasty] 元西域人華化考
Yüan Hsü Wen-cheng kung
Chih-cheng chi
元許文正公至正集
Yüan-nien hsin-fa [First Year
New Code] 元年新法
Yüan shih [Yüan History] 元史

Yüan-tai she-hui chieh-chi chih-tu [Social Classes in China under the Yüan Dynasty] 元代社會階級制度

Yüan-tai ti-fang cheng-fu [Local Governments in the Yüan Period] 元代地方政府

Yüan tien-chang [Institutions of the Yüan Dynasty] 元典章

Yüan tien-chang hsin-chi [New Supplements to the Yüan tien-chang] 元典章新集

yüan-wai-lang (Vice Director of a Bureau of a Board) 員外郎

yüeh (music) 樂

yün 運

yün-shih (commissary of salt transportation) 運使

Yung-hui fa-ching [The Yung-hui Code] 永徽法經

Yung-lo 永樂

Yung-lo ta-tien [Great Institutions of the Yung-lo Reign] 永樂大典

BIBLIOGRAPHY

PRIMARY SOURCES

Chan-ch'ih [*Jamči*]. [*On the Postal Relay System*]. *Kuo-hsüeh wen-k'u* edition; *Pien* No. 28 & No. 30, Peking, 1936.

Chang Yang-hao. *Yüan Chang Wen-cheng kung Kuei-t'ien lei-kao* (1790).

Chin shih [*Chin History*]. *Po-na-pen*, Yüan, Chih-cheng edition; reprinted by The Commercial Press, Shanghai, 1931.

Ch'in-ting Hsü Wen-hsien t'ung-k'ao. Che-chiang shu-chü, 1887.

Chiu T'ang shu. *Po-na-pen*, Sung edition; reprinted by The Commercial Press, Shanghai, 1936.

Chou li chu-shu. *Ssu-pu pei-yao* edition, 1930.

Hsieh Ying-fang. *Kuei ch'ao kao*. *Ssu-pu ts'ung-k'an san-pien* edition; The Commercial Press, Shanghai, 1936.

Hsin-pien shih-wen lei-yao ch'i-ta ch'ing-ch'ien. Jih-hsin shu-t'ang, 1324; reprinted by Koten kenkyūkai, Tokyo, 1963.

Hsü Ho-fu. *Ch'iang-tung lei-kao*. *Ch'ang-chou hsien-che i-shu* edition. 1899.

Hsü Yu-jen. *Yüan Hsü Wen-cheng kung Chih-cheng chi*. *Chung-chou ming-hsien wen-piao nei-chi* edition.

Hsü Yüan-jui. *Li-hsüeh chih-nan* [*Guidance to the Bureaucratic Studies*]. Original preface dated 1301; reprinted and incorporated in the *Chü-chia pi-yung shih-lei ch'üan-chi hsin-chi*, Ming, *Ssu-li-chien* edition.

Hu Chih-yü. *Tzu-shan ta-ch'üan-chi*. Ho-nan kuan-shu-chü, 1932.

Huang Chin. *Chin-hua Huang hsien-sheng wen-chi*. *Hsü Chin-hua ts'ung-shu* edition.

Kuo-ch'ao wen-lei [*Specimens of Our Dynastic Literature*]. Shanghai: The Commercial Press, 1929.

Lao Ch'i-ta yen-chieh (*Nogŏltae Ŏnhae*). Originally printed in Korea; reprinted in Kyoto?, 1972?.

Li Yüan-pi. *Tso-i tzu-chen.* Original preface dated 1117; reprinted by The Commercial Press, Shanghai, 1934.

Liao shih [*Liao History*]. *Po-na-pen*, Yüan edition; reprinted by The Commercial Press, Shanghai, 1931.

Ma Tuan-lin. *Wen-hsien t'ung-k'ao.* Che-chiang shu-chü edition, 1896.

Ou Yang-hsüan. *Kuei-chai wen-chi. Ssu-pu ts'ung-k'an* edition.

P'u T'ung-shih yen-chieh (*Pak T'ongsa Ŏnhae*). Originally printed in Korea; reprinted in Kyoto?, 1972?.

Shen Chung-wei, *Hsing-t'ung-fu shu* [*Commentaries on the Unified Code in Rhyme*]. *Chen-pi-lo ts'ung-shu* edition, Peking, 1913.

Ssu-k'u ch'üan-shu tsung-mu t'i-yao. Shanghai: The Commercial Press, 1933.

Su T'ien-chüeh. *Tz'u-hsi wen-kao. Shih-yüan ts'ung-shu* edition.

Sun Ch'eng-tse. *Ch'un-ming meng-yü lu. Ku-hsiang-chai hsiu-chen shih-chung* edition.

Ta Ming hui-tien [*Institutions of the Great Ming Dynasty*]. Reprint of 1587 edition, Taipei, 1963.

Ta Yüan ma-cheng chi. [*On the Aaministration of Imperial Stud of the Great Yüan*]. *Kuo-hsüeh wen-k'u* edition; *Pien* No. 49, Peking, 1937.

Ta Yüan sheng-cheng kuo-ch'ao tien-chang (*Yüan tien-chang*). Yüan edition; reprinted by National Palace Museum, Taipei, 1972.

Ta Yüan sheng-cheng kuo-ch'ao tien-chang (*Yüan tien-chang*). *Sung-fen-shih ts'ung-k'an* edition, Peking, 1908.

T'ao Tsung-i. *Cho-keng lu.* Shih-chieh shu-chü edition, Taipei, 1963.

T'ung-chih t'iao-ko [*Code of Comprehensive Institutions*]. Peking: Kuo-li Pei-p'ing t'u-shu-kuan, 1930.

Wang Hao-ku. *Hai-ts'ang lao-jen Yin-cheng lüeh-li. Shih-wan-lo ts'ung-shu* edition; incorporated in the *Pai-pu ts'ung-shu chi-ch'eng*, I-wen yin-shu-kuan, Taipei, 1968.

Wang Yün. *Ch'iu-chien hsien-sheng ta-ch'üan wen-chi. Ssu-pu ts'ung-k'an* edition.

Wei Ch'u. *Ch'ing-ya chi. Ssu-k'u ch'üan-shu chen-pen ch'u-chi ti-erh-chi* edition. Shanghai: The Commercial Press, 1934.

Wu Ch'eng. *Wu Wen-cheng kung wen-chi*, 1756.

BIBLIOGRAPHY

Wu Shih-tao. *Wu Li-pu chi. Hsü Chih-hua ts'ung-shu* edition.
Yang Shih-ch'i. *Li-tai ming-ch'en tsou-i* [*Memorials Submitted by Eminent Ministers in Various Dynasties*]. Ming, Yung-lo, *Nei-fu* edition.
Yao Nai. *Hsi-pao-hsien shu-lu. Hsi-pao-hsien i-shu* edition, 1879.
Yao Sui. *Mu-an chi*. Shanghai: The Commercial Press, 1929.
Yeh Tzu-ch'i. *Ts'ao mu tzu*. Original preface dated 1378; reprinted in 1762.
Yü Chi. *Tso-yüan hsüeh-ku lu. Ssu-pu ts'ung-k'an* edition.
Yüan ch'ü hsüan [*Selection of Yüan Dramas*]. *Ssu-pu pei-yao* edition; reprinted by Chung-hua shu-chü, Taipei, 1968.
Yüan shih [*Yüan History*]. *Po-na-pen*, Ming, Hung-wu edition; reprinted by The Commercial Press, Shanghai, 1935.

SECONDARY SOURCES

Chinese Works

Chao I. *Erh-shih-erh shih cha-chi* [*Notes on the Twenty-Two Histories*]. Shanghai: The Commercial Press, 1958.
Ch'en Yüan. *Shen-k'o Yüan tien-chang chiao-pu*. Peking: Peking University, 1931.
———. *Yüan Hsi-yü-jen hua-hua k'ao* [*Studies on the Sinicization of Central Asians of the Yüan Dynasty*]. *Li-yün shu-wu ts'ung-k'o* edition, 1934.
Hsüeh Yün-sheng. *T'ang Ming lü ho-p'ien* [*A Combined Text of the T'ang and Ming Codes*]. *Wan-yu wen-k'u* edition; Shanghai: The Commercial Press, 1937.
K'o Shao-min. *Hsin Yüan shih* [*New Yüan History*]. Fu-keng-t'ang edition, Tientsin, 1922.
Meng Ssu-ming. *Yüan-tai she-hui chieh-chi chih-tu* [*Social Classes in China under the Yüan Dynasty*]. Peking: The Harvard-Yenching Institute, 1938.
P'eng Hsin-wei. *Chung-kuo huo-pi-shih* [*History of Chinese Money and Credit*]. Shanghai: Jen-min ch'u-pan she, 1965.
Shen Chia-pen. *Shen Chi-i hsien-sheng i-shu chia-pien* [*Bequested Writings of Mr. Shen Chi-i, First Series*]. Peking, 1929.
Tai Yen-hui. *T'ang lü t'ung-lun* [*On the General Principles of the*

T'ang Code]. Taipei: Cheng-chung shu-chü, 1970.

Weng Tu-chien. "Meng-yuan shih-tai ti fa-tien pien-chuan" ("The Codification during the Mongol-Yüan Period"), *Yen-ching she-hui k'o-hsüeh*, 1 (1948), 155–174.

Yang P'ei-kuei. *Yuan-tai ti-fang cheng-fu* [*Local Governments in the Yüan Period*]. Taipei: Hao-han ch'u-pan she, 1975.

Yeh Ch'ien-chao. *Chin-lü chih yen-chiu* [*A Study of the Statutes of the Chin Dynasty*]. Taipei: The Commercial Press, 1972.

Japanese Works

Abe Takeo. *Gendaishi no kenkyū* [*Historical Studies on the Yüan Period*]. Tokyo: Sōbunsha, 1972.

Akai Setsu. "Heburaihō ni okeru dōgai hōhuku no keibatsu ni tsuite" ("Lex Talionis in the Pentateuch"), *Hōseishi kenkyū*, 5 (1954), 32–78.

Azia rekishi jiten [*Dictionary of Asian History*]. Tokyo: Heibonsha, 1959–1962.

Haneda Tōru. "Shina no hakuzoku shochō to kanbunmei" ("La civilisation chinoise et les dynasties barbares du Nord de la Chine"), *Haneda hakushi shigaku ronbunshū jōkan rekishihen* [*Historical Essays of Dr. Haneda*, Volume One: *On History*]. Kyoto: Kyoto University Press, 1957, 697–715.

Harada Keikichi. *Kusabigata moji hō no kenkyū* [*Study of Cuneiform Law*]. Tokyo: Kiyomizu kōbundō shobō, 1967.

Higashigawa Tokuji. *Shina hōseishi ron* [*On Chinese Legal History*]. Tokyo: Rinji Taiwan kyūkan chōsakai, 1916.

Ichimura Sanjirō. *Shinashi kenkyū* [*A Study of Chinese History*]. Tokyo: Shunjūsha, 1939.

Iwai Hirosato. "Gendai keizaishi jō no ichi shin shiryō" ("A New Historical Document Concerning Economic History of the Yüan Dynasty"), Baikeikai, ed., *Yamashita sensei kanreki tōyōshi ronbun shū* [*Collected Essays on Oriental History in Honor of Mr. Yamashita on the Occasion of His 60th Birthday*] Tokyo: Rokumeikan, 1938, 81–168.

Iwamura Shinobu. "Gen tenshō keibu no kenkyū" ("Criminal Procedure under the Yüan Dynasty"), *Tōhō gakuhō* (Kyoto), 24 (1954), 1–114.

———. *Mongoru shakai keizaishi no kenkyū* [*Studies in the Social and Economic History of the Mongols*]. Kyoto: Kyoto University Press, 1968.

Iwamura Shinobu and Tanaka Kenji. *Gen tenshō keibu dai issatsu* [*Board of Punishments in the Institutions of the Yüan Dynasty*, Volume One]. Kyoto: Kyoto University Press, 1964.

———. *Gen tenshō keibu dai nisatsu* [*Board of Punishments in the Institutions of the Yüan Dynasty*, Volume Two]. Kyoto: Kyoto University Press, 1972.

Kobayashi Takashirō. "Gendai hōseishi zakkō" ("Some Remarks on the Codes of the Yüan Dynasty"), *Kanagawa Kenritsu Gaigo Tankidaigaku kiyō: Jinbum shakai hen* (*Humanities and Social Sciences, Bulletin of the College of Foreign Studies, Yokohama*), 1 (1968), 1–33.

Kobayashi Takashirō and Okamoto Keiji. *Tsusei jōkaku no kenkyū yakuchū dai issatsu* [*An Annotated Translation of the Code of Comprehensive Institutions*, Volume One]. Tokyo: Chūgoku keihōshi kenkyūkai, 1964.

Kōraishi (*Koryŏsa*) [*Korean History*], Volume Two. Tokyo: Kokusho kankōkai, 1908.

Kotake Fumio and Okamoto Keiji, eds. *Genshi keihōshi no kenkyū yakuchū* [*An Annotated Translation of the "Treatise on Punishment and Law" in the Yüan shih*]. Tokyo: Kyōiku shoseki, 1962.

Kurata Junnosuke. "Gen tenshō no ryūden" ("Bibliographical Notes on the *Yüan tien-chang*"), *Tōhō gakuhō* (Kyoto), 24 (1954), 443–460.

Kuwabara Jitsuzō. *Kuwabara Jitsuzō zenshū dai go kan* [*Collected Works of Kuwabara Jitsuzō*, Volume Five]. Tokyo: Iwanami shoten, 1968.

Matsumoto Yoshimi. "Gendai ni okeru shasei no sōritsu" ("Foundation of the *She* in the Yüan Period"), *Tōhō gakuhō* (*Tokyo*), 11 (1940), 328–337.

Miyashita Saburō. "Sō-Gen jidai no iryō" ("Medical Science in the Sung and Yüan Periods"), Yabuuchi Kiyoshi, ed., *Sō-Gen jidai no kagaku gijutsushi* [*History of Science and Technology in the Sung and Yüan Periods*]. Kyoto: Kyoto

University Press, 1967, 123–170.

Miyazaki Ichisada. "Sō-Gen jidai no hōsei to saiban kikō" ("Law and Judicial System in the Sung-Yüan Period"), *Tōhō gakuhō* (Kyoto), 24 (1954), 115–226.

Nakada Kaoru. *Hōseishi ronshū dai ikkan* [*Collected Studies of Legal History*, Volume One]. Tokyo: Iwanami shoten, 1929.

Niida Noboru, *Chūgoku hōseishi kenkyū: hō to kanshū, hō to dōtoku* [*A Study of Chinese Legal History: Law and Customs, Law and Morality*]. Tokyo: Tokyo University Press, 1964.

———. *Chūgoku hōseishi kenkyū: keihō* [*A Study of Chinese Legal History: Criminal Law*]. Tokyo: Tokyo University Press, 1959.

———. *Chūgoku hōseishi kenkyū: tochihō, torihikihō* [*A Study of Chinese Legal History: Law of Land and Law of Transaction*]. Tokyo: Tokyo University Press, 1960.

———. *Chūgoku no nōson kazoku* [*Chinese Peasant Families and Clans*]. Tokyo: Tokyo University Press, 1952.

———. "Shina kinsei no gikyoku shōsetsu ni mietaru shihō" ("Civil Law as Reflected in Pre-Modern Chinese Plays and Novels"), Ishii Ryōsuke, ed., *Nakada sensei kanreki shukuga hōseishi ronshū* [*Collected Essays on Legal History in Honor of Mr. Nakada on the Occasion of His 60th Birthday*]. Tokyo: Iwanami shoten, 1937, 315–517.

———. *Tōryō shūi* [*Remnants of the T'ang Ordinances*]. Tokyo: Tokyo University Press, 1933.

———. *Tō-Sō hōritsu bunsho no kenkyū* [*The Critical Study on Legal Documents of the T'ang and Sung Eras*]. Tokyo: Tokyo University Press, 1937.

Okamoto Keiji. "*Rigaku shinan* no kenkyū" ("A Study of *Li-hsüeh chih-nan*—The Historical Significance of Law in the Yüan Dynasty"), *Tōkyō kyōiku daigaku bungakubu kiyō* (*The Bulletin of the Tokyo Kyoiku University Literature Department*), 36 (1962), 1–31.

Otagi Matsuo. "Gendai toshi seido to sono kigen" ("L'état et l'origine du système municipal dans la Chine sous les Mongols"), *Tōyōshi kenkyū*, 3 (1938), 265–292.

Shimada Masao. "Mindai Mōko no hōkanshū" ("The Legal

Customs of the Mongols in the Ming Dynasty"), Nihon daigaku hōgakkai (Society of Legal Studies, Japan Univ.), ed., *Hōseishigaku no shomodai* [*Various Problems Concerning the Scholarship of Legal History*]. Tokyo: Nihon daigaku hōgakkai, 1971, 641–662.

Sogabe Shizuo. *Chūgoku ritsuryōshi no kenkyū* [*A Study of the History of Statutes and Ordinances of China*]. Tokyo: Yoshikawa kōbunkan, 1971.

Sudō Yoshiyuki. *Tō-Sō shakai keizaishi kenkyū* [*Studies in the Social and Economic History of the T'ang and Sung Dynasties*]. Tokyo: Tokyo University Press, 1965.

Tai En-fui (Tai Yen-hui). "Tōritsu ni okeru jomen tōzokuhō" ("The Provision for 'the Expulsion-Dismissal and Atonement' in T'ang Law"), *Hōseishi kenkyū*, 13 (1962), 53–92.

Tamura Jitsuzō. *Chūgoku seihuku ōchō no kenkyū: chū* [*Dynasties of Conquest in China*: Part Two]. Kyoto: Kyoto University Press, 1971.

Tayama Shigeru. *Mōko hōten no kenkyū* [*Study of Mongolian Codes*]. Tokyo: Nihon gakujutsu shinkokai, 1967.

Uematsu Tadashi. "Ishū *Shigen shinkaku* narabini kaisetsu" ("Restoration of the *Zhi-yuan xin-ge* and Its Comment"), *Tōyōshi kenkyū*, Vol. 30, No. 4 (1972), 1–29.

Yanai Watari. *Mōkoshi kenkyū* [*Studies on Mongolian History*]. Tokyo: Tōkō shoin, 1930.

Yeh Sen-sho (Yeh Ch'ien-chao), *Kinritsu no kenkyū* [*A Study of the Statutes of the Chin Dynasty*]. Tokyo?, 1971?.

Yoshikawa Kōjirō. "Gen tenshō no buntai" ("The Style of Documentary Chinese in the *Yüan tien-chang*"), *Tōhō gakuhō* (Kyoto), 24 (1954), 367–396.

———. *Yoshikawa Kōjirō zenshū dai jūgo kan* [*Collected Works of Yoshikawa Kōjirō*, Volume Fifteen]. Tokyo: Chikuma shobō, 1969.

———. *Yoshikawa Kōjirō zenshū dai jūyon kan* [*Collected Works of Yoshikawa Kōjirō*, Volume Fourteen]. Tokyo: Chikuma shobō, 1968.

Western Works

Amos, Sheldon. *The History and Principles of the Civil Law of*

Rome. London: Kegan Paul & Trench Co., 1883.

Blackstone, Sir William. *Commentaries on the Law of England.* London: John Murray, 1857. Vol. IV.

Bodde, Derk and Clarence Morris. *Law in Imperial China.* Cambridge, Mass.: Harvard University Press, 1967.

Brunner, Heinrich. *Deutsche Rechtsgeschichte.* Leipzig: Verlag von Duncker & Humblot, 1906. Buch I.

———. *Deutsche Rechtsgeschichte.* München and Leipzig: Verlag von Duncker & Humblot, 1928. Buch II.

Chan, Hok-lam. "Liu Ping-chung (1216–74): A Buddhist-Taoist Statesman at the Court of Khubilai Khan," *T'oung Pao,* 53 (1967), 98–146.

Ch'en, Fu-mei Chang. "Local Control of Convicted Thieves in Eighteenth-Century China," Frederick Wakeman, Jr. and Carolyn Grant, eds., *Conflict and Control in Late Imperial China.* Berkeley and Los Angeles: University of California Press, 1975, 121–142.

Ch'ü T'ung-tsu. *Law and Society in Traditional China.* The Hague: Mouton & Co., 1961.

Cleaves, Francis Woodman. "The 'Fifteen "Palace Poems"'" by K'o Chiu-ssu," *Harvard Journal of Asiatic Studies,* 20 (1957), 391–475.

———. "The Sino-Mongolian Inscription of 1362 in Memory of Prince Hindu," *Harvard Journal of Asiatic Studies,* 12 (1949), 1–133.

———. "The Sino-Mongolian Inscription of 1338 in Memory of Jigüntei," *Harvard Journal of Asiatic Studies,* 14 (1951), 1–104.

Franke, Herbert. "Aḥmed, Ein Beitrag zur Wirtschaftsgeschichte Chinas unter Qubilai," *Oriens,* 1 (1948), 222–236.

———. "From Tribal Chieftain to Universal Emperor and God: The Legitimation of the Yüan Dynasty" (paper prepared for the Conference on Legitimation held under the auspices of the American Council of Learned Societies in June 1975, Asilomar Conference Grounds, Monterey, California).

———. *Geld und Wirtschaft in China unter der Mongolenherrschaft.* Leipzig: Otto Harrassowitz, 1949.

————. "Seṅ-ge, Das Leben eines uigurischen Staatbeamter," *Sinica*, 17 (1942), 90–113.

Golstunskij, K. *Mongolo-Oiratskije Zakony 1640*. St. Petersburg, 1880.

van Gulik, R. H. *T'ang-Yin Pi-Shih*. Leiden: E. J. Brill, 1956.

Hummel, Arthur W., ed. *Eminent Chinese of the Ch'ing Period*. Washington. D.C.: United States Government Printing Office, 1943. Vol. I.

Hunter, Alexander. *A Systematic and Historical Exposition on Roman Law*, 3rd ed. London: Sweet & Maxwell Limited, 1897.

Jahn, Karl. "Some Ideas of Rashid al-Dīn on Chinese Culture," *Central Asiatic Journal*, 14 (1970), 134–147.

Legge, James. *The Chinese Classics*. Hong Kong: Hong Kong University Press, 1960. Vol. II.

McKnight, Brian. "Sung Justice: Death by Slicing," *Journal of the American Oriental Society*, Vol. 93, No. 3 (1973), 359–360.

Milsom, S. F. C. *Historical Foundations of the Common Law*. London: Butterworths, 1969.

Mote, Frederick. "China under Mongol Domination: 1234–1367." draft prepared for *The Cambridge History of China*, Vol. IV.

Moule, A. C. and Paul Pelliot. *Marco Polo: The Description of the World*. London: George Routledge & Sons Ltd., 1938. 2 vols.

Pollock, Frederick and Frederic Maitland. *The History of English Law*. 2nd ed. Cambridge: Cambridge University Press, 1968. 2 vols.

de Rachewiltz, Igor. "Yeh-lü Ch'u-ts'ai (1189–1243): Buddhist Idealist and Confucian Statesman," Arthur Wright and Denis Twitchett, eds., *Confucian Personalities*. Stanford, Ca.: Stanford University Press, 1962, 189–216.

Ratchnevsky, Paul. "Die mongolische Rechtsinstitution der Busse in der chinesischen Gesetzgebung der Yüan-Zeit," Herbert Franke, ed., *Studia Sino-Altaica, Festschrift für Erich Haenisch zum 80. Geburtstag*. Wiesbaden: Franz Steiner Verlag GMBH, 1961, 169–179.

———. "Die Yasa (J̌asaq) Cinggis-khan und ihre Problematic," *Sprach, Geschichte und Kultur der Altaischen Völker* (Protokollband der XII. Tagung der Permanent International Altaistic Conference 1969 in Berlin). Berlin: Akademie-Verlag, 1974, 471–487.

———. *Un Code des Yuan.* Paris: Librairie Ernest Leroux, 1937.

Riasanovsky, V. A. *Fundamental Principles of Mongol Law.* Tientsin, 1938.

Schurmann, Herbert Franz. *Economic Structure of the Yüan Dynasty.* Cambridge, Mass.: Harvard University Press, 1956.

Schwartz, Benjamin I. "The Chinese Perception of World Order, Past and Present," John K. Fairbank, ed., *The Chinese World Order.* Cambridge, Mass.: Harvard University Press, 1968, 276–288.

Vernadsky, George. "The Scope and Contents of Chingis Khan's Yasa," *Harvard Journal of Asiatic Studies,* 3 (1938), 337–360.

Yang Lien-sheng. *Excursions in Sinology.* Cambridge, Mass.: Harvard University Press, 1969.

———. "Historical Notes on the Chinese World Order," John K. Fairbank, ed., *The Chinese World Order.* Cambridge, Mass.: Harvard University Press, 1968, 20–30.

———. "Marginalia to the *Yüan tien-chang*," *Harvard Journal of Asiatic Studies,* 19 (1954), 42–51.

———. *Money and Credit in China.* Cambridge, Mass.: Harvard University Press, 1952.

———. "Schedules of Work and Rest in Imperial China," *Harvard Journal of Asiatic Studies,* 18 (1955), 301–325.

Yule, Henry. *Travels of Marco Polo.* London: John Murray, 1929. 2 vols.

INDEX

A-ho-ma, *see* Aḥmad
Abe Takeo, 17 n.64, 29, 35–36, 102–104
adjudication: ethnic, 69, 81–84; military, 84–86; professional, 69, 87–88; religious, 69, 86–87
administration, *see* adjudication; *Chih-yüan hsin-ko* (translation of); civil administration; official administration; and *names of specific administrative bodies and responsibilities*
Aḥmad, 46
ao-lu (a'uruγ) (camp), 84
Azia rekishi jiten [Dictionary of Asian History], 104

beating, with sticks, 42, 49–51
Bible, *talio* in, 61
Blackstone, William, 47 n.17
Bodde, Derk, xviii–xix, 43, 51
business brokers, 93–94, 124
Busse (redemption), 54

capital punishment, *see* death sentences
cattle theft, punishment for, 58–60
cha-lu-hua-ch'ih, see Jaryuči
cha-sa, see Jasaγ
chan (decapitation), 42–43
Chan-ch'ih [Jamči] [On the Postal Relay System], 7
chan-hu (households of the postal relay system), 86
chang (beating with a heavy stick), 42, 49–51
Chang Ju-chi, 91 n.89
chang-kuan (leading officials), 131
Chang-tsung, 11
Chang Yang-hao, 46
Chao I, 39
Chao I-chai, 92

Chao Liang-pi, 16
Chao Shih-yen, 25–28
Che-yü p'i-shih [Precedents Selected from Legal Trials], 91, 96 n.111
Ch'en, Paul Heng-chao, 17, 101–106
Ch'en Ssu-ch'ien, 38–39
Ch'en Yüan, 40. *See also Chih-yüan hsin-ko*
Cheng-kuan (principal officials), 75, 119, 131
Ch'eng-chi-ssu (Činggis). *See* T'ai-tsu
Ch'eng-hsien kang-yao [Essential Outlines of Established Principles], 36
Ch'eng-tsung (Temür Qaγan), 10, 19–21, 44–45
chia (wooden cangue, collar), 74–75
chiao (strangulation), 42–43
chiao-ch'ien (foot money), 127
Chieh Hsing-t'ung fu [Annotated Unified Code in Rhyme], 90
chieh-lan (farming the taxes), 127 n.62
chieh-yu (certificate of discharge), 116
chien-ch'a yü-shih (investigating censors), 25, 107. *See also* investigation; *su-cheng lien-fang ssu*
chien chih-na (supervising cashier), 138
ch'ien-hsi (forced removal from one's residence), 48
Ch'ien tzu wen [The Thousand Character Essay], 134 n.86
Chih-cheng t'iao-ko [Chih-cheng Code], 36; codification of, 38; revision of, 39
chih-chung (assistant prefect), 75
chih-kuan (appointed officials), terms of office for, 114–16
Chih-yüan ch'ao (chih-yüan note), 60
Chih-yüan hsin-fa [Chih-yüan New Code], 8–9, 17, 101

197

LIBRARY OF CONGRESS CATALOGING IN
PUBLICATION DATA

Ch'en, Paul Heng-chao, 1944–
  Chinese legal tradition under the Mongols.

  (Studies in East Asian law, Harvard University)
  Includes chinese text and English translation of Chih-yüan
hsin ko.
  Bibliography: p.
  Includes index.
    1. Law—China—History and criticism. 2. Law, Mongolian
3. Chih-yüan hsin Ko, I. Chih-yuan hsin ko. II. Title.
III. Series: Harvard studies in East Asian Law.
340'.0951   78-70283
ISBN 0-691-09238-9

GPSR Authorized Representative: Easy Access System Europe - Mustamäe tee
50, 10621 Tallinn, Estonia, gpsr.requests@easproject.com

www.ingramcontent.com/pod-product-compliance
Lightning Source LLC
Chambersburg PA
CBHW050431280326
41932CB00013BA/2065

9780691627953